The Power of Pawns

Jörg Hickl

The Power of Pawns

Chess Structure Fundamentals for Post-beginners

New In Chess 2016

Cover design: Volken Beck
Translation: Ian Adams
Supervisor: Peter Boel
Proofreading: Frank Erwich
Production: Anton Schermer

Have you found any errors in this book?
Please send your remarks to editors@newinchess.com. We
will collect all relevant corrections on the Errata page of our
website www.newinchess.com and implement them in a
possible next edition.

ISBN: 978-90-5691-631-2

Contents

Explanation of Symbols

**The chessboard
with its coordinates:**

!	good move
!!	excellent move
?	bad move
??	blunder
!?	interesting move
?!	dubious move
±	White stands slightly better
∓	Black stands slightly better
±	White stands better
∓	Black stands better
+−	White has a decisive advantage
−+	Black has a decisive advantage
=	balanced position
∞	unclear
⇄	counterplay
⧾	compensation
#	mate
corr.	correspondence
jr	junior
sr	senior

☐ White to move
■ Black to move
♔ King
♕ Queen
♖ Rook
♗ Bishop
♘ Knight

Introduction

What every club player desires is to reach an acceptable playing level with a reasonable expenditure of time and effort. That is the point of the present book 'The power of the pawns'. An overview of basic pawn structures, together with a lot of practical hints, helps to improve one's understanding of chess at a deep level.

Chess players require a broad spectrum of knowledge. A game seldom works out as planned – new, frequently unknown positions suddenly crop up and demand great flexibility. One has to transform experience into a positional evaluation which is as accurate as possible. Profound knowledge is of course an advantage, but frequently unnecessary. This book is intended to make a contribution to turning a club player into an all-rounder, who can feel at home in any situation. It is important to recognise the strengths and weaknesses of a pawn structure, in order to bring their advantages to bear in practice. The study of this volume will help you with that.

In the middle of the 90s, when in addition to top-level sport I focussed more of my chess activity on the organisation of chess holidays and chess training, the needs of the majority of club players were foreign to me. The demands of top-level chess are too different from those of occasional tournament players. In more than ten years of intensive work and communication with the participants in my holidays, the same questions about structures and evaluation of positions kept coming up. I became aware that club players have to struggle with a similar approach and similar problems.

These reflections led among others to the following questions: 'Can I do something to improve this situation? Where can my experience help to make learning easier for chess players? And how can they make progress?'

During my training I kept having my attention drawn to the difficulties participants had with pawn structures and the related evaluation of positions. 'Pawns are the soul of the game' – this was already recognised by François-André Danican Philidor, the world's best player in the 18th century. Their particular way of moving is of decisive significance: they are the only pieces which cannot move backwards. A careless pawn move can have important consequences, which can be seen with subjects such as the good/bad bishop, the open file or the eternal piece.

To clarify these specific effects on the other pieces, the introductory part of the book is dedicated to the minor pieces and the rooks. Those pieces which move both in straight lines and diagonally, the king and the queen, are far less dependent on the structure and thus are not considered separately.

There are many 'typical' pawn structures – too many. Even for experienced grandmasters their study involves lifelong learning. No single book can provide an exhaustive treatment and would in any case demand too much of the student. So the main part is limited to the most frequently met and basic structures: from 'hanging pawns' via 'isolated pawns' to 'weak squares'.

Working with this book

It is not sufficient to read chess books. Their contents must be studied intensively and worked through, so as to consolidate the knowledge in a lasting manner. This demands a certain amount of personal initiative and unfortunately also a not inconsiderable investment of time. That, however, is the only way in which the knowledge can be assimilated and also recalled without problem at a later date in order to be of use in your own games.

Every structure dealt with in the second part is first explained in general terms by means of a diagram. In order to lay the accent on their particularities, no pieces have been included – in certain circumstances, however, not a single piece has yet left the board. All the structures of course can occur with reversed colours.

Basically you should be working with a chessboard of tournament dimensions! Through their practice chess players are very strongly influenced by three-dimensional thinking and achieve noticeably better results at the board than they do when working with a chess program or a computer monitor.

Important positions are highlighted by diagrams and provided with an exercise. Solving these will be easier for you if in doing so you answer the following questions:
- What are the specific characteristics of the position? Pay attention to different pawn majorities, king safety and important peculiarities concerning the minor pieces, like for example good or bad bishops or eternal squares for pieces.
- Where should I play? Queenside, kingside, or the centre?
- Are different evaluations valid for different phases of the game? Should you neglect in the opening or middlegame a pawn weakness, which will constitute a serious defect in the endgame?
- Where are there pawn levers? Is there a possibility of altering the structure? By advancing my own pawn, can I open a line or create a weakness?

And never forget an extremely important point:
- What are the opponent's intentions? If you can answer this question then you are one step ahead of him!

But *The Power of the Pawns* does not just offer an overview of various structures. In many places you will find, in italics, practical tips, e.g. how to behave in time trouble, finding candidate moves and classic mistakes.

Independent study of the model games listed at the end of each chapter will round off the subject matter and deepen the knowledge you have acquired. All the games mentioned in the book are available on the internet in electronic form for a free download at www.joerg-hickl.de.

I would like to express my great gratitude to my co-author Erik Zude for his outstanding cooperation and to Uwe Schupp for his editorial work on the book. I would also like to mention specially the participants in the chess holidays, whose constructive questions and suggestions in the long run were the driving force behind this book.

Jörg Hickl

Part 1

Pieces and pawns

Chapter 1
The bishop

*My secret for success: with every move I force my opponents
to think for themselves!*
Dr Alexander Alekhine

The bishop, which moves exclusively diagonally, is more dependent on the structure than any other piece. If a pawn is in its way it can be considerably limited in its radius of influence. If that is its own pawn, and fixed to boot, then we call it a bad bishop – a factor which can decide a game. This motif is central to whole opening systems (e.g. the King's Indian or even the French Defence).

We recommend that you look into this subject in depth. In the majority of all games of chess it plays an important role, but it is often only marginally dealt with by chess theory.

The bad bishop seen for example in the Advance Variation of the French Defence after the moves 1.e4 e6 2.d4 d5 3.e5

We speak of a bad bishop when the latter is restricted by its own pawns fixed on the same colour of squares as the bishop. Here, structures with central pawns are very much to the fore, since that is where the effects are the greatest. However, even a single rook's pawn can make a bishop a bad one.

In the diagram the e6- and d5-pawns restrict the black bishop on c8. Of course this problem also exists to a slightly lesser extent on the white side for the bishop on c1. But the latter can, however, still be deployed actively on the kingside to a certain extent.

How can we remedy this shortcoming?

Playing with the bad bishop

Basically three options are available:
- Exchange it off: here e.g. via the manoeuvre ...b7-b6 and ...♗a6.
- Change the position of the pawns: in our diagram the white central pawns had to be eliminated in order for us to be able to move our own. So the correct plan consists of an attack on the white pawn chain with the levers ...c7-c5 and ...f7-f6.
- Get the bishop in front of the pawn chain: in our example the idea consists of ...f7-f6, followed by ...♗d7-e8-g6/h5. A protracted plan, but since in closed positions time often plays a subordinate role, such a procedure is very common in practice.

Playing against the bad bishop

Of course we try to prevent the scenarios mentioned above. The great weakness of the bad bishop, however, makes itself felt on squares of the other colour. The more defenders (in our example of the dark squares) disappear, the more clearly this factor moves into the foreground.

Good bad or bad good bishop?

The terminology is not simple and transitions are fluid. The only way to get a feel for how to weigh up what is involved is through the study of this characteristic of the position over numerous practical examples. What is by definition a bad bishop can also represent a positive criterion in a game!

The bad bishop

Taken from a simultaneous game Jarchov-Hickl during a chess trip to Mallorca, 2001:

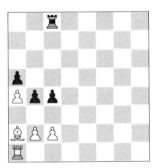

It is obvious that the bishop on a2 is largely excluded from the action. White's desire to activate this weak minor piece is all the more understandable. It would have been correct to move the a1-rook out of the corner and to go on to adapt the pawn structure to the minor piece by means of c2-c3. The tempestuous **1.b3** meant that after the unforeseen reply **1...c3** White had written his name into the history of my chess travels. The phenomenon of a bishop shut in on a2 became known as the 'Jarchov bishop'.

The good bad bishop

It goes without saying that the bishop on g4 is a very active piece. It is, however, restricted by its own pawns on e6 and d5, with the consequence that it cannot help out on the queenside. This may not be relevant for the moment, but it might have a part to play at a later stage of the game. The bishop on d3, on the other hand, is unreservedly good.

The bad good bishop

After the moves **1.c4 e6 2.♘f3 d5 3.g3 ♘f6 4.♗g2 ♗e7 5.0-0 0-0 6.b3 c5 7.e3 ♘c6 8.♗b2 d4 9.exd4 cxd4 10.♖e1 ♘e8 11.d3 f6** we reach the following position.

Black is planning to follow up with ...e6-e5. Thereafter, according to our definition, the bishop on e7 is bad on account of the fixed d4-pawn and the one on b2 is good. But at a second glance we notice that the white queen's bishop can hardly achieve much at all and it will even be difficult to find a sensible task for it in the long run. Actually, all it is doing is getting in the way, and after all the ♗e7 on its diagonal is inhibiting the thematic counterplay on the queenside, b3-b4. Based on this consideration, the early exchange of the actually good bishop via 12.♗a3 is also seen, in addition to the most frequently played standard manoeuvre ♘a3-c2, intending to become active by means of b3-b4.

Conclusion

In judging the quality of a bishop, white and black are meaningless. We must learn to recognise the subtle differences and their relevance to the evaluation of the position.

Years of practice and the study of many games are required for this. So all this chapter can do is draw your attention to the problem.

1 Réti Opening

Jörg Hickl	2545
Sergey Tiviakov	2680

Germany Bundesliga B 2006/07 (7)

1.g3 ♘f6 2.♗g2 d5 3.♘f3 e6 4.0-0 ♗e7 5.c4 0-0 6.b3 b6 7.♗b2 ♗b7 8.e3 ♘bd7 9.♕e2 dxc4 10.bxc4 ♘c5 11.♗d4 ♘fd7 12.♖d1

I had dim memories of a game played a year previously against the Lithuanian Rozentalis, in which I had a slight advantage. Why had my opponent chosen that variation? What had he prepared? As the player with the higher Elo rating he would certainly want to try for a win.

During a tournament game lots of thoughts (often too many thoughts) run through one's head, and emotions play a significant role. My decades of experience teach me that it is rarely a good idea to set out to avoid your opponent's preparation. You must absolutely stick to tried and tested structures and avoid unnecessary risks! Your opponent will deviate sooner or later. Games are rarely won by brilliant play, but by tactical blunders and a rush of blood to the head — no matter what the Elo level.

Despite thinking for a long time, I could not see the light here and unintentionally I deviated from the previous game, which had gone 12.♘c3 ♘a6 13.♘a4 c5 14.♗b2 ♗f6 15.d3 ♗xb2 16.♕xb2 ♕f6 17.♕xf6 ♘xf6 18.♘e5 ♗xg2

19.♔xg2±, Hickl-Rozentalis, Germany Bundesliga 2001/02.

12...♖e8 13.d3 ♗d6 14.♘c3

Giving up the bishop. However, in return Black has to place a pawn on a square of the same colour as his own bishop and, as long as White still has the pawn block f2/e3, there is little his opponent's dark-squared bishop can do.

14...e5 15.♗xc5 ♘xc5 16.♘d2 ♗xg2 17.♔xg2 ♗f8 18.♘de4 ♘e6

In which part of the board should White play?
Take a few minutes and explore the demands of the position!

The white pawn structure has no weaknesses, the d3-point can be sufficiently defended. But Black does not have any obvious problems either. There is, however, the imbalance of bishop against knight. The following plans are possible:

- Play on the queenside with a2-a4
- Play in the centre with d3-d4 or f2-f4
- Play on the kingside with e.g. g3-g4

Here are a few possible approaches to a solution:

1) What can I achieve on the queenside? Even a pawn on a5 does not really advance my cause. In addition I have to

reckon on Black playing ...a7-a5, which secures the b4-square for his bishop.

2) Both pawn thrusts fail for tactical reasons: 19.d4? exd4 20.exd4 f5 or 19.f4 exf4 20.gxf4 f5, after which the knight on e4 must move and the vis-à-vis of the queen on e2 and rook on e8 leads after ...♘f4+ to the loss of the queen. Independently of that, the opening of the position unexpectedly turns Black's only weakness, the bishop on f8, into a strength, and in addition a file is cleared for the inactive rook on e8.

3) What would the opponent like to do? *This reflection should always occupy a central position.* Here it immediately leads us to a plausible solution. Black is planning ...f7-f5 and ...c7-c6, after which our knights no longer have outposts. In what follows, the bishop comes to g7, the queen to d7 and the a-rook to d8. The advantage in space will slightly favour Black. So we have to prevent ...f7-f5 in order to maintain the most important minor piece in the centre!

19.♕f3 c6 20.h4

In order to keep the number of tactical errors down, current chess engines were used to help with the production of this publication. A procedure which I do not recommend to readers on the first analysis of their own games!

Here my feeling for the position could never imagine White to be at a disadvantage. The computer on the other hand already sees Black ahead by a good half a pawn.

One can learn too little from the programs and there is too great a danger that they wean us off thinking. Only one's own work can lead to an improvement in playing strength!

The computer is, however, a useful tool for seeking out tactical mistakes in our own analysis... afterwards.

20...♖b8 21.♕f5 f6?!

Putting another pawn on the same colour as the bad bishop. A better idea was 21...g6 22.♘f6+ (22.♕xe5 loses a piece after 22...♗g7 23.♕d6 f5) 22...♔h8 23.♕f3 ♘f4+ 24.gxf4 ♕xf6 25.♘e4 with approximately level chances.

22.g4 ♕c8

Offering a draw, but White can play on without any risk.

23.h5 ♗e7

Here I spent a certain amount of time looking into the tactical solution 24.h6 and the position which would arise after 24...g6 25.♘xf6+ ♔f7 26.♕f3 ♗xf6 27.♘e4 ♕d8 28.g5 ♘xg5 29.♘xg5+. White is better here because of the eternal e4-outpost for his knight. But in this liquidation one is above all behind in material. So it has to be correct!

After repeated calculation, disillusionment set in. I discovered the move 26...♘g5−+. A typical blunder in calculating variations. Fortunately there was a quiet alternative: the inactive knight on c3 should support the play on the kingside.

24.♘e2 ♘d8 25.♕f3

25.♘2g3 was on offer here.

25...♘f7 26.♘2g3 ♕e6 27.♖h1 ♖bd8 28.♖ad1 h6?!

Understandable, to remove from the position a possible h5-h6 for White, but, just like move 21, ...h7-h6 also weakens the light squares. The bishop will continue to remain bad!

29.♕f5 ♕xf5 30.♘xf5

White has obtained a clearly superior position. But how should he continue? I was planning to bring the king over to protect the d3-pawn, to activate the h1-rook and then, after a line opening on the queenside, to look out for a chance to bring the rooks into the game. There was no need for me to be any more specific in my considerations, and in a game of chess you should also take into account the opponent, who will not usually be sitting there idly. This is the case here too.

30...b5?!

After this the c-file which opens will be occupied for good by White. A better try was 30...♗a3.

31.cxb5 cxb5 32.♖c1 ♖d7 33.♖c6 ♖xd3 34.♖c7 ♗f8 35.♖hc1

The activity of the rooks is more important than recovering the pawn. After 35.♖xa7 ♖c8 the control of the c-file passes to Black.

35...♖ed8 36.♖b7

The b-pawn is more valuable than the a-pawn, if it finds a safe haven on b4 and fixes a2.

36...♖3d7

In view of the threat of 37.♖cc7, this is forced.

37.♖xb5 ♘d6 38.♘fxd6 ♗xd6 39.♖c6

On account of the fixed black pawns the d6-bishop is irremediably bad – there is nothing for it to attack anywhere on the board. White is dominating on the light squares. After all his pieces have been brought into their ideal positions, the a-pawn advances to a6, and at a suitable moment the rook will invade on b7. Black is powerless and can only play a waiting game. The open d-file has no role to play. White is probably already winning, but the computer, on the other hand, still considers the position almost level.

39...♗e7 40.♔f3 ♔f7 41.♘g3 ♗f8 42.a4 ♗d6 43.♘f5 ♗b8 44.a5 ♗c7 45.♘g3 ♗d6 46.♔e4 ♗c7 47.♘f5 ♗b8 48.a6 ♔e8 49.♖b2 ♗d6 50.♖b7 ♗f8 51.♖cc7 ♖xc7 52.♖xc7 ♖d7 53.♖xd7?

53.♖b7 with *zugzwang* would have ended the game straight away, but a lot can happen in the sixth hour of play! I had not seen a continuation after 53...♔d8. However, the simple 54.♖b8+ wins the ♗f8.

53...♔xd7 54.♔d5 ♔c7 55.♔e6 ♔b6 56.♔f7

56...♗c5 57.♔xg7 ♔xa6 58.♘xh6

The bishop, which is still bad, cannot even sacrifice itself for a pawn.

58...♔b5 59.♘f5 a5 60.h6 a4 61.h7 1-0

For a player with an Elo rating approaching 2700 this was not really an overwhelming performance. Did he not recognise the danger of the bad bishop? Or was he totally bent on winning against the weaker player and went too far?

Too much can be read into chess games without any proof being offered for the conclusion. Always bear in mind: chess is boxing on an intellectual level, man against man — and we are fallible. You always have a chance!

A good year later GM Tiviakov deservedly became European champion.

Model games

Hickl-Rozentalis (Germany Bundesliga 2001/02)

Carlsen-Van Wely (Foros 2008), good against bad bishop

Kasparov-Svidler (Moscow 2004), good bad bishop

Karjakin-Shirov (Heraklion 2007), passive bad bishop

What outsiders underestimate is the degree of resistance which really good players can put up.

Nigel Short

Training exercises

After a lot of general advice, we should like to bring the chapter on the bishop to a conclusion with a practical unit. In the following diagrams the g2-pawn is under attack.

Should White play f2-f3 or g2-g3?

Your judgement here should not concern only the endgame. Does your evaluation change somewhat if there are even more pieces on the board?

Exercise 1

Exercise 2

Instead of a knight White has a bishop on d3.

Exercise 3

Instead of the knight White has a bishop on e3.

Exercise 4

White has the bishop pair.

When playing against a bishop there are two basic rules:

Rule 1

Arrange the pawn structure to suit your own bishop.

Rule 2

Limit the radius of action of the opposing bishop.

It is important to observe a clear hierarchy with these basic principles: rule 1 always comes before rule 2!

And now we have the solutions which follow:

Solution to Exercise 1

1.f3 Since we do not have a bishop of our own we play against the opposing minor piece. 1.g3 would surrender control of the light squares.

A g2-pawn which would later tend to be a weakness constitutes an exception: the opposing bishop would be in a position to attack the pawn (in this case from f1). But this would only represent a threat if g2-g3 were no longer possible, e.g. if the pawn were fixed by ...f5-f4 or ...h5-h4. On the way there Black, for his part, breaks Rule 1, since these pawns could be blocked on the light squares.

Solution to Exercise 2

1.g3 Our own bishop leads us to Rule 1. Pawns and bishop have to complement each other! On d3 the bishop controls the light squares, meaning that the pawns must look after the maintenance of the dark ones. 1.f3 limits the mobility of our own minor piece, which can lead to the problem of the bad bishop.

Solution to Exercise 3

1.f3 Just like in Exercise 2 the important thing here is to control the light squares.

Solution to Exercise 4

When you have the two bishops, there is no way to avoid restricting one of them. In our diagram the balance of the position will be decided by the relationship between the dark-squared bishop and the knight. It is probable that the light-squared ones will be exchanged at some point. Thus it is important to arrange our structure to suit the dark-squared bishop: **1.f3**

Basically these solutions remain valid in all phases of the game. The few exceptions can for the moment be put to one side and need be taken into account only by players of a clearly higher Elo level.

Moreover, our rules also cover the subject of the 'airhole'. If you want to remove the possibility of a back-rank mate from the position and are thinking about h2-h3 or g2-g3, simply remember Rule 2.

To be fair – when your opponent has the bishop pair, the whole business is anything but simple.

In addition:

Exercise 1 led to heated debate between the authors. Is it not possible to play 1.g3 too? Of course it is, because it will scarcely be possible to prove that in this specific (endgame) position it is worse than **1.f3**. Nevertheless, this book is addressed to 'normal' club players and aims to make chess more comprehensible, so that the knowledge acquired can be transferred to your own games. Let us imagine diagram 1 with a few more pieces:

Here one would not waste a single second considering 1.g3. The weakness of the light squares after 1...♕f3 would be really annoying.

Follow the rules and playing chess becomes simpler.

Chapter 2
The knight

It is not about looking for the best move, but about playing according to a sensible plan.

Savielly Tartakower

The minor pieces, bishops and knights, have been considered since time immemorial as being of almost equal value. At the start of the 70s, the eccentric American chess genius Robert James Fischer (1943-2008, World Champion 1972-75) expressed some doubt about this evaluation and gave precedence to the bishop. He valued it at 3.25 pawns compared to 3 for the knight. But this opinion did not hold good for long. Nowadays a consensus has come about for the evaluation of the bishop depending on the types of position.

The long-legged bishop shows its clear superiority in certain situations, above all in endgames with passed pawns on both flanks, but the advantages of the knight are not to be despised. It can be active on squares of both colours, it is the ideal blockading piece and the way it moves makes it unpredictable. There is one tactical factor which is often of considerable significance in practical games with limited thinking time. All too often, one 'simply did not see' a knight fork.

The outpost

2 Sicilian Defence
Patrick Wolff   2570
David Bronstein   2465
Wijk aan Zee 1992 (9)

**1.e4 c5 2.♘f3 ♘c6 3.d4 cxd4
4.♘xd4 ♘f6 5.♘c3 e5 6.♘db5 d6
7.♗g5 a6 8.♘a3 b5 9.♗xf6 gxf6
10.♘d5 f5 11.♗d3 ♗e6 12.0-0 ♗g7
13.♕h5 f4 14.c4 bxc4 15.♗xc4 0-0
16.♖ac1 ♖b8 17.b3 ♗xd5 18.♗xd5
♘b4 19.♖fd1 ♘xa2 20.♖c6 ♕e7
21.♘c4 ♘b4 22.♖xd6 ♘xd5
23.♖6xd5 ♖xb3**

White to move

Evaluate the situation.

White is a pawn down but can help himself to the one on e5. That would, however, solve Black's main problem of the bad bishop on g7. An aspect which basically has to be taken into account. Frequently more can be achieved on the weakened squares of the other colour. After 23...♖b5 the position would in no way be clear. A good moment to be keeping an eye open for alternatives.

Knights need outposts! This statement has been attributed to the first official chess World Champion, Wilhelm Steinitz (1836-1900, World Champion 1886-1894). What he meant are the squares on which the short-range piece can find solid support from its own troops, usually pawns. Exchanging it or driving it away ought to be difficult for the opponent or only possible under unfavourable circumstances.

The search for such a square in the position in the diagram quickly leads us to f5, and the game continuation suddenly appears easy to understand.

No doubt Patrick Wolff, twice US-Champion, had also looked into the capture on e5. So it is important first of all to spot the sensible moves, called in chess jargon 'candidate moves', and to work through them in order of priority: firstly those options which require a forced reply, such as capturing or giving check. One then turns to the alternatives, takes them quickly into account, compares them one with the other, rejects some options, goes more deeply into others and finally selects one of them. A diffuse process, which is not always well structured even in the case of top grandmasters.

Alexander Kotov (1913-1981), one of the best players in the world during the post-war era and a representative of the much-praised Russian school of chess, suggested another way of proceeding: look for the candidate moves, calculate the first one out till you get a result, go to the second and calculate, go to the third, etc. At the end you choose the move with the best evaluation. Like that there are no cross-links and no jumping about between individual candidate moves. That appears to be a desirable plan which saves time, however it is not a very human way of going about things. One frequently does not discover till candidate move three tactical possibilities or positional subtleties which require a change in or a re-evaluation of the first two moves. Nobody, except perhaps a computer, can calculate like that!

But many club players fail before they get there because of a certain tunnel vision. One discovers an impressive move and on doing so forgets the rest of the world. If the result of the calculation is satisfactory, the move is made. Thus, presented in exaggerated fashion, candidate move one can win us a pawn, candidate move two a piece and candidate move three is mate. But if numbers two and three are not considered because we are euphoric about the result of move one, many good possibilities will remain unexamined.

But back to our exercise. The correct evaluation of the significance of an outpost means that the gain of material resulting from the first candidate move can quickly fade into the background.

24.♘d6 h6

With the clear intention of continuing with the relieving 25...♕g5.

25.h4

Prevents Black's plan and removes from the position a possible back-rank mate (an important concern with major pieces on the board).

25...♖fb8?

The decisive error. The only way to defend the kingside was with 25...♕f6 26.♘f5 ♖e8.

26.♘f5 ♕f8

26...♕f6 27.♖d6.

27.♕g4

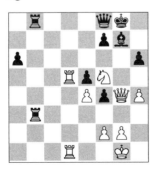

This threatens not only to take the pawn on h6, but also the immediately decisive 28.♖d8.

27...♖b1 28.♘xh6+ ♔h7 29.♘f5 ♗f6 30.♖xb1 ♖xb1+ 31.♔h2 ♖b7

Black prevents White's idea of hitting on the f7-pawn with ♖d7, ♕h5 and ♘h6, but there is already no longer a way to save the game.

32.♖d6 ♗g7

And we now have the motif we already know:

33.♖d8   **1-0**

3 Sicilian Defence
Herman Pilnik
Efim Geller
Gothenburg 1955 (15)

1.e4 c5 2.♘f3 ♘c6 3.d4 cxd4 4.♘xd4 ♘f6 5.♘c3 d6 6.♗e2 e5 7.♘b3 ♗e7 8.0-0 0-0 9.♗e3 ♗e6 10.♗f3 a5 11.♘d5 ♗xd5 12.exd5 ♘b8 13.c4 ♘a6 14.♗d2 b6 15.♗c3 ♘c5 16.♘xc5 bxc5 17.♕e1 ♘d7 18.♗d1 a4 19.♗c2 f5 20.♖d1 g6 21.♕e2 ♗f6 22.f3

Black to move

The very first glance conveys the impression that Black is clearly better. Good pieces, the pawn pair f5/e5 which controls the central squares, and the semi-open b-file with a space advantage on the queenside leap to the eye.

But how should he continue? The breakthrough ...e5-e4 is for the moment being prevented by White and on the b-file the otherwise inactive white bishop pair is keeping an eye on the entry squares.

22...e4

At the cost of a pawn Black gets the ideal square for his knight, e5, as well as a pawn majority on the kingside which nothing is stopping him from advancing.

23.♗xf6 ♕xf6 24.fxe4 f4 25.♖f2 ♘e5

Of course, capturing the b2-pawn cannot be the idea: 25...♕xb2? 26.♕g4 ♘e5 27.♕e6+ leads to an advantage for White.

Black's strategy has clear outlines: the extra white pawn and the majorities on the queenside and in the centre do not have any part to play. The bishop on c2 has no future and remains demoted to the role of onlooker until the end of the game.

26.♖df1 ♕h4 27.♗d1 ♖f7

A typical way in which strong players go about things: they always make sure that all their forces are engaged in the struggle. Since White does not even have a whiff of counterplay, Geller prepares the later deployment of the as yet inactive a-rook, before starting operations on the kingside.

28.♕c2 g5 29.♕c3 ♖af8 30.h3 h5

31.♗e2?

Under all circumstances White had to take on a4 here. Black's attack after 31...g4 32.♗d1 ♕g5 33.♔h1 does look threatening, but there is no forced win in sight.

The basic rule is: if your opponent leaves something en prise, the first thing to do is to check the possible capture. If you cannot find a refutation, you must start from the point of view that your opponent has blundered the material! Never believe that he has made a correct sacrifice. That holds true, whatever the playing strength of your opponent may be. Well, if his name is Komodo or Stockfish, you can have confidence in the tactical developments!

31...g4 32.♖xf4?

This loses immediately. It would have been better to concede the exchange with 32.a3 ♕g5 33.♔h1 g3 34.♖f3. But after 34...♖b8 35.♗d1 ♘xf3 36.♕xf3 ♖xb2 Black infiltrates via the b-file, hardly something about which White can be enthusiastic.

32...♖xf4 33.♖xf4 ♖xf4 34.g3 ♘f3+ 35.♔f2 ♕xh3 36.gxf4 g3+ 37.♔xf3 g2+ 38.♔f2 ♕h2   0-1

In chess I always seek something which suits me. Risky play in the style of chess musketeers is not my thing, even though it pleases many friends of sharp twists and turns.

Anatoly Karpov

The blockading piece

The knight is well positioned on any square from which it cannot be driven away. A particularly important square of this type is the one in front of an opposing pawn. The latter works like a shield, but does not limit the action of the knight. We call this the blockading square.

4 Old Indian Defence

Suat Atalik	2599
Jörg Hickl	2560

Chalkidiki 2003 (8)

1.d4 d6 2.♘f3 ♘f6 3.c4 ♘bd7 4.♘c3 e5 5.e4 ♗e7 6.♗e2 0-0 7.0-0 c6 8.♕c2 a6 9.♖d1 ♕c7 10.♗g5 ♖e8 11.♖ac1 h6 12.♗h4 ♘h7 13.♗xe7 ♖xe7 14.♕d2 ♘hf6 15.♘h4 ♘f8 16.d5 c5 17.g3 ♘8h7 18.f3 ♘g5 19.♕e3 g6 20.♖b1 ♗d7 21.b4 b6 22.a4 ♖ee8 23.a5 cxb4 24.♖xb4 b5 25.♖a1 ♕c5 26.♕xc5 dxc5 27.♖bb1 b4 28.♘d1

Black to move

Find a plan.

The position is of a closed character and not very dynamic on account of the lack of open lines and pawn levers which are hard to make use of. What strikes us first of all is the bad white bishop. Both sides have a protected passed pawn, which, however, cannot be activated for the moment, but which naturally represents an asset for the endgame. Pressure on e4 will permanently rule out the lever f3-f4. Black, on the other hand, would like to play ...f7-f5, but both the knight on f6 and the weakness of the g6-pawn are getting in the way of that. For the present, the mighty white passed pawn has no support whatsoever. Nevertheless, it should be kept under precautionary observation. *Whoever controls the square in front of the passed pawn has the advantage!*

Back in 1925, Aaron Nimzowitsch (1886-1935) wrote in his masterpiece *My System*: 'the passed pawn is a criminal which belongs under lock and key!'. For the time he was coming up with revolutionary theses about the importance of the centre and the pieces. Even today all our chess is based on these. In more than 80 years, little has changed. There is hardly a top player who when learning the game did not read this milestone work, and compulsory reading of the book must still be absolutely encouraged for every club player.

Based on our reflections, in the position in the diagram a transfer of the knight from f6 to d6 suggests itself. On the other hand, in what follows White will bring his knight from d1 to d3 and attack the c5- and e5-pawns. Black will need both rooks to defend them. On account of the closed character of the position, these can confidently be entrusted with such a lowly task.

To get the knight to its ideal d6-square, the only way is via e8. Therefore

28...♖e7 29.♘b2 ♘e8 30.♘d3 ♖c8 31.♗d1 ♔g7

It was more accurate to complete the plan and place the knight on its target square d6. In retrospect, I cannot explain what stopped me from doing so: greed, euphoria, carelessness or time trouble – teachers are not always the best students.

32.♗b3 f5

The alternative 32...♘d6 was still worth considering.

33.f4

I had not paid sufficient attention to this advance, which had not been possible for the whole time! A chess player's typical excuse, is it not? To tell the truth, I had not even seen it!

33...♘f7

I was fortunate that this move was still available. Of course not 33...exf4? 34.e5 and the pawns decide the day.

34.♖e1

White is threatening to take first on f5 and then on e5. The only possibility to protect the square one more time consists of:

34...♔f6

In the endgame the king is a powerful piece – unfortunately, however, very susceptible to tactical motifs.
34...fxe4 35.♖xe4 ♗f5? (at this point the computer solution is more exact: 35...♘f6 36.♖xe5 ♘xe5 37.fxe5 ♘xd5 38.e6 ♘c3 39.exd7 ♖xd7 with

equality and an uneven distribution of material. But human beings cannot play like that. The time trouble, which is usual at this point, also dramatically raised the error quotient) 36.♘xf5+ gxf5 37.♖xe5 ♘xe5 38.fxe5 and once more we see the rise of the dominating pawn pair.

35.♘f3

35...fxe4 36.fxe5+?

Only now is White on the way to a loss. He had to play 36.♖xe4 exf4 37.♖xe7 ♔xe7 38.♘xf4 ♗f5 39.♖e1+ ♔f6 with approximate equality.

36...♘xe5 37.♘dxe5 ♖xe5 38.♘xe5 ♔xe5 39.♖e3 ♘d6

But that too is computer chess: both Atalik and I consider this position to be won. The centralised king is overpowering. The computer coyly suggests that Black is ahead only by the value of a pawn.

40.♖ae1 ♔d4

The remainder of the game was played at the merciless Fischer thinking time of 30 seconds per move and thus does not merit any more comments.

41.♖3e2 ♗g4 42.♖f2 ♗f3 43.♖c1 ♖f8 44.♖d2+ ♔e5 45.♖e1 ♖f6 46.♗a2 ♘b7 47.♔f2 ♘xa5 48.♖b1 b3 49.d6 bxa2 50.♖xa2 ♘xc4 51.♖c1 e3+ 52.♔e1 ♘xd6 53.♖xc5+ ♔d4 54.♖c7 ♗d5

White resigned.

5 Queen's Gambit Declined
Tigran Petrosian   2635
John Peters   2370
Lone Pine 1976 (2)

1.c4 ♘f6 2.♘c3 c5 3.g3 ♘c6 4.♗g2 e6 5.♘f3 ♗e7 6.d4 d5 7.cxd5 ♘xd5 8.0-0 0-0 9.♘xd5 exd5 10.dxc5 ♗xc5 11.a3 a5

This prevents b2-b4, but places a pawn on a square of the same colour as that of the bishop on c5 and weakens the b5-square, which White later turns to his advantage several times during the game. So 11...♗f5 was better.

Various continuations have been tried out at this point, e.g. 12.♕c2 and 12.♗g5. The move in the game, however, is much better:

12.♘e1

White opens the diagonal of the bishop and will put the knight on an 'eternal' square, where it effectively blockades the opposing isolated pawn. We shall meet this copy-book procedure again in the chapter on 'hanging pawns'.

What is remarkable is that once it gets there the knight will not be moved again till the end of the game on move 60.

12...d4

A procedure which is often desirable in isolani positions; it fixes the e2-pawn but it also reduces the bishop on c5 to the status of a bad bishop.

13.♘d3 ♗b6 14.♗d2 ♖e8 15.♖c1 ♗g4 16.♖e1 ♖c8 17.h3 ♗f5 18.♕b3 ♗e4 19.♗xe4 ♖xe4 20.♕b5 ♘a7 21.♖xc8 ♘xc8 22.♗g5 ♕d6 23.♖c1 ♘a7 24.♕f5 ♖e8 25.♗f4 ♕d8 26.♖c2 ♘c6 27.h4 h6 28.♕b5 ♘a7 29.♕f5 ♘c6

White to move

Find the candidate moves.

Up until here we have seen the course a game can take between two players of differing strengths. White goes about things carefully and waits for his chance. He has learned that it is seldom to his advantage to use a crowbar and in doing so conforms to an important principle: 'Do not be over-hasty!'.

Tigran Petrosian (1929-1984, World Champion 1963-69) was considered a master of prophylaxis, i.e. the anticipatory thinking that the opponent's plans at first deserve a higher weighting than his own. Of course, decades spent refining such a technique also lead to the subordinating of one's own activity to the opponent's threats, something which is not always desirable.

There is no doubt that he knew that he held the advantage in this position, but it is not possible to spot an obvious plan at first. It would be good to exchange the bishop on f4 for the c6-knight, which would further emphasise the weakness of the black bishop or the strength of his own knight. Moreover, White's last two queen moves are typical of such phases of play. Without changing the character of the position, pieces are moved back and forward and the opponent is given the opportunity to ruin his own position. If that does not work, one has to strike out in a different direction – as happens here.

The positioning of the pieces cannot be improved any further. Should one make some sort of change in the pawn structure? Perhaps start some action on the kingside? No, in certain circumstances that would bring the white king into danger. Advancing the b-pawn on the queenside is nice, but it relieves Black of his weakness on a5 and concedes both c3 and the a-file.

30.♔f1!

This move does not, of course, change the evaluation of the position. So the exclamation mark is only being awarded for the plan. Since ideas are in short supply, all that seems to be left is to become active on the kingside. Previously, however, the king is brought

to safety on the other flank. In addition, on its way there it also protects the e2-point. However, care must be taken in order not to offer any targets to the opposing pieces. Please note that Petrosian does not do anything committal. If he no longer likes his idea, he could return to g1 at almost any point and look round for another way to proceed.

30...♖e6 31.♕b5 ♘a7 32.♕b3 ♘c6 33.h5 ♘e7 34.♔e1 ♘d5 35.♕b5 ♘f6 36.♔d1 ♘d5 37.♗e5 ♘e7 38.g4 ♘c6 39.♗g3 ♘a7 40.♕b3 ♘c6 41.♔c1 ♖e4 42.f3 ♖e3 43.♔b1

43...♘e7?

Black cannot find a way to change anything about the position and makes a momentous mistake. The bishop on b6 has no prospects. Up till now, however, the disadvantage had been kept within acceptable limits. It is only this knight move which clearly tips the balance in favour of White. Now it is possible to exchange the minor pieces!

A wait-and-see policy, e.g. 43...♖e6, was indicated. The desired opening on the kingside is not easy to engineer. At the end of all this one might get the impression that White won by doing nothing. Doing nothing in superb style!

44.♗h4   ♕d6   45.♗xe7   ♖xe7 46.♖c8+ ♔h7 47.♖f8 ♕c7 48.f4 ♗c5

Black to move

49.♕d5

Centralisation is always good and there are many routes to success. But there was a more forcing way, though it involved tactics: 49.♘xc5 ♕xc5 50.♕d3+ g6 51.♖xf7+ ♖xf7 52.♕xg6+ ♔h8 53.♕xf7.

49...♖e5 50.♖xf7

Black resigned.

Knights can also be bad!

This is especially true in endgames with passed pawns on both wings, where their short-range nature can be fatal. And in the middlegame too they can represent a serious encumbrance if they do not have outposts and targets.

6 Réti Opening

Jörg Hickl	2589
Andreas Huss	2393

Switzerland tt 2008

1.g3 d5 2.♗g2 c6 3.♘f3 ♗g4 4.c4 e6 5.b3 ♘d7 6.♗b2 ♘gf6 7.0-0 ♗e7 8.d3 0-0 9.♘bd2 a5 10.a3 ♕c7 11.♕c2 ♖ac8 12.♖fe1 ♖fd8 13.e4 dxe4 14.dxe4 ♘c5 15.♗c3 ♕b6 16.♖e3 ♗h5 17.h3 ♖a8 18.♖b1 ♗g6 19.♘e5 ♘a6 20.♕b2 ♗c5 21.♖e2 ♗d4 22.♘xg6 hxg6 23.e5 ♘e8 24.♘e4 ♗xc3 25.♕xc3

Here the fat is already in the fire. Even after they have been moved several times, it remains unclear what is to be done with the black knights. White, on the other hand, has the d6-outpost, the idea of playing b3-b4 in order to shut the knight on a6 completely out of the game, as well as some possibilities on the kingside. It is understandable that in serious time trouble my opponent wanted to reduce the attacking potential with

25...♕d4

but after

26.♕xa5

that gives away a pawn without any compensation. But it was hard to come up with a good suggestion. There is the not much better 25...♘c5 26.♕e3 ♘d7,

analysis diagram

after which there are several ways for White to hold on to the advantage, e.g.: 27.♕f4 ♕c7 28.♘g5 ♘f8 is the complex continuation but on a full board, which is not wrong when the opponent is in time trouble. The computer solution 27.c5 surrenders the d5-square: 27...♕a7 28.♖d2 ♘xe5 (here 28...♘c7 is also worth considering) 29.f4 ♖xd2 30.♕xd2 f5 31.fxe5 fxe4 32.♕d4. In view of how time was running out, I would nevertheless clearly have chosen the simple 27.♕xb6. After 27...♘xb6 28.♘c5 ♖ab8 29.f4 there is no doubt about White's advantage. The black knights still have no prospects.

In general, preference should be given to a solution which does not require tactics. You reduce the risk of making a mistake and save valuable thinking time. In desperate time trouble there were only a few remaining moves:

26...b6 27.♕c3 ♖ac8 28.b4 ♕xc3 29.♘xc3 ♖d3 30.♖c1 c5?? 31.♗b7 1-0

The technique of moving a piece several times which has been mentioned is moreover an outstanding help in finding a plan. When using it, ask yourself the following questions:

1) What could be achieved hypothetically if my opponent did not make a move and I was allowed to make several moves in a row? Goals might be: opening a file for a rook, creating a pawn weakness, setting things in motion for a tactical motif, improving the positions of pieces, etc., etc.

2) Is the desired scenario achievable or can the opponent prevent it without any problem?

Knights are often bad because the opposing bishop dominates them. In

the next game interaction with other pieces plays hardly any role. The knight has no outposts and there is nothing it can attack.

7 Sicilian Defence
Jonathan Speelman 2605
Margeir Petursson 2550
Novi Sad ol 1990 (13)
1.e4 c5 2.♘f3 d6 3.♗b5+ ♗d7 4.♗xd7+ ♘xd7 5.0-0 ♘gf6 6.♖e1 e6 7.d3 ♗e7 8.♘bd2 0-0 9.h3 b5 10.♘f1 c4 11.♘g3 cxd3 12.cxd3 ♘e5 13.d4 ♘xf3+ 14.♕xf3 d5 15.e5 ♘d7 16.♘h5 ♔h8 17.♕g4 ♖g8 18.♗d2 ♘b6

A better move would have been 18...♖c8 followed by ...♘b8-c6. That is where the knight belongs!

White to play

We find ourselves confronted with a French structure. The pawns on d4/e5 give White space for action on the kingside, but they turn his dark-squared bishop into a bad one. Overlapping with this factor is the even worse knight on b6. We can see that the latter is hard to activate. White goes on to play specifically against this weak point. In any case the remainder of Black's position is sound. There are neither pawn weaknesses nor inactive pieces. So White's advantage must be considered as tiny. Since Black would love to play 19...♘c4, the next move is obvious.

19.b3 ♖c8 20.♖ac1 ♗a3

He tries to contest his opponent's right to the c-file. But in only a few moves a white rook will pop up on it again. The alternative consisted of 20...g6, which however weakens the dark squares. A typical dilemma in positions with no counterplay. The first player's advantage is still clear, but the choice of the correct move is difficult.

21.♗g5 ♖xc1 22.♗xc1 ♗e7 23.♗e3 ♘d7 24.♖c1 a5 25.g3 a4

Black is suffering from being able neither to strengthen his position nor to relieve it by exchanging. He has to keep still, the skirmish on the queenside does not change the situation. Since in any case White cannot come up with anything concrete either, everything is still hanging in the balance.

26.h4 axb3 27.axb3 ♕b6 28.♘f4 ♖d8 29.♘h3 ♖a8 30.♘g5

30...♗xg5?!

An inaccuracy. Black may not be able to avoid the exchange of the bishop for the knight, but after 30...♔g8 31.♕h5 ♗xg5 32.♕xg5 it is his move and with 32...♔f8 he can prevent the unpleasant invasion of the opposing queen on e7.

31.♕xg5 ♔g8 32.♕e7 ♕b7 33.♗d2

Improves the bad bishop. Since Black cannot move, an operation on the kingside with h4-h5, which forces ...h7-h6, ♔g1-g2 and then g4-g5 could be seriously considered.

33...♖c8 34.♖a1 ♘c5

The only relieving move, but where will it be able to go to from b7?

35.♕xb7 ♘xb7 36.♗b4

White prevents the approach of the opposing king and after a knight move he would like to close the c-file with the bishop.

36...f6 37.f4 fxe5 38.fxe5

Black to move

How would you continue?
Decide between the candidate moves 38...♔f7, bringing up the king, and 38...♘d8. Also evaluate the continuation 38...h5.

38...♔f7?

Black is obviously in a critical situation. Basically the king is the piece which should be activated at once in the endgame if the position allows it. Here, however, the badly posted knight is more important. The continuation chosen in the game leads to an unpleasant pin on the seventh rank. What was indicated was the immediate activation of the knight by 38...♘d8, and amazingly Black can still fight on!

After the logical 39.♗c5 he has at his disposal a surprising trick:

analysis diagram

39...b4! 40.♗xb4 ♘c6 41.♖c1 (41.♗c5 ♘xe5 42.b4 ♘d3 43.♖a3 ♘xc5 44.dxc5 ♔f7 and Black is still in the game; 41.♗c3? promises even less: 41...♘xe5 and Black is slightly better) 41...♖b8 42.♖xc6 ♖xb4 43.♖xe6 ♔f7 44.♖a6 ♖xd4 45.♖a7+ ♔e6 46.♖xg7 ♖d3 47.♔f2 (47.♔g2!?) 47...♖xb3 48.♖xh7 ♔xe5. This has resulted in a rook ending in which White is a pawn up. The basic rule is that connected passed pawns win against a single one. Black can, however, develop considerable activity, for which reason he can still reckon on having really good chances of a draw.

The aforementioned 38...h5 was a good alternative. The pin on the knight is avoided and above all White cannot, as in the game, hold the king to the kingside with g3-g4.

39.♖a7

The pin is more than unpleasant.

39...♖c7 40.g4 ♔g6

Things now come to a rapid conclusion.

41.♔g2 h5 42.♔g3 ♖f7 43.♖a6 ♖f1 44.♖xe6+ ♔f7   **1-0**

Even at a high level and at least in most games one gets a second chance. What is required is to hold on long enough. Tenaciousness is a characteristic of good players. They never throw the towel in early. This is one reason why after their game against a strong player many players often regretfully finish with the words 'but I was winning'.

For it is the minority of games which are decided in the opening. Playing strength shows through principally at an advanced point in a tournament game.

Model games:

Geller-Najdorf (Zurich 1953) and **Smyslov-Rudakovsky** (Moscow 1945), which are both explained further in the chapter on backward pawns. These games explore in more depth the subject of a central knight which cannot be dislodged against a bad bishop **Speelman-Ehlvest** (Linares 1991), on the problem of bad knights.

Chapter 3

The rook

It is really a superior man who can watch a game of chess
and remain silent.
Chinese proverb

Though they are mostly of slight use in the opening, the effectiveness of the rooks grows the longer the game progresses. They need open files to develop their high potential. The goal here is above all the seventh or even the eighth rank of your opponent: there they can achieve extra horizontal impact and attack opposing pawns and the king.

To get there one's own pawns are often sacrificed in order to open files.

The opening and occupation of a file

The position is closed in character. In order to activate the major pieces a file needs to be opened. For that there is **1.a4**, intending a4-a5.

The following replies are available: allow 2.a5 and then take it, advance past it or stay in position, and also the ugly 1...a5, which turns the b6-pawn into a lasting weakness and degrades the black queenside majority.

How would you react?

Let us take a closer look at the first option: White gets in a4-a5. Capturing 2...bxa5 can be quickly excluded – it leaves the two weaknesses a7 and c5. By-passing with 2...b5 (after e.g. 1...♖ab8) leads after 3.cxb5 to a c5-pawn in need of protection. Black has three pawn islands, White only two. So what about doing nothing? But there is no way of hanging on to the a-file: 1.a4 ♔g7 2.a5 ♔f6 3.♖a4 (or 3.♖fb1 ♖ab8 4.axb6 axb6 5.♖a6/7) followed by ♖fa1. After that White infiltrates on the seventh or eighth rank and has the clearly more active pieces.

In his 1956 manual, *Pawn Power in Chess*, which is highly recommended, Hans Kmoch describes the distance between the back rank and the pawns as the 'rearspan'. A greater rearspan generally leads to the seizing of the file. White has a superiority in space and can determine when he will play axb6. The doubling of rooks forces Black into moving away.

After it has become clear to us that in all cases b6 is weak, the unpleasant 1... a5 will feel somewhat easier. In any case, by playing it we can prevent White from also getting the a-file. The b6-weakness can be covered horizontally with the rooks or also later by the king.

The enumeration of pawn islands which was mentioned is a simple procedure which almost always leads to a rapid and frequently very reliable evaluation of the structure.

White or Black to move

White continues with 1.♗h3, which forces Black to give up the c-file. The white rook arrives powerfully on c7. If it is Black to move, he must prevent this in all circumstances. In order to close the h3-c8 diagonal, both 1...h5, intending 2.♗h3 ♘g4, and 1...g5 2.♗h3 g4 come into consideration. However, White can continue to hope for an advantage by transferring the bishop to the a6-c8 diagonal. E.g. 1... h5 2.♖fe1 a5 3.♗h3 (or also the immediate 3.♗f1) 3...♘g4 4.♗f1 ♖ad8 5.♗a6 ♖a8 6.♗b7 ♖a7 7.♗c8 ♖a8 8.♗xg4 hxg4 9.♖c6 and White does finally possess the only open file.

Openings in which pawn chains have a part to play, such as the French or the King's Indian, are characterised by their closed nature. So both sides try to open lines for their major pieces.

One of the basic structures in the King's Indian Defence

White is planning c4-c5 and, after the opening of the c-file, penetrating to c7 with a rook. His advantage in space allows him to double his major pieces before the exchange on d6, which is not possible for Black. You will find more on this subject in Chapter 10, 'Pawn chains'.

8 Czech System

Paul Motwani	2520
Michael Adams	2640

Moscow 1994 (3)

1.e4 d6 2.d4 ♘f6 3.♘c3 c6 4.f4 ♕a5

The Czech System enjoyed great popularity in the 90s. It was considered to be an opening with a slightly dubious reputation, which had been little explored theoretically. Decent results could be obtained with a relatively slight amount of work. Gradually, however, some weaknesses became apparent, so that it has almost disappeared from grandmaster practice.

5.e5 ♘e4 6.♕f3 ♘xc3 7.♗d2 ♗f5 8.♗d3 ♗xd3 9.cxd3 ♕d5 10.bxc3 dxe5

The opening is going White's way. 10...e6 now or on the next move would have been a little better. Nevertheless the powerful centre guarantees White a solid advantage.

11.fxe5 ♕xf3 12.♘xf3 e6 13.♔e2 ♘d7

The doubled pawns not only help White to a considerable influence in the centre, but also to an additional semi-open file. White has an advantage in space; he is better off. To confirm the advantage the rooks must be brought into the action and lines opened.

14.♖hb1

Shuts in the rook on a1, but the recurring weakness in the b-file, b6, should be attacked with the a-pawn – for which the rook is ideally placed.

14...b6 15.a4 ♗e7 16.a5 b5 17.c4 a6

How would you continue?

After having read the first chapter, you would have to take into consideration the exchange of the mediocre bishop on d2 for the opposing one by means of ♗b4. But who does that help? The action costs time but creates no real weaknesses in the black camp. Above all, Black gets some space for his pieces. *When you have an advantage in space you should avoid exchanges!*

The knight and king could hardly be better placed. The rook, however, has done its duty on the b-file. After a possible cxb5 the neighbouring file will be opened.

18.♖c1 0-0

Black cannot keep the c-file closed. The strange-looking 18...♘b8, so as to cover c6 and to be able to recapture on b5 with the a-pawn, is refuted by 19.cxb5 axb5 20.a6 (with the threat of 21.a7) 20...♖xa6? (the correct move is 20...♖a7) 21.♖xa6 ♘xa6 22.♖xc6+–.

19.cxb5 cxb5 20.♖c7

Mission accomplished, the rook has penetrated to the seventh rank.

20...♖fd8 21.♖ac1

This brings the other rook into the game. White has a clear advantage.

21...♔f8

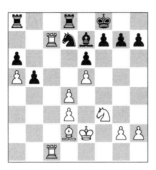

The white rooks are very actively posted, however they cannot decide the game on their own.

How can the replacement troops, the ♗d2 and ♘f3, get into the game? How can we create space for them? Since the d-pawn is not blockaded, the possibility of the clearance sacrifice d4-d5 must of course be considered at any point.

Precise calculation is the basis of tactics.
Never sacrifice simply 'because it looks
good'. An experienced player tends to take
the material and to hang on to it!
'It is always better to sacrifice your
opponent's pieces.'
Savielly Tartakower

22.d5 exd5 23.e6

The logical follow-up to the previous move.

23...♘f6?!

The capture on e6 was slightly better: 23...fxe6 24.♘d4 ♗d6 25.♘xe6+ ♔g8 26.♖7c6 ♗a3 27.♘xd8 ♗xc1 28.♗xc1 ♖xd8, even if White's advantage after 29.♖xa6 is incontestable.

24.♘g5 h6

25.♖xe7! hxg5

25...♔xe7 26.♗b4+ ♔e8 27.♖c7 fxe6 28.♖e7+ ♔f8 29.♘xe6+ ♔g8 30.♖xg7+ ♔h8 31.♖g6 with a win for White.

26.♗b4?!

And here 26.♖cc7 would have underlined the strength of the rooks on the seventh rank: 26...♘e8 and only now 27.♗b4 (or even 27.exf7 ♘xc7 28.♖xc7 ♖d6 29.♗b4 ♖d8 followed by 30.♖a7xa6xd6+−) 27...♘xc7 28.exf7

analysis diagram

28...♖e8 29.♖xe8+ ♔xf7 30.♖e7+, winning a piece.

26...♖e8 27.♖xe8+ ♔xe8 28.♖c7 fxe6 29.♖e7+?!

The immediate 29.♖xg7 would have been better, followed by ♖e7+ and ♖xe6.

29...♔d8 30.♖xg7 ♘e8 31.♖xg5 ♖a7 32.♖g6?!

There was nothing wrong with the immediate activation of the connected passed pawns with 32.h4.

32...♖h7 33.♖xe6 ♖xh2 34.♔f3 ♖h4?

And here the final chance consisted of 34...♘c7. After 35.♖d6+ ♔c8 36.♗d2 ♖h7 37.♗f4 b4 38.♖b6 b3 39.♖xb3 White's advantage is considerable, and possibly sufficient for a win, but Black is still in the game.

35.♗e1 ♖h1 36.♗g3 ♖d1 37.♗h4+ ♔d7 38.♖e7+ ♔c6 39.♖xe8 b4 40.♔e2

Black resigned.

In the following example the file has already been opened:

9 King's Indian Defence
Mikhail Botvinnik
Bent Larsen
Leiden 1970 (2)

1.c4 g6 2.♘c3 ♗g7 3.d4 d6 4.e4 ♘f6 5.f3 0-0 6.♗e3 a6 7.♕d2 c6 8.♗d3 b5 9.♘ge2 ♘bd7 10.0-0 ♖b8 11.cxb5 axb5 12.b4 ♘b6 13.a4 bxa4 14.♘xa4 ♘xa4 15.♖xa4 ♗d7 16.♖a5 ♕b6 17.♖b1 ♖fc8 18.♘c3 ♕d8 19.♕a2 ♗e6 20.♕a3 d5 21.e5 ♘d7 22.♘a4 ♗f5 23.♗xf5 gxf5 24.♖a6 ♖c7 25.♖c1 ♕c8 26.♖a5 e6 27.♗d2 ♗f8 28.f4 ♔h8 29.♘c5 ♘xc5 30.dxc5 ♕d8 31.♕d3 ♕d7 32.♖ca1 ♖cb7 33.♖a8 ♕c8 34.♖xb8 ♕xb8 35.♕a3 ♔g8 36.♕a4 ♕c7 37.♖a3 h6 38.♕a8 ♖b8 39.♕a5 ♕c8 40.♕a6 ♗e7 41.♕xc8+ ♖xc8 42.♔f2 ♔f8 43.♔f3

Now let us take a close look at this position.

Black to move

White has a bad bishop, but his superiority in space, the weakness of the c6- and h6-pawns and, above all, the possession of the a-file constitute more than sufficient compensation. White is better.

Bent Larsen (1935-2010) lost this game quickly due to an over-estimation of his chances. He wrote: 'I am probably slightly better and, if my king makes it into the centre, I will get prospects of a win.' Such boundless optimism helps players make progress, but also causes many to lose the feel for danger. But nevertheless, his fresh, creative chess brought the Dane to the top of world chess. At the end of the 60s he was considered the best player in the western hemisphere and a hot contender for the world title. His harsh 6:0 defeat at the hands of the future World Champion Fischer in the Candidates' match in Denver in 1971, however, was an abrupt end to Larsen's title ambitions.

43...h5?!

Striving for activity leads to a further weakening. The pawn was easier to defend on h6. He had to play 43...♔e8 44.♖a7 (44.h3!?) 44...♔d8 45.g4 fxg4+ 46.♔xg4 ♖c7 47.♖a6 ♔d7 48.f5 h5+

49.♔f4 exf5 50.♔xf5 with a long and arduous struggle for the draw (Kasparov).

44.♔e2

Opens the third rank for a possible rook lift to h3.

44...♔g7 45.♗e1 ♔g6 46.♖a7

The rook on the seventh rank!

46...♗d8 47.♗c3 h4 48.♔d3

48...h3?!

This fits in with Larsen's style, but here too it can be seen that material is the most important element in chess. He will not see the pawn again. Such action is often based on the fact that one can spot a threat by the opponent, but can find no defence to it. White would like to go to a4 with the king and then set his queenside majority in motion. A plan an opponent would not like to witness helplessly.

It was preferable to play 48...f6 49.♔e3 (49.♖a6 ♔f7 (49...fxe5 50.♗xe5 ♗f6 51.b5!? is dangerous for Black)) 49...fxe5 50.♗xe5 ♗f6 51.g3 ♗xe5 52.fxe5 hxg3 53.hxg3. White is better here too, but Black is still alive.

49.gxh3 ♗h4 50.♔e2 ♗d8 51.♔f3 ♗h4 52.♔g2 ♖d8 53.♔f3 ♖c8 54.♔e2 ♗d8

54...f6 is now obviously bad on account of 55.♖e7 fxe5 56.♖xe6+. But the preparatory 54...♗d8 also reveals itself

to be insufficient. What was required was the waiting move 54...♔g7. After 55.♔d3 ♔g6 56.♖b7 ♗d8 57.♗e1 there is no doubting White's advantage, but creating a passed pawn is not so easy as it is in the game.

55.♗e1 f6

The logical carrying out of the black plan weakens the e6-point, which comes back to haunt him some moves later.

56.♔f3 fxe5 57.fxe5 ♖c7 58.♖a8 ♗g5 59.♖g8+ ♔h5 60.h4 ♗h6 61.♖h8 ♔g6 62.h5+ ♔g7 63.♖a8 ♗g5 64.♖a6 ♖c8

Around 20 moves after our starting diagram, the picture appears to have changed only in unimportant details. Almost all the pawns are on the starting squares and there is hardly any change regarding the rooks. But the (extra) white h-pawn is decisive. It ties down Black's pieces and secures an outpost on g6. A white rook would cut a good figure there.

After long positional manoeuvring, the time is ripe for a tactical solution. This is somewhat typical of a game of chess: advantages obtained by good strategy constitute the foundations for tactics which work.

65.b5 cxb5 66.♖xe6 ♗c1 67.♗b4 d4 68.♖g6+ ♔h7 69.♖d6 ♗b2

70.♖d7+ ♔g8 71.e6 ♗c3 72.e7 ♖e8
73.♖d8 ♔f7 74.♖xe8 ♔xe8 75.c6
1-0

*A blitz game or a time trouble duel is like
a boxing match; artistry goes out of the
window, the struggle comes to the fore.*

Bent Larsen

The semi-open file

The diagram shows a weakness of the
d6-pawn which strikes us at once.
An outstanding target for our major
pieces, which here too have the greater
rearspan.

Moreover, the effects of this are not
confined to the pushing forward of
our rooks. The greater manoeuvrability
which goes with the advantage in space
means that a rook can also be employed
horizontally on d3, e.g. on the kingside
or also in the attack on the queenside
pawns. That can be seen in the model
game Shirov-Topalov, Morelia/Linares
2008.

Rooks which are on the defensive on
d7 or d8, on the other hand, do not do
much damage.

Things are somewhat more difficult in
the following example:

Let us restrict our consideration to the
pawn skeleton, which can arise in one
form or another from various openings,
e.g. the Old Indian or the King's Indian
Defence (with a black pawn on g6) –
or even from the Ruy Lopez and the
Scotch, in each case with a white pawn
on c2 instead of c4. White is slightly
better on account of his advantage in
space, but also there are no weaknesses
in the opposing camp.

The pieces in our diagram position
change the situation slightly. By playing
1.♘d5 White occupies the outpost. The
annoyingly placed knight will sooner
or later force Black to play 1... c6, after
which White simply replies 2.♘c3 and
goes on to lay siege with his rooks to
the new target which has arisen on d6.
In an endgame without major pieces
this would be practically meaningless!

Let us quickly deal with Black's attempt
to do without playing ...c7-c6: a rook
move to c8 would be obligatory, but
how do things continue? Even if we
manage to swap off the knight on d5,
we would then have to deal with the
new problem of the backward pawn in
the c-file, which is going to be opened.
White's advantage in no way decides
the game, but in view of its long-lasting
nature and of the lack of counterplay for
Black, it is really unpleasant.

The seventh and eighth ranks

10 Tarrasch Defence
Mikhail Botvinnik
Alexander Alekhine
Netherlands 1938 (7)

1.♘f3 d5 2.d4 ♘f6 3.c4 e6 4.♘c3 c5 5.cxd5 ♘xd5 6.e3 ♘c6 7.♗c4 cxd4 8.exd4 ♗e7 9.0-0 0-0 10.♖e1 b6 11.♘xd5 exd5 12.♗b5 ♗d7 13.♕a4 ♘b8 14.♗f4 ♗xb5 15.♕xb5 a6 16.♕a4 ♗d6 17.♗xd6 ♕xd6 18.♖ac1

White has occupied both open files. Black must resist as quickly as possible. However 19...♘d7 neglects the c6-square, so:

18...♖a7 19.♕c2 ♖e7

The identical distribution of material and the symmetrical pawn structure give us the impression that all is well with the black position. But appearances can be deceptive. An important difference can be found in the activity of the pieces and, linked to that, the possession of the c-file.

20.♖xe7 ♕xe7 21.♕c7 ♕xc7 22.♖xc7 f6

This deprives the white knight of important squares and opens up for his own rook the possibility of putting up some resistance on the seventh rank.

23.♔f1

After the desirable 23.♖b7, the move 23...♖c8 reminds White of the weakness of his back rank, and by taking control of the c-file Black has survived the worst.

23...♖f7 24.♖c8+ ♖f8 25.♖c3

Of course White does not exchange the rooks, which differ so much in value. He is ready to return to c7 as soon as ...♖f7 is no longer possible.

25...g5 26.♘e1 h5

White to move

Evaluate the position and find plans for White.

It is not difficult to see that White has the advantage and can hardly go wrong. Black's options are, on the other hand, limited. Ideas might consist of ...♔g7-g6-f5, ...♔f7-e6 or even ...a6-a5-♘a6, but that hardly changes the evaluation of the position at all.

So what is the most precise way to cash in on the positional advantage? Well done if you thought of the transfer of the knight ♘e1-c2-e3! And the standard manoeuvre of activating the king with ♔f1-e2-d3 is also not bad. But did you also consider 27.h4 ? 27...gxh4 splits up the pawns and the white knight gets into the game via f3. After 27...g4 White will win material with the fork ♘d3-f4. What is left is not moving the g-pawn, but then White can decide whether he fights to clear the e5-square for his knight with 28.hxg5 fxg5 or, as in the game, he continues to play around f4.

27.h4 ♘d7 28.♖c7 ♖f7 29.♘f3 g4 30.♘e1 f5 31.♘d3 f4

The only way to prevent the deadly ♘f4.

32.f3

32.♘b4 would have won a pawn, but the positional advantage obtained after the game continuation is at least as important.

32...gxf3 33.gxf3 a5 34.a4 ♔f8 35.♖c6 ♔e7 36.♔f2 ♖f5

37.b3

Would you also have played that? Don't be over-hasty. Be patient and wait until the opponent makes a mistake – these are virtues which are foreign to many chess players. Our students keep on telling us, 'I must exert some pressure'. What that means, however, is rarely clear. Whenever you see in your mind's eye this word 'must', it should alarm you and encourage you to check your thoughts.

Positions with complete control should first be improved to the maximum before forcing things and transforming the advantage.

A clever man does not make all the
mistakes himself. He gives others a chance.
Winston Spencer Churchill

In our example White is in no hurry. He exploits Black's desperate situation.

37...♔d8 38.♔e2 ♘b8

39.♖g6!

He plays against the opposing minor piece. After the greedy 39.♖xb6? ♔c7 and then ...♘c6, the knight would get into the game on a reasonable square for the first time.

39...♔c7 40.♘e5 ♘a6 41.♖g7+ ♔c8 42.♘c6 ♖f6 43.♘e7+ ♔b8 44.♘xd5 ♖d6 45.♖g5 ♘b4 46.♘xb4

With a transition to an easily won rook ending.

46...axb4 47.♖xh5 ♖c6 48.♖b5 ♔c7 49.♖xb4 ♖h6 50.♖b5 ♖xh4 51.♔d3

Black resigned.

A frustrating defeat for the reigning World Champion Alekhine (1892-1946, World Champion from 1927-35 and 1937-46) against the up-and-coming Mikhail Botvinnik (1911-95, World Champion from 1948-57, 1958-60 and 1961-63).

The importance of the eighth rank is often linked to a direct attack on the opposing king and not infrequently ends in a back-rank mate.

Take half an hour to solve the following exercise:

White to play and win
(Adams-Torre, New Orleans 1920)

There are many rumours surrounding this game. The two friends are supposed to have played it for training purposes, but the tactics are too beautiful and too complex for Edwin Adams to have been thought capable of finding the solution over the board.

Neither side yet has an airhole, so the theme of the back-rank weakness and, linked to it, a diversion of the queen, which is protecting the e8-rook, immediately leaps to the eye. The e-file, on which White has already doubled his rooks, plays the decisive part.

We still have to find out how to start: **1.♕g4** Since the black queen is tied to the rook on e8, all that is left is **1...♕b5 2.♕c4** Once again the queen is taboo. **2...♕d7 3.♕c7** and the diversionary motif works for the third time. **3... ♕b5** 3...♕a4 4.b3 ♕b5 5.a4+−. We could get so far without any risk and − if we could not continue − we could always hit the emergency brakes with the perpetual pursuit of the queen on the g4-, c4- and c7-squares. But our goal is not a draw and even less to lose after 4.♕xb7 ♕xe2 5.♖xe2 ♖c1+ 6.♘e1 ♖xe1+ 7.♖xe1 ♖xe1#. White too does not have an airhole. Painfully confronted with the opposing defensive

idea, we are the ones who have to find a solution. **4.a4** A pawn sacrifice, the idea of which becomes clear on the next move. **4... ♕xa4 5.♖e4! ♕b5** and now, after there is nothing left to take on e2, White wins with **6.♕xb7**.

The unimportant file

Before the opening of a file, it needs to be weighed up which side will get the most from it. If it only means the exchange of the major pieces, perhaps the tempi would be more sensibly employed at some other point. It is, however, especially unpleasant, if at the end the file falls into the hands of our opponent. It is also not worth striving to open a file if there are no entry squares on it.

11 Ruy Lopez
Anatoly Karpov
Ulf Andersson
Stockholm 1969 (3)
1.e4 e5 2.♘f3 ♘c6 3.♗b5 a6 4.♗a4 ♘f6 5.0-0 ♗e7 6.♖e1 b5 7.♗b3 0-0 8.c3 d6 9.h3 ♘a5 10.♗c2 c5 11.d4 ♕c7 12.♘bd2 ♗b7 13.d5 ♗c8 14.♘f1 ♗d7 15.b3 ♘b7 16.c4 ♖fb8 17.♘e3 ♗f8 18.♘f5 ♘d8 19.♘h2 ♘e8 20.h4 f6 21.h5 ♘f7 22.♖e3 ♘g5 23.♘h4 ♕d8 24.♖g3 ♘c7 25.♘2f3 h6 26.♘g6 a5

White to move

Evaluate the position.

The position is of a closed character. There are pawn levers in f2-f4 and the less probable ...f6-f5, as well as a2-a4. One notices especially the two bad bishops on f8 and c2; the light-squared one could possibly, under certain circumstances, and at some point far in the future, be exchanged on g4. There is no salvation in sight for the dark-squared one.

Like in our opening example, we cannot prevent a weakening on the queenside, though here too

27.a4

stops the black plan of opening a further file and thus activating the second rook. The b-file on its own is not really dramatic, since the black rooks do not have any entry squares into the opposing camp.

In what follows Black has no active options available to him, and he must wait and see how the white initiative develops on the kingside. However, Andersson's position is solid and still capable of being defended. White has the advantage since he has a plan available to him. Or in other words: playing without a plan puts you at a disadvantage!

27...bxc4 28.bxc4 ♞a6 29.♕e2 ♜a7 30.♗d2 ♜ab7

An imposing advance of the black rooks, which does not achieve anything! There are no target squares.

31.♗c3 ♞b4

And the knight has no future either.

32.♗d1 ♞a6 33.♞d2 ♞b4 34.♜e3 ♗e8 35.♞f1 ♕c8 36.♞g3

Anatoly Karpov (*1951, World Champion from 1975-85, FIDE World Champion from 1993-99) first prevents any hint of counterplay with the push ...f6-f5.

White's plan is clear: queen and bishop change positions, the knight goes to h2 to enable the exchange of the bishops on g4. Thereafter the newly freed f5-square will be occupied by ♞f1-g3-f5 and finally any of the knights on g5 can be prised off with g2-g3 and f2-f4. If required, the white major pieces can swing over to the kingside at the appropriate moment.

How simple chess is! At least for commentators and some spectators. If you are sitting at the board, everything looks quite different, and a good player (in the ideal case) is only certain at the moment when his opponent resigns!

36...♗d7 37.♕d2 ♞h7 38.♗e2 ♚f7 39.♕d1 ♗e7 40.♞f1 ♗d8 41.♞h2 ♚g8 42.♗g4 ♞g5 43.♗xd7 ♕xd7 44.♞f1

44...f5

Pre-empting the plan which was sketched out, but the white rooks are more mobile after the opening of the position.

45.exf5 ♕xf5 46.♘g3 ♕f7 47.♕e2 ♗f6 48.♖f1 ♕d7 49.f4 exf4 50.♖xf4 ♗xc3 51.♖xc3 ♖e8 52.♖e3 ♖bb8 53.♕f2 ♘h7

After this things come to a speedy end. There was, however, the more tenacious if unpleasant 53...♕xa4 54.♖xe8+ ♕xe8 55.♖f8+ ♕xf8 56.♘xf8 ♖xf8 57.♕e3±.

54.♘f5	**♖xe3**	**55.♕xe3**	**♘f6**
56.♘ge7+	**♔h8**	**57.♘xh6**	**♖e8**
58.♘f7+	**♔h7**	**59.♖e4**	**♖xe7**
60.♖xe7			**1-0**

Supporting the passed pawn

'Rooks belong behind passed pawns – behind one's own as well as behind the opponent's.' This statement by the dogmatic Dr. Siegbert Tarrasch (1862-1934), one of the best players in the world around the turn of the previous century, is still valid today. As the pawn advances, the rearspan – and with it the manoeuvrability – of the rook behind the pawn becomes greater, and that of the other rook smaller.

You will find more on this subject in Part 2 in the chapter 'The passed pawn'.

Model games

Shirov-Topalov (Morelia/Linares 2008)

Kramnik-Naiditsch (Dortmund 2007)

Topalov-Vallejo-Pons (Dos Hermanas 2008)

Aronian-Kramnik (Yerevan 2007)

Kramnik-Svidler (Wijk aan Zee 2005)

Karpov-Unzicker (Nice 1974)

Part II

Basic pawn structures

Chapter 4

Hanging pawns

In ten murders there are fewer mysteries than in a
game of chess.

Sir Arthur Conan Doyle

The isolated pair of pawns c4/d4 (more rarely e4/f4) on semi-open central files are described as 'hanging pawns'.

Particular characteristics

The structure derives its name from the vulnerability of the pawns. They are hanging in the air without support from neighbours, and that makes them vulnerable.

However, they also offer many advantages: White has strong central control, an advantage in space and the permanent threat of advancing one of the pawns. That is precisely where the danger lies: if one of them moves, the other becomes backward. This often brings about a transformation to other basic pawn structures. The advance c4-c5 or d4-d5 leads us on to the territory of the related themes 'passed pawn' and 'backward pawn'.

Plans for White

The advantage in space allows White to post his pieces actively. That means that there is the ever-present threat of a pawn breakthrough by means of c4-c5 or d4-d5. The option of d4-d5 is of particular significance since in addition to the creation of a passed pawn there is also the opening of diagonals in the direction of the black king. So the breakthrough is not infrequently carried out with the sacrifice of the d-pawn.

The dynamism of the central pawns is a clear plus in a position, but nevertheless one which loses significance as the number of pieces decreases. Simplifications which involve the exchange of pieces should be avoided.

Plans for Black

Black, on the other hand, finds himself on the defensive at first. Just like when playing against the isolated pawn, it is advantageous to reduce the opponent's attacking potential by exchanges. Playing on the semi-open files will exert pressure on the central pawns, which require protection. A typical plan consists of transferring the knight from f6 via e8 to d6, from where it puts pressure on the c4-pawn, followed by ...♘f5, with an attack on d4. This can be effectively supported by a dark-squared bishop on g7, or on the f6-square which has been freed. In this way a transition to a structure with an isolated or backward pawn under favourable circumstances can be aimed for.

If Black forces the advance of one of the hanging pawns – possibly by the advance of his own e-, or more rarely b-pawn – the other one immediately becomes weak, as does the square in front of it.

Conclusion

The diagram shows a very unbalanced formation which is not easy to judge. On account of possible transformations, a profound study of the chapters on 'Passed pawns' and 'Backward pawns' is of great advantage in the evaluation of this position. Because of its complexity many players avoid this structure. For someone whose approach to chess is dynamic, they can represent a dangerous weapon.

The breakthrough with d4-d5

12 Nimzo-Indian Defence
Svetozar Gligoric
Paul Keres
Zagreb 1958 (2)

1.d4 ♘f6 2.c4 e6 3.♘c3 ♗b4 4.e3 c5 5.♗d3 b6 6.♘f3 ♗b7 7.0-0 0-0 8.♗d2 cxd4 9.exd4 d5 10.cxd5 ♗xc3 11.bxc3 ♕xd5 12.c4 ♕d6 13.♗c3 ♘bd7 14.♖e1 ♖ac8 15.h3 ♖fd8 16.♖e3 ♘h5?

There is no doubt that the opening went favourably for the top Yugoslavian player. He has central pawns, which would be hard to attack, and also the bishop pair, which is aiming in the direction of the black kingside. The main unbalancing factor, however, consists of the dark-squared bishop, for which Black has no counterpart. Since White will be aiming to activate this in the meanwhile mediocre piece, d4-d5 is constantly an option.

Because of his lack of counterplay Black should here be accepting that he has the worse position and playing a waiting game. It was worth considering 16... h6, or even the transfer of the d7-knight to g6 via f8. The game move betrays the lack of a sense of danger. The tactical motif of the 'unprotected minor piece' forms the basis of White's breakthrough:

17.d5! ♘c5

17...exd5 allows the thematic strike on h7: 18.♗xh7+! ♔xh7 19.♘g5+ ♔g8 (the alternative 19...♔g6 is also unsatisfactory: 20.♘xf7! ♔xf7 21.♕xh5+ ♔g8 (21...♔g6? 22.♖e7+) 22.♗xg7 ♔xg7 23.♖ae1 with deadly threats) 20.♕xh5 ♕g6 21.♕xg6 fxg6 22.♖e7. The c3-bishop which has been set free decides matters: 22...d4 23.♗xd4 ♘f6 24.♗xf6 gxf6 25.♘f7, winning material.

18.♘g5 g6

18...♘xd3? 19.♕xh5 and f7 and h7 are hanging at the same time. With the move in the game Black, of necessity, breaks our rule from Chapter 1, always putting pawns on the squares of the colour of the opposing bishop. He has to pay the bill straight away.

19.♗e2

With the unpleasant threat of bringing the queen to d4.

19...♘g7

19...♘f4? 20.♕d4+−; 19...exd5 20.♕d4 (here it is important to observe the order of moves. The immediate 20.♗xh5 allows 29...d4!) 20...f6 21.♗xh5 gxh5 (and 21...dxc4 is hardly any better: 22.♕xc4+ ♗d5 23.♕d4 gxh5 24.♖g3 with threats which cannot be warded off) 22.♖e6+−.

20.♕d4 ♕f8 21.♕h4 h5 22.♗g4!
The bishops dominate.

22...f5?

22...♘f5? 23.♗xf5! exf5 24.♖ae1 and ♕d4 can no longer be prevented: 24...f6? 25.♘e6 ♘xe6 26.♖xe6+−. A better way was 22...♖e8 23.♖ae1±.

23.♘xe6 ♘gxe6?

With 23...♘cxe6 24.dxe6 Keres could have put up stiffer resistance.

24.dxe6 ♖e8

24...fxg4 25.e7+−.

25.♗xh5! ♕h6

25...gxh5 26.♕g5+ ♔h7 27.♕xh5+ ♕h6 28.♕f7++−; 25...♖xe6 26.♗xg6 ♖xg6 27.♕h8+ ♔f7 28.♕h7+ ♖g7 29.♗xg7 ♕xg7 30.♖e7++−.

26.♕f6 f4 27.♕f7#   **1-0**

Model games for the breakthrough with d5

Reshevsky-Donner (Los Angeles 1963)
Nimzowitsch-Tarrasch (St Petersburg 1914)
Keres-Taimanov (Moscow 1951)

The plan with c5

13 Réti Opening
| **Jörg Hickl** | 2530 |
| **Leif Erlend Johannessen** | 2519 |

Hofheim 2005 (8)

1.g3 d5 2.♘f3 ♘f6 3.c4 e6 4.♗g2 ♗e7 5.b3 0-0 6.♗b2 c5 7.0-0 ♘c6 8.e3 b6 9.♘c3 dxc4 10.bxc4 ♗b7 11.♕e2

11...♘b4?!

Here I felt provoked. What does the steed want from me? The desire to occupy the weakish d3 does not justify putting the knight on a square from which it doesn't achieve much. My internal chess adviser kicked in and demanded the punishment of this strange move.

Basically, as optimism rises and at the latest when the state of euphoria has been reached, every chess player should hear the alarm bells ringing.

But even grandmasters do not always have this faculty. Here I remembered a poem from my schooldays: 'Das Büblein auf dem Eise' ('The little boy on the ice') by Friedrich Güll. Without having read it you can certainly imagine how things turn out: as a chess player, one has fallen through thin ice too often. Fortunately the danger was not too great here; so off we go into a pawn structure I had mostly avoided on account of ignorance on my part! Later I learned that Kramnik had continued with 11...♘b4, but that did not make me like the move any more.

12.d4!

The knight moves to e1 or e5 prevent ♘d3 and the hanging pawns, but they lead to an exchange of pieces and hardly offer White any prospects of an advantage.

12...cxd4 13.exd4

Here we have our hanging pawns on c4 and d4, with all their advantages and disadvantages!

13...♖c8 14.♖fd1 ♖e8

14...♕c7 15.a3 ♘a6 16.d5 exd5 17.cxd5 ♖fe8 18.♕f1 ♕b8 19.♘d4 ♘c5 20.♘c6 with advantage to White in Kharitonov-Dvoirys, Hoogeveen 2000.

15.♖ac1

15.a3 ♘c6 16.♘e5 ♕c7 17.♘b5 ♕b8 and once again we come to the pawn breakthrough 18.d5 with a slight advantage for White.

15...♗f8 16.a3 ♘c6 17.♘e5 ♕c7 18.♘b5

Pursuing a strategically dubious idea, but here it has a concrete justification. Of course the exchange on c6 cannot be in White's interest. After 18.♘xc6 ♗xc6 19.♘e4 ♘xe4 20.♗xe4 ♗xe4 21.♕xe4 ♕c6 Black already had a comfortable game in Bogza-Meijers, La Fère 2004. Prospects for an attack by White have disappeared. The pawns are starting to become weak.

18...♕b8 19.c5!?

This continues logically the idea begun on move 18. White obtains the initiative, but to a certain extent he burns his bridges. Should this temporary advantage evaporate, then he can be left with the bad bishop on b2. If 19.♘xc6 ♗xc6 20.♗xc6 ♖xc6 21.♕f3 ♖cc8 22.d5 e5=.

19...♘d5?

A better move was 19...♘xe5! 20.dxe5 ♗xg2 (20...♘d5 21.♘d6 ♗xd6 22.cxd6±) 21.♔xg2 ♘d5 (21...♕b7+ 22.♔g1 ♘d5 23.♘d6 ♗xd6 24.cxd6) 22.♘d6 ♗xd6 23.cxd6 ♕b7 24.♔g1 with a slight advantage to White: a mighty passed pawn on d6, but a bad bishop on b2 against a knight on d5 which cannot be driven away.

20.♘d7 ♕a8 21.♕g4 ♖cd8 22.♘xf8 ♖xf8 23.♘d6 ♘a5 24.♘xb7 ♕xb7

White to move

How should White continue?

The position has taken on fixed contours. 19.c5 has led to a backward pawn. This, however, is more than compensated for due to White's superiority in space and the strong bishop on g2, which fits in perfectly with the central structure. The bishop pair plays a secondary role. In any case, having the two bishops is an element in chess which is often over-estimated. As is the case in the present example, usually one of the two is not particularly good.

The central pawns are effectively blockaded. As for the rooks, at first sight we can think of no better options for deploying them. However, one of our pieces is standing inactive in the corner. After joining up these individual parts of the puzzle, it should be easier to form a plan for the future: the dark-squared bishop must be activated! As a target, square d6 catches the eye. Of course we have no need to fear its being swapped along the way for the d5-knight, the pride of the black position.

25.♗c3! ♘c6

25...♘c4? 26.♗b4+−.

26.♗d2 ♔h8 27.♗f4 ♖fe8

27...♘xf4 28.♕xf4±.

28.♗d6±

White has active play for his pieces and considerable chances on the kingside. Both players now slowly drifted into serious time trouble. Although there was still an exciting finish for the spectators, at many points the quality of play left a lot to be desired.

Even though it makes sense to make maximal use of your thinking time, you should take strict care to avoid any extreme shortness of time. Otherwise the door is left wide open to chance!

28...♘ce7 29.♕h5 ♔g8 30.♗e4 h6

30...g6 31.♕f3±.

31.g4 f6 32.♖e1?!

32.h4!.

32...♕d7 33.h4 bxc5

33...e5 34.g5.

34.dxc5 e5 35.g5 ♘f4 36.♕f3 hxg5 37.hxg5

37...♘f5?

37...♘h3+ 38.♔h2 ♘xg5 39.♕b3+ ♔f8 (39...♔h8 40.♖h1=) 40.♗g2=.

38.gxf6 ♘d4 39.♗d5+ ♔h8?

39...♘xd5 40.♕xd5+ ♕f7 41.♕e4 ♕xf6 (41...gxf6 42.♖e3+−) 42.♖c3±.

40.♕h1+ ♘h3+

40...♕h3 41.♕xh3+ ♘xh3+ 42.♔h2 ♘f4 43.♖xe5 ♖xe5 44.fxg7++−.

41.♔f1 ♕f5 42.fxg7+

42.♕h2 gxf6 (42...♕d3+ 43.♔g2+−) 43.♖e3+−.

42...♔xg7 43.♕g2+ ♔f6 44.♗e4

44.♕g3+−.

44...♕h5 45.♕h2 ♖g8 46.♗g2 ♖xd6 47.cxd6 ♖xg2 48.♕xg2 ♘f4 49.d7 ♘de6 50.♖c6 ♔f7

50...♘xg2 51.d8♕++−.

51.d8♕ ♘xd8 52.♖c7+ ♔e6 53.♕g8+ ♘f7 54.♕xf7+

The simplest way to the win. 54.♕e8+ ♔f6 55.♕e7+ ♔g7 56.♕xe5+ may well be more precise, but *as far as possible, avoid complicated tactical variations! The risk of overlooking something is too great. Be aware that the inner desire to impress the spectators around your board or to become immortal, can lead to disaster! Come back to earth and your Elo rating will thank you for it!*

54...♕xf7 55.♖xf7 ♔xf7 56.♖xe5

Black resigned.

14 Queen's Gambit Declined
Osip Bernstein
José Raul Capablanca
Moscow 1914

A model game which is often quoted, but unfortunately not an error-free example. Chess literature often looks back to the games of former masters, but without checking them properly. It is not always a demonstration which suits the subject, but often too great a difference in playing strength plays the decisive role. That is the case in the present example. Nevertheless, we would not like to deprive you of it, above all on account of its beautiful finish.

1.d4 d5 2.c4 e6 3.♘c3 ♘f6 4.♘f3 ♗e7 5.♗g5 0-0 6.e3 ♘bd7 7.♖c1 b6 8.cxd5 exd5 9.♕a4 ♗b7 10.♗a6 ♗xa6 11.♕xa6 c5

12.♗xf6

White unnecessarily exchanges his bishop. Even if both minor pieces are of more or less equal value, advanced players tend to prefer the bishops. They might turn out to be superior to the knights in a future stage of the game which cannot yet be foreseen, for example in the endgame. But also, even if one is not a fan of the bishops this exchange seems unnecessary. Because of the weakness of d5 the knight on f6 was going nowhere. The natural move is of course to castle kingside, with a slight advantage.

12...♘xf6 13.dxc5?!

White deliberately brings about the hanging pawns, but this turns out to be unfavourable.

13...bxc5 14.0-0 ♕b6 15.♕e2

The position has changed. After somewhat the worse opening, Black now has control in the centre and active play for his pieces.

It was now possible to play on with his superiority in space and not to force matters, e.g. bring the queen to the central e6-square and complete the development of his rooks.

15...c4?!

The continuation chosen by Capablanca leads to a backward pawn and allows the opponent to equalise comfortably: 16.e4 dxe4 (but 16...d4 is worse: 17.♘d5 ♘xd5 18.exd5 ♗f6 19.♕xc4 ♕xb2 20.d6 with advantage to White) 17.♘xe4 ♘xe4 18.♕xe4 ♗f6 19.♕xc4 ♗xb2 20.♖c2.

But White defends passively and quickly finds himself in a threatening situation.

16.♖fd1 ♖fd8 17.♘d4 ♗b4 18.b3 ♖ac8 19.bxc4 dxc4 20.♖c2 ♗xc3 21.♖xc3 ♘d5 22.♖c2 c3

A passed pawn which almost inspires fear, but which is under control. The powerful knight on d4 still holds everything together. In what follows, however, White neglects to make an airhole for the king and later perishes because of the weakness of the back rank.

23.♖dc1 ♖c5 24.♘b3 ♖c6 25.♘d4 ♖c7 26.♘b5?!

This is the introduction to a tactical blunder. After the simple 26.h3 White is still in the game.

26...♖c5 27.♘xc3??

And even here it was possible to play on with 27.♘d4. The move in the game loses immediately.

27...♘xc3 28.♖xc3 ♖xc3 29.♖xc3

Black to move

Bernstein had probably only counted on 29...♕b1+, since after 30.♕f1 Black cannot play 30...♖d1, as he also has a back-rank problem.

But what followed was the surprising deflectionary move

29...♕b2

And White resigned.

Only after the forced 30.♖c2 does Black play 30...♕b1+, which wins the rook after 31.♕f1.

Model game for the plan with ...c7-c5

Bertok-Fischer (Stockholm 1962)

The weakness of hanging pawns

15 Queen's Gambit Declined
Garry Kasparov 2740
Lajos Portisch 2605
Brussels 1986 (5)

Garry Kasparov (*1963, World Champion from 1985-2000) dominated the world of chess for two decades, from 1985 to his surprising withdrawal from the tournament scene in 2005.

It is impressive to see the ease with which he gets an advantage over a world-class Hungarian grandmaster in the following game and how he then converts it to the full point.

His opponent, Lajos Portisch (*1937), can also point to a unique career on the chess scene. Between 1958 and 2000 he represented his country in 20 chess olympiads and qualified seven times for the Candidates' tournament for the World Championship.

Chess is a lifelong passion!

1.d4 ♘f6 2.c4 e6 3.♘f3 d5 4.♘c3 ♗e7 5.♗g5 0-0 6.e3 ♘bd7 7.♕c2 h6 8.cxd5 exd5 9.♗f4 c5 10.♗e2 b6 11.0-0 ♗b7 12.♖fd1 ♖c8 13.dxc5 bxc5

With his last move Kasparov brought about a structure with hanging pawns.

57

White to move

Evaluate the position and consider as many sensible candidate moves as possible.

Tip: *also take into account ideas for Black.*

Black seems developed and d5 appears well defended. Only the knight on d7 and the rook on f8 are not yet fully involved in the struggle and could be put on better squares. A possible move is 14...♘b6 and then ...♕d7 and ...♖fd8. But first of all it is up to White to come up with an idea. For the moment it is apparently not worth considering using a lever against the hanging pawns with b2-b4 or e3-e4. The standard manoeuvre ♘f3-e1-d3 looks slightly strange, since the target square f4 is also still blocked by the bishop. The vis-à-vis of queen and rook in the c-file could make possible tactical operations with ...d5-d4. Doubling rooks on the d-file does not substantially increase the pressure against d5.

So the options appear to be limited to the minor pieces. Where would our knights be well placed and where are the weaknesses in the opposing camp? The advance of the black h-pawn 8...h6 has weakened the light squares g6 and f5. Hans Kmoch describes the formation g7/h6 in his *Pawn Power in Chess* as a 'staircase'. A knight on f5 would be almost impossible to drive away. It puts pressure

on the rear step of the staircase, which cannot be moved since the front one would be hanging. But the target square does not appear to be reachable: the candidate move 14.♘h4 unfortunately fails to the pawn fork 14...g5. However, the preparatory 14.♗g3 is possible.

14.♘b5 is also worth considering. The knight is threatening both to take on a7 and also to invade on d6. But after the logical 14...a6 15.♘d6 ♗xd6 16.♗xd6 ♖e8 there is no sign of any further advantage for White. The pawn sacrifice 14...♘h5 was also possible. After 15.♘xa7 (15.♗e5 ♕b6=) 15...♘xf4 16.exf4 ♖a8 17.♘b5 ♕b6 Black has considerable positional compensation with his powerful centre in conjunction with his active pieces

In this complex situation Kasparov comes up with a surprising and creative continuation.

Superficially,

14.a4!?

is aimed only against the move ...♘b6 by Black and voluntarily makes the b-pawn backward. One can understand that Portisch stops it advancing further.

14...♕a5

But now the hidden idea becomes visible: the ♗e7 has lost its protection, which makes possible:

15.♘h4 ♖fd8 16.♘f5 ♗f8 17.♘b5 ♘e8

18.♗d6!

Threatening 18.♘e7+, winning the exchange, for which reason Portisch is obliged to let a knight on to d6.

18...♘xd6 19.♘fxd6 ♖b8 20.♘xb7 ♖xb7

White's advantage manifests itself in the winning of a pawn and the better bishop.

21.♖xd5 ♖db8 22.♕d2 ♕xd2 23.♖xd2 ♘f6

24.♖a2?!

The knight should be transferred to c4. Kasparov would not like to allow any counterplay and even temporarily concedes the d-file. Also worth considering was 24.♗f3.

24...♘e4 25.♖c2 ♖d7 26.g3 a5 27.♔g2 g6 28.♗f3 ♘f6 29.♘a3

At last the knight can be set in motion. The first goal is the ideal blockading square c4. From there it protects b2 and attacks a5. The Hungarian is working against that.

29...♗d6 30.♗c6 ♖dd8 31.♖a1 ♗e5 32.♗b5 ♘d5 33.♖b1 ♗d6 34.♖d2 ♘b6

After Black has accepted a less favourable position for his knight in order to make ♘c4 impossible, White changes direction. From b3, his knight will attack two weak pawns. As White's knight is stronger than Black's, of course White does not exchange it on c4.

35.♖c1 ♗e7 36.♖e2

The white rook is the better one and avoids the exchange.

36...♖bc8 37.♘b1 ♔g7 38.♘d2 ♖a8 39.♘b3 ♖dc8 40.♖ec2 c4 41.♘d2 ♖a7 42.♘xc4 ♘xc4 43.♖xc4 ♖xc4 44.♖xc4 f5

White is two pawns up, but the queenside majority is devalued and the bishops of opposite colours constitute a high risk of a draw. Basically they favour the attacking side. However, should the rooks disappear, Black can justifiably cherish some hopes.

45.h3

White creates a passed e-pawn.

45...h5 46.g4 hxg4 47.hxg4 fxg4 48.♔g3 ♗d6+ 49.♔xg4 ♖c7 50.♗c6 ♖f7 51.f4

Kasparov took a long time thinking about this committal move. With the block f2/e3 intact, there were no targets for the black bishop.

51...♔h6 52.♗d5 ♖f6 53.♖c1 ♔g7 54.b3

Don't be too hasty, White is not in a hurry.

54...♖f8 55.♖d1 ♗c5 56.♖d3 ♗a3 57.♗c4 ♗c1

Basically, this is the ideal diagonal for the bishop. The pawns are attacked from behind, 58.e4 is not possible. But if the f-pawn moves, it can come down to a blockade on the dark squares.

However, White's advantage is already too great.

58.♖d7+ ♔h6 59.♖e7 ♗d2 60.♔f3 ♗b4 61.♖b7 ♗c3 62.♗d3 ♖f6 63.♔g4 ♗d2 64.f5   1-0

Did you consider that 14.a4 was not obvious and wonder how you could ever come up with such a solid idea? Then you are certainly in good company, in that of many clearly more highly-rated players. BUT:

Chess players live on what they have experienced. What they have once experienced and suffered widens their horizons and makes them stronger. For that the study of numerous grandmaster games and your own games is absolutely indispensable.

Nor did Kasparov himself pull the move out of his hat by magic. Two years previously, on the occasion of the World Championship match in Moscow, there had been the following encounter:

16 Queen's Indian Defence
Garry Kasparov   2715
Anatoly Karpov   2705
Moscow 1984 (14)

1.d4 ♘f6 2.c4 e6 3.♘f3 b6 4.g3 ♗a6 5.b3 ♗b4+ 6.♗d2 ♗e7 7.♗g2 0-0 8.0-0 d5 9.cxd5 ♘xd5 10.♘c3 ♘d7 11.♘xd5 exd5 12.♖c1 c5 13.dxc5 bxc5 14.♘e1 ♘b6

White to move

What do you think of the knight on b6?
Guess how Kasparov continued here!

Of course he continued with the move we know:

15.a4

Only, one move later, after

15...♖c8 16.a5

he offered a draw (which was accepted). Why Kasparov offered the draw will probably remain a mystery, but in the final position Black has already equalised in any case. The badly posted knight was driven on to better squares. Via a8, c7 and possible e6 it finds its way back into play. White's weakened queenside structure is of a permanent nature.

17 Queen's Gambit Declined
Viktor Kortchnoi   2660
Efim Geller   2630
Moscow 1971 (5)

1.d4 d5 2.c4 e6 3.♘c3 ♗e7 4.♘f3 ♘f6 5.♗g5 0-0 6.e3 h6 7.♗h4 b6 8.♗e2 ♗b7 9.♗xf6 ♗xf6 10.cxd5 exd5 11.0-0 ♕e7 12.♕b3 ♖d8 13.♖ad1 c5 14.dxc5 ♗xc3 15.♕xc3 bxc5

A type of position which has already been tested hundreds of times in practice. Neither of the sides has so far managed to demonstrate an advantage.

16.♖c1 ♘d7 17.♖c2 ♖ab8 18.b3 ♕e6 19.♖d1 ♕b6 20.♘e1

This introduces a typical manoeuvre in the struggle against hanging pawns. The knight on f3 and also the bishop on e2 (in fianchetto systems the g2-bishop) are nicely placed, but are not contributing much to the position. On its way to the target square f4, from d3 the knight has in addition an influence over c5. The light-squared bishop exerts pressure on d5 or, as in the following example, becomes active on the h3-c8 diagonal. Things are still okay for Black, but in what follows Geller cannot find a clear line. Kortchnoi prevents any pawn breakthroughs and slowly begins to attack the centre.

20...♖bc8 21.♗g4 ♕g6?!

Black was probably dreaming of unmasking the bishop with ...d5-d4 and giving mate on g2. But, as the game shows, the queen has no place on the kingside. It was stronger to unpin immediately with 21...♖c7.

22.♗h3 ♖c7?!

It was not too late to admit the mistake and ruefully return to the queenside. But who can manage that? For example, 22...♕b6 23.♘d3 could have been played. Then the pawn duo can no longer be stopped, but after 23...c4 24.bxc4 ♖xc4 25.♕b2 ♕c7 Black has almost complete equality thanks to

the outpost on c4, which is typical of isolani positions.

23.♘d3

23...♘f6?

The possession of the centre is always a major commitment. The opponent will try everything possible to destroy it. With our shaky structure something will soon be overlooked. The knight move blocks the route to the queenside for its own queen, and in view of the unprotected position of the rook on c7 Black loses the c5-pawn. Even after the better 23...c4 24.♘f4 ♕e4 25.♖cc1 White retains a lasting positional advantage. The undesirable transition to a position with a weak pawn on d5 has taken place.

But, as is so often the case: having a weak pawn is better than being a pawn down. Material is the most important thing in chess!

24.♕a5   ♘e8   25.♖xc5   ♖xc5
26.♕xc5   1-0

Model games

Fischer-Spassky (Reykjavik 1972)
Hickl-Sokolov (Switzerland tt 2007), transformation of the hanging pawns into an isolated queen's pawn structure
Brynell-Spraggett (Tarragona 2006)
Georgiev-Grooten (Gibraltar 2007)

Chapter 5

Isolated pawns

*I pity anyone who does not know the game of chess. It
already brings pleasure to the student, and the heights of
enjoyment to the connoisseur.*

Lev Nikolaievich Count Tolstoy

'Isolani? That is a pawn weakness which one should avoid if possible!' This point
of view is widespread amongst club players and sometimes even met with in
experienced tournament players. But chess is not as simple as that.

An isolated pawn no longer has neighbours. It can occur in all areas of the board.
But the term 'isolani' is usually applied to a white pawn on d4 or a black one on
d5 – the 'isolated queen's pawn'. This can arise from numerous openings and thus
happens frequently in practice.

In this connection an extremely important topic is 'free play for the pieces versus
pawn weakness', to the study of which the examples with isolated queen pawn
positions lend themselves very well. But what you learn there about the initiative
and about attack and defence on the kingside is also applicable to many other types
of position.

In this chapter we shall consider the three most important positions with an
isolated queen's pawn (IQP).

In the first, IQP (I), there is a black pawn on e6, which makes the timely
development of the latter's queen's bishop harder.

In IQP (II) Black has instead a pawn on c6 or c7. The queen's bishop can easily
be brought into play on the c8-g4 diagonal.

Finally, IQP (III) deals with Black's bishop fianchetto with ...g7-g6.

IQP (I)

Specific characteristics

The white queen's pawn is separated from the remaining pawns. It is not protected by a neighbour and is thus a welcome target for the black pieces. The square in front of it, d5, cannot be controlled by white pawns. It serves as an active outpost for opposing blockading pieces. As compensation for this weakness White obtains an advantage in space on the kingside and the central outposts e5 and e4 for his pieces.

The e6-pawn somewhat cramps the black position. The queen's bishop cannot be developed on the c8-h3 diagonal. If it is fianchettoed, however, the e6-point loses its support, so that attacking motifs such as ♘f3-e5xf7 and then ♗ or ♕xe6 come into consideration. In any case Black requires several moves to develop the bishop. This means that White as a rule obtains a lead in development. In addition, the pawn on e6 gets in the way of a transfer of the black pieces to the kingside.

Plans for White

White disposes of perfect squares for the development of his minor pieces. ♘c3 and ♘f3 are obligatory; according to the situation the king's bishop will be actively developed to c4 or d3 and the queen's bishop to g5 or f4. White tries to exert pressure on the d5-square (♗c4). Alternatively, there might be an attack on the kingside, frequently with the queen-bishop battery ♕d3-♗c2 in conjunction with ♗g5 or even with the manoeuvre ♘e5 and then ♕f3(d3)-h3. We will go into this later in the game Smyslov-Karpov.

Sample game: Smyslov-Karpov, Leningrad 1971

White usually does without creating an airhole with h2-h3 or g2-g3, so as to be able to bring the major pieces into position on the third rank for an attack against the black kingside.

A frequently recurring motif is the advance of the IQP, often involving a pawn sacrifice:

Sample game: Kramnik-Anand, Dos Hermanas 1999

With the help of 13.d5 the pieces develop their full effect. At the same time the coordination of the black forces is disrupted. Later we will analyse the problems which result from this.

Plans for Black

As so often in cramped positions, one main idea involves simplifications: by exchanging minor pieces, the opposing attacking potential and the influence exerted over the square in front of the pawn are reduced. The major pieces exert pressure on the IQP. An optimal set-up can be seen in the following diagram:

Model game: Kortchnoi-Karpov, Meran m(9) 1981

The black queen's pawn is besieged by the major pieces, whereas the white pieces are tied to its defence and passive. Nevertheless, in pure minor piece endgames an IQP represents a static weakness. As soon as White's attacking chances have been neutralised, Black can make use of the d5-square for manoeuvring and attempts to invade the white position. The game Flohr-Capablanca demonstrates a typical ideal endgame:

Model game: Flohr-Capablanca, Moscow 1935

The black queen's bishop is weak, since the d-pawn is being blockaded on the square of the same colour as its bishop. On the other hand, the knight on d4 cannot be driven away and is dominant. White can also occupy the square with the king.

Endgame theoreticians have found out through extensive analyses that the position can be held. The defence is, however, complicated and protracted. What is important for it is to optimise the coordination between the queenside pawns and the bishop by means of ...♗d7, ...b7-b6 and ...a6-a5, so that the IQP remains the only weakness. In the model game it was only with great difficulties that Capablanca reached the safe haven of a draw.

Conclusion

The IQP structure enables a rapid and active development of the pieces – White obtains prospects of an attack. However, if Black manages to neutralise the opposing initiative, without simplifying the pawn structure, there are prospects of a lasting positional advantage.

The astonishing logic and the mathematical precision place the game of chess on the same level as any exact science, whereas the beauty and vividness of expression linked with artistic fantasy allow it to be classified on the same footing as the other arts.

Gottfried Wilhelm Leibniz

The plan with d4-d5

18 Queen's Gambit Declined
Vassily Smyslov 2620
Anatoly Karpov 2540
Leningrad 1971 (6)
**1.c4 c5 2.♘f3 ♘f6 3.♘c3 d5 4.cxd5
♘xd5 5.e3 e6 6.d4 cxd4 7.exd4
♗e7 8.♗d3 0-0 9.0-0 ♘c6 10.♖e1
♘f6 11.a3 b6 12.♗c2 ♗b7 13.♕d3
♖c8?**

Black ignores a major threat in IQP positions. No matter how gifted a player is in positional play, overlooking tactics can nullify this – and this can happen to anybody! Karpov was considered the world's best connoisseur of this type of position. He frequently put fans of the IQP in their place by patiently neutralising the opposing initiative and then cashing in on a tiny advantage in the later part of the game. In the section IQP (III) we shall be looking more closely at how he outplayed Garry Kasparov in an endgame which has become famous. It consoles us to see how even such a connoisseur can commit a clear mistake in variations which were meat and drink to him.

14.♗g5?

And ex-World Champion Vassily Smyslov (1921-2010, World Champion 1957-58), known for his extremely harmonious playing style, fails to take the chance being offered him! In the Candidates' tournament of 1983, Smyslov, at an advanced age, won two IQP games against the world-class Hungarian player Zoltan Ribli with energetic attacking play (see model games). But here he misses an opportunity to turn the game in his favour with a sharp attack: 14.d5! ♘a5 15.♗g5 ♖xc3 (15...g6 16.dxe6 ♕xd3 17.♗xd3 ♗xf3 18.gxf3 ♘b3 19.♖ad1± or 16.d6±) 16.♕xc3 ♕xd5 17.♖ac1±.
After 14...exd5 White also retains an advantage: 15.♗g5 ♘e4 (15...g6 16.♖xe7) 16.♘xe4 dxe4 17.♕xe4 g6 18.♗xe7 ♕xe7 19.♕xe7 ♘xe7 20.♖xe7 ♗xf3 21.♗b3±.

14...g6 15.♖ad1 ♘d5 16.♗h6 ♖e8

There is no real way to achieve anything on the kingside. Smyslov, however, exploits the greater activity of his pieces, eliminates the blockade and thus creates the pre-conditions for the advance of the IQP.

**17.♗a4 a6 18.♘xd5 ♕xd5 19.♕e3
♗f6 20.♗b3**

Controlling the important blockading square.

20...♕h5?

He neglects his weak back rank. The correct way was 20...♕d7 21.d5 exd5 22.♕xb6±.

21.d5!

The pawn cannot be taken because of the back-rank mate. Thus the weak IQP turns into a strong passed pawn.

21...♘d8 22.d6

Here it massively disrupts the coordination of the black pieces. Karpov can no longer defend the position.

22...♖c5

On b8, c8 or a8 the rook would be ineffectual. Now, however, the eighth rank loses its final protection with the result that the penetration by the white queen is decisive.

23.d7 ♖e7 24.♕f4 ♗g7

24...♗xf3 25.♕xf6 ♕xh6 26.♕xe7 ♕g5 27.♕xg5 ♖xg5 28.♖d3 ♖xg2+ 29.♔f1 ♗b7 30.♗d5 ♗xd5 31.♖xd5 ♖xh2 32.♖d6+–.

25.♕b8	**♕xh6**	**26.♕xd8+**	**♗f8**
27.♖e3	**♗c6**	**28.♕xf8+**	**♕xf8**
29.d8♕			**1-0**

Four years later, recently crowned World Champion Karpov committed the same error:

19 Nimzo-Indian Defence

Lajos Portisch	2635
Anatoly Karpov	2705

Milan 1975 (5)

1.c4 ♘f6 2.♘c3 e6 3.d4 ♗b4 4.e3 c5 5.♗d3 0-0 6.♘f3 d5 7.0-0 cxd4 8.exd4 dxc4 9.♗xc4 b6 10.♖e1

♗b7 11.♗d3 ♘c6 12.a3 ♗e7 13.♗c2 ♖e8 14.♕d3

The situation is reminiscent of the game against Smyslov.

14...♖c8? 15.d5 exd5 16.♗g5 ♘e4 17.♘xe4 dxe4 18.♕xe4 g6 19.♕h4

With a strong attack for White. Karpov miraculously (or was it the tenaciousness that is the hallmark of a good player?) escaped with a draw.

And since we are discussing the fallibility of one of the greatest players of all time, there is another short example we would not like you to miss:

20 Queen's Indian Defence

Larry Christiansen	2620
Anatoly Karpov	2725

Wijk aan Zee 1993 (2)

1.d4 ♘f6 2.c4 e6 3.♘f3 b6 4.a3 ♗a6 5.♕c2 ♗b7 6.♘c3 c5 7.e4 cxd4 8.♘xd4 ♘c6 9.♘xc6 ♗xc6 10.♗f4 ♘h5 11.♗e3 ♗d6??

Black's last move represented an 'innovation', based on a solid positional foundation. Black is playing against the bad white bishop on f1 and planning 12...♕f6 and then ...♗e5 or ...♗f4 and possibly even ...g7-g5, with control of the dark squares. However, this deep strategic thought disregarded the laws of tactics.

Any unprotected piece constitutes a combinatory motif!

When there are two of them things get tight. Where is the intersection point?

12.♕d1   **1-0**

Unlike our pawns the queen can also move backwards!

21 Queen's Gambit Accepted
Vladimir Kramnik   2751
Viswanathan Anand   2781

Dos Hermanas 1999 (3)

1.d4 d5 2.c4 dxc4 3.♘f3 e6 4.e3 ♘f6 5.♗xc4 c5 6.0-0 a6 7.♗b3 cxd4 8.exd4 ♘c6 9.♘c3 ♗e7 10.♖e1 0-0 11.a3 ♘a5 12.♗c2 b5

Black has – temporarily – badly positioned his knight on a5 in order to activate his queen's bishop on the a8-h1 diagonal. Is it really only temporary? He certainly intended to renew the coordination between his pieces within the next few moves. But, as so often happens, he did not manage to do so: White exploits the bad coordination between the black pieces for a direct attack on the kingside.

13.d5

13.♕d3 ♗b7 14.♗g5 g6 15.♗h6 ♖e8 16.♘e5 was an alternative.

13...♖e8

But 13...exd5 is followed by 14.♕d3 with good attacking prospects for White. Taking with the knight, on the other hand, is problematic: 13...♘xd5?! 14.♘xd5 exd5 15.♕d3. Now White's initiative swells into a violent attack. Black has to reply to every white threat with a move which is either passive or weakening. He does not manage to bring into play those pieces which are stranded on the queenside. For example: 15...g6 16.♗h6 ♖e8 17.♕c3 f6 18.♘h4 with a strong attack. The build-up of material in front of the black king looks worrying.

14.♗g5 h6

14...♘xd5 is risky: 15.♘xd5 ♗xg5 16.♘xg5 ♕xg5 17.♕d3 f5 (17...g6 18.♕c3 ♕xd5 19.♗e4±) 18.♘c7 ♖d8 19.♕f3 ♖a7 20.♘xe6 ♗xe6 21.♖xe6±. White has brought about a serious weakening of Black's kingside.

15.♗h4 ♘xd5

15...♘c4 16.♘d4, intending 17.♘c6.

16.♘xd5 exd5 17.♕d3 g6 18.♕e3 ♗e6 19.♕xh6 ♗xh4

Since the advance in the centre Kramnik has created serious threats with almost every move, whilst all that Anand could do was react to them. White has recovered the sacrificed pawn, Black, on the other hand, has been able to develop his queen's bishop solidly to e6. He is now just on the point of bringing his pieces on the queenside into the game. Kramnik, however, can obtain an advantage with some energetic play.

20.♗xg6! ♕f6 21.♗h7+ ♔h8 22.♗g6+ ♔g8 23.♕h7+ ♔f8 24.♘xh4 ♕g7

Kramnik gives this move a question mark and prefers 24...♕xb2 25.♗d3 ♕g7 26.♕h5 ♘c4!. After 27.♘f3, however, the exposed black king position is hard to defend.

25.♕xg7+ ♔xg7 26.♗d3±

White has won a pawn. But in the meantime the black pieces have become active, which makes it hard to achieve the win.

26...♘c4 27.b4 ♘b2 28.♗f1 d4 29.♘f3 ♖ad8 30.♖eb1 ♘c4 31.♖d1 ♗g4 32.♖d3!

32.♖xd4 ♗xf3 33.♖xd8 ♖xd8 34.gxf3 ♘d2 'with good chances of a draw' (Kramnik).

32...♘b2 33.♖xd4 ♗xf3 34.♖xd8 ♖xd8 35.gxf3

Unlike in the variation after 32.♖xd4 Black does not here have the resource 35...♘d2.

35...♖c8 36.♖a2 ♘a4 37.♖d2 ♖c6 38.f4 ♘b6 39.♔g2 ♘c4 40.♖d3 ♘b2 41.♖g3+ ♔h8 42.♗e2 ♖c2 43.♗h5 ♖c7 44.f5?

44.♔f3 was indicated. The activity of the king is a significant factor in endgames!

44...♔h7 45.♗e2 ♔h6 46.h4 ♖c2 47.♗f3 ♘c4 48.♗d5 ♘d6 49.♖d3 ♔g7 50.♗f3 ♘xf5 51.♗b7 ♘xh4+ 52.♔g1 ♖e2 53.♗xa6 ♖e5 54.♖c3 ♘f5 55.♖c5 ♖xc5 56.bxc5 ♘d4 57.c6 ♘xc6 58.♗xb5 ♘a5 59.♔g2 ♔f6 60.♔f3 ♔e5 61.♔e3 ♘b7 62.♗c4 f6 63.a4 ♘a5 64.♗f7 ♘c6 65.♔d3 ♔d6 66.♔e4 ♘e7 67.a5 ♔c5 68.a6 ♘c8 69.♗h5 ♔d6 70.♗f3 1-0

The advance d4-d5 – at a moment when the black pieces were not cooperating well – gave Kramnik a dangerous attack on the kingside.

Attacking the king

22 Caro-Kann Defence
Borki Predojevic 2609
Boris Golubovic 2441
Vogosca 2007 (9)

1.e4 c6 2.d4 d5 3.exd5 cxd5 4.c4 ♘f6 5.♘c3 e6 6.cxd5 ♘xd5 7.♘f3 ♗b4 8.♗d2 ♘c6 9.♗d3 0-0 10.0-0 ♘f6 11.♗g5 h6

Golubovic would perhaps have done better to prepare the desired exchange of the white queen's bishop with 11...♗e7.

The inconspicuous move 11...h6 has a similar provocative effect on the attacking side in IQP positions as has waving a red rag to a bull. Black does do everything right: he creates an airhole for his king – with tempo – and prepares the exchange of the dark-squared bishop. After ♗g5-h4, ...♗b4-e7 and ...♘h5 the white one can no longer escape.

Simplifying is a good plan for Black, but the other side of the coin is that at the same time there is a weakening of the position of the king; this is a frequently recurring motif. Golubovic does exchange the bishop, but Predojevic goes on to show that White has other ways of achieving his goal.

12.♗h4 ♗e7 13.♖e1 ♘h5?!

Black remains true to his plan. However, there was the more prudent 13...b6 14.a3 ♗b7, in order to further his development.

14.♗xe7 ♘xe7 15.♘e5 ♘f6 16.♖e3 ♗d7

Black has lost a lot of time with his elaborate exchanging operation: his whole queenside is still not involved.

17.♕d2!

Threatening ♖e3-g3 and then ♕xh6.

17...♘f5

After 17...♗c6 there follows 18.♖ae1! ♕b6 19.♖g3 ♔h8 20.♖h3 ♔g8.

analysis diagram: position after 20...♔g8
White to move

How does the attack get going?

21.♖xh6!. That is Predojevic's beautiful idea. The queen's bishop, which, according to plan, was to be used to take on h6, had to be surrendered. So instead, he uses the rook! Its substitute is already warming up on e1. Here you can see how dangerous it can be if White brings a lot of attacking pieces to the kingside. Black is restricted by the e6-pawn and the knight on e5 and cannot bring over defenders quickly enough. One of the numerous attacking pieces is sacrificed to destroy the black king position, but after that White is left with much superior might to deploy against the exposed king.

21...gxh6 22.♕xh6 ♘f5 23.♗xf5 exf5 24.♕g5+ ♔h7 25.♖e3+−. Analysis by Predojevic in the jubilee edition of *Chess Informant* 100.

18.♗xf5 exf5 19.d5±

Black has pulled the emergency cord and left White with a well supported passed pawn in the centre. Finding a defence against its advance is, however, very difficult.

19...♕b6 20.♘xd7 ♘xd7 21.d6 ♘f6 22.♘d5 ♘xd5 23.♕xd5

It is now established that the pawn will push forward to the seventh rank. In endgames with queen and rook that is usually enough for a win.

23...♕xb2 24.♖d1 b5

The queenside pawns will arrive too late. But even a passive defence is condemned to failure. With queens and rooks on the board, the black king cannot intervene in the struggle for the queening square. White will succeed in forcing access to the eighth rank.

25.h3 a5 26.d7 ♕c2 27.♖de1 ♖ad8 28.♖e8 ♕c7 29.♖xd8 ♕xd8 30.♕xb5 ♕c7 31.♖e8 ♕c1+ 32.♕f1 1-0

Predojevic demonstrated how to turn a lead in development and an advantage in space into a dangerous attack on the king.

Besieging the IQP

23 Queen's Gambit Declined

Vassily Ivanchuk 2750
Levon Aronian 2744

Morelia/Linares 2007 (7)

1.d4 ♘f6 2.c4 e6 3.♘f3 d5 4.♘c3 ♗b4 5.♗g5 ♘bd7 6.cxd5 exd5 7.♕c2 c5 8.a3 ♗xc3+ 9.♕xc3 h6 10.♗xf6 ♕xf6 11.e3 0-0 12.♗e2 b6 13.0-0 ♗b7 14.♖fc1 ♖ac8 15.dxc5 ♕xc3

15...bxc5 would have made the transition to hanging pawns.

16.♖xc3 ♖xc5

This time Black has the IQP. The position has been slightly simplified, with White nevertheless being able to retain his structural advantage. However, a double rook exchange on the open c-file looks likely. If Black can then avoid the exchange of the white bishop against his knight, all he has to do is to bring the king to d6, with a position which is easy to defend.

17.♖cc1!

17.♖ac1 ♖fc8 18.♖xc5 ♖xc5 19.♖xc5 bxc5= (Ivanchuk).

17...♖fc8

The desirable exchange of rooks 17...♖xc1+ 18.♖xc1 ♖c8 19.♖xc8+ (19.♖d1 ♖c2 20.♗b5 ♘c5 21.♖b1 a6 22.♘d4 ♖d2 23.♘f3 ♖c2=) 19...♗xc8 is not sufficient for equality, since White is able to exploit the bad position of the black bishop. After 20.♘d4 White threatens to win a pawn with 21.♘c6: 20...♔f8 (20...♘f6 21.♘c6 or 20...♘e5 21.f4) 21.♗g4± and after the exchange 22.♗xd7 we reach a constellation similar to the model game Flohr-Capablanca. Black is facing an uphill struggle.

18.♖d1!

That took some imagining: Ivanchuk, a world-class player famed for his constantly amazing creativity, allows Aronian to invade the second rank with his rook, only in order to avoid any further exchanges of major pieces. The unwelcome guest on c2 is then to be politely ushered out, after which the white rooks will besiege the IQP on the d-file in text-book fashion.

18...♖c2 19.♗b5 ♘f8 20.♖ab1 ♖2c7 21.♗a4

Preventing further visits by the black rook, but also preparing ♗b3, with an attack on the only weakness on the board. Moreover, the white pawns on the dark squares b2, a3, e3 and f2 harmonise very well with the light-squared bishop.

21...♘e6 22.♗b3 ♔f8

23.h3

Black should not be freed from his weak IQP 'only' for the sake of a slight gain in material. Instead of prematurely gobbling up a pawn, White first consolidates the position. He does not want to collect the pawn until all his pieces are well placed and Black's counterplay can be reduced to a minimum.

It is precisely this patience which is often lacking in amateurs. Masters always try to include the whole of their army in their considerations and avoid being left with one or more passive pieces after winning a pawn.

After 23.♗xd5 ♗xd5 24.♖xd5 ♖c1+ 25.♖d1 ♖xd1+ 26.♖xd1 ♖c2 27.♖b1 Black would have some compensation for the pawn. It is now no longer so easy to shift the rook from the second rank: 27...♘c5 28.♘d4 ♖d2 and things become complicated.

23...♖c5 24.♔h2 ♔e7 25.♖d2 ♖b5 26.♗a2 ♖bc5 27.♘e1 a5 28.♖bd1 ♖d8 29.♔g3 ♖b5

Putting pressure on b2. But here the rook gets into difficulty. 29... g5, which takes the wind out of the sails of the idea of ♘d3-f4, was better.

30.f3 ♖c8?

After 30...♘c5 31.e4 or 30...♖c5 31.♘d3 ♖c7 32.♘f4 ♘xf4 33.♔xf4± Black's disadvantage remains within limits.

31.♘d3±

Threatening a3-a4, winning the exchange. Now Aronian has to surrender his IQP without any compensation.

31...d4 32.♗xe6 ♔xe6 33.♘f4+ ♔e7 34.♖xd4 ♖c7 35.♖1d2 ♖bc5 36.e4

Ivanchuk is a sound pawn up and has the better minor piece: the bishop is biting on granite in the form of f3 and e4 and is simply depriving the knight of one square or another. On the dark squares, on the other hand, Black is totally helpless. That is the advantage of the knight compared to the bishop. It can control squares of both colours.

36...♖c4 37.♖d6 ♖4c6 38.e5 ♖c2 39.♖xc2 ♖xc2 40.♖xb6 ♗c6 41.b4 g5 42.♘h5 axb4 43.axb4 ♗d5 44.♘g7 ♖e2 45.♘f5+ ♔e8 46.♘xh6 ♗e6 47.♖b5 ♖b2 48.♖b8+ ♔d7 49.♖g8 **1-0**

24 Réti Opening
Mikhail Botvinnik
Evgeny Zagoriansky

Sverdlovsk 1943 (6)

1.♘f3 d5 2.c4 e6 3.b3 ♘f6 4.♗b2 ♗e7 5.e3 0-0 6.♘c3 c5 7.cxd5 ♘xd5 8.♘xd5 exd5 9.d4

A transition to an IQP position is on the cards, the white d-pawn will probably be exchanged for the black c-pawn. Zagorianski could, however, also offer a transformation to a position with hanging pawns: 9...b6 and then ...♗b7.

9...cxd4?!

A typical inaccuracy. Black makes the required exchange too soon and presents White not only with a tempo but also with the important d4-square.

10.♕xd4 ♗f6 11.♕d2 ♘c6 12.♗e2 ♗e6

Black adopts a very passive set-up. 12...♗f5 was preferable

13.0-0 ♗xb2 14.♕xb2±

White has the blockading square d4 firmly under control. Since Black has no active options, White has a long-lasting advantage. Such positions are the nightmare for fans of the IQP. Possible piece activity has not materialised.

Black has the worse structure with no prospects of activity. Nevertheless, all is not yet lost. A defence is possible, though it will require much patience and tenacity.

14...♕a5 15.♖fd1

White begins siege operations with the major pieces.

15...♖ad8 16.♖d2 ♖d7 17.♖ad1 ♖fd8 18.h3 h6

19.♘e5

Generally an exchange of minor pieces quite suits White, as we have already seen. In addition, the knight is more active here, and over and above that it clears the f3-square for the bishop, which can attack the weak pawn from there.

19...♘xe5 20.♕xe5 ♕c5 21.♗f3 b6

The correct pawn formation. Black so far has only one weakness in his position: d5. He must avoid a second one. On b7 the pawn could become a target for the white bishop.

22.♕b2 ♖c8 23.♕e5 ♖cd8

Despite the difference in activity between the white and black pieces it is not easy for the first player to make any progress. The d5-pawn is reliably protected and the pin on the d-file is not leading anywhere, since the rook on d7 is also protected. The bishop on e6 appears to be bad, but it is holding the black position together. Further examples of such 'bad' pieces, which are passively defending a weakness and thus allowing the other pieces to become active, will be seen in the next chapter.

24.♖d4 a5

This game is quoted in numerous manuals as an object lesson in how to exploit the passive set-up of opposing pieces, force a second weakness and then win by laying siege to the two weaknesses. Nevertheless, in what follows we see that Zagorianski's defence was not the best possible one. Here he was probably somewhat inferior to his mighty opponent. Botvinnik was especially feared for his systematic scientific preparation, his endgame ability and also for his tenacious defence of inferior or even lost positions. In numerous encounters with top players Botvinnik was able to save something from totally unpromising positions. His less well-known opponent was unable to display comparable resistance in this game.

25.g4

By advancing the pawn to g5 Botvinnik wanted to force a second weakness in the black camp. Of course, in so doing he also compromises his own position. But he reasons that the passive black major pieces cannot exploit this.

25...♕c6 26.g5

26.h4 looks more natural.

26...hxg5 27.♕xg5 f6 28.♕g6 ♗f7 29.♕g3

The weakening of the black kingside has only been moderately successful. It is possible to defend the g7-point.

29...f5?!

It is only after this move that the black position becomes very difficult. A better one was 29...♕c2. The disadvantage is limited if Black manages with active play to make the coordination of the white forces difficult. It would not then be so easy for Botvinnik to obtain the desired battery on the g-file: 30.♖1d2 ♕c1+ 31.♔g2 ♖e7±.

The following moves are anything but forced – White does not win by force.

30.♕g5 ♕e6 31.♔h1 ♕e5 32.♖g1 ♖f8?!

Here too, 32...♔f8, 32...♗e6 and 32...♖d6 offered Zagorianski much more promising alternatives.

33.♕h6 ♖b8?

It is only after this mistake that Black is finally lost. He still had at least practical chances with the more active 33...♖c8. The following sample variations illustrate tough defence: 34.♕xb6 (34.♖h4 ♔f8 35.♕h8+ ♗g8 36.♖f4 ♖c6±) 34...c2 35.♕xa5 ♖xf2 36.♕a8+ ♗e8 37.♗xd5+ ♖xd5 (37...♔f8 38.♗g2 ♖xd4 39.exd4

♕xd4 40.♖e1 ♖e2 41.♖xe2 ♕d1+
42.♔h2 ♕xe2 43.♕d5+−) 38.♕xd5+
♕xd5+ 39.♖xd5 ♗c6 40.e4 ♗xd5
41.exd5 ♖xa2 and there is no win in
sight. Compared to that, the text move
is too passive. Zagoriansky can no longer
withstand Botvinnik's attack on his king.

34.♖h4   ♔f8   35.♕h8+   ♗g8
36.♖f4+−   ♖bb7   37.♖g5   ♖f7
38.♕h5 ♕a1+ 39.♔g2 g6 40.♕xg6
♗h7 41.♕d6+ ♖fe7 42.♕d8+   1-0

Model games
Polugaevsky-Tal (Tbilisi 1956)
Flohr-Capablanca (Moscow 1935)
Botvinnik-Vidmar (Nottingham 1936)
Portisch-Karpov (Milan 1975)
Smyslov-Ribli (London m(5) 1983)
Smyslov-Ribli (London m(7) 1983)

> *Nature has given us the chess board, from*
> *which we neither can nor wish to deduce*
> *anything; she has carved for us the pieces,*
> *of which the values, motions and power*
> *gradually become known to us; it is now*
> *up to us to make such moves as promise us*
> *a win; everyone tries to do this in his own*
> *way and does not like to be persuaded.*
> Johann Wolfgang Goethe in 'Schrift zur
> Naturwissenschaft' ('Writings on science')

IQP (II)

This structure can also arise from many
different openings, and once again also
with reversed colours.

Specific characteristics
White usually has two central squares
(e4 and e5) at his disposal, Black
only one – the blockading square d5,
which he often supports with ...c7-c6.
But unlike in the position for IQP (I),
here the black queen's bishop has free
rein and is developed to e6, f5 or g4.
Additionally, Black is not hemmed in
on the kingside and can more easily
assemble pieces for the defence. Though
in return the b3-f7 diagonal is open,
which favours tactical motifs against f7.

Plans for White
As is most often the case in IQP structures, White attacks here too. In addition
to the plans described in the section IQP
(I), he can often exert pressure on f7,
frequently by means of ♘e5 and ♗c4.

Plans for Black
The free c8-g4 diagonal gives Black
chances to exchange his queen's bishop
against a white attacker, either the
knight on f3 or even the king's bishop.
He will have slight problems with the
development of the queen's knight. On
c6 it can come under pressure down the
semi-open c-file:

On d7, however, the knight is less active. As previously, Black tries to exchange minor pieces, without relieving White of his pawn weakness.

Conclusion
Both sides follow similar ideas to those in the IQP (I) structure. The free diagonal for the queen's bishop and the open e-file, however, give Black more possibilities for simplifying the game.

The advance d4-d5

25 Queen's Gambit Declined
Garry Kasparov 2740
Nigel Short 2615
Brussels 1986 (9)
1.d4 e6 2.♘f3 ♘f6 3.c4 d5 4.♘c3 ♗e7 5.♗g5 h6 6.♗xf6 ♗xf6 7.e3 0-0 8.♖c1 c6 9.♗d3 ♘d7 10.0-0 dxc4 11.♗xc4 e5 12.h3 exd4 13.exd4 ♘b6 14.♗b3 ♗f5 15.♖e1

Black has been able to develop his queen's bishop freely to f5. He has, however, a problem with the vulnerability of the f7-point. In addition, the white pieces are more active. The black knight on b6 may be controlling d5, but will find it hard to occupy the square. White would then be able to play ♗b3xd5 and bring about a transformation of the structure which favours him. The

black queen's bishop will be hindered by the fixed pawn which will appear on d5. In the variation in the text White would now like to position his pieces actively on the kingside, e.g. by means of ♕d1-d2-f4 and then ♖e3. Black must not allow that.

15...♗g5?!
The e5-square had to be taken under surveillance, so 15...♖e8 was on offer. At this point opening theory later found long forced variations which only just achieved equality.

16.♖a1 ♘d7?!
He now over-protects e5, but in return allows White to get in his d4-d5 break-through.

17.d5 ♖c8?
After 17...♘c5 the neglect of the central e5-square becomes noticeable: 18.♖e5 ♗g6 19.♘xg5 hxg5 20.dxc6 ♘xb3 21.♕xb3 bxc6 22.♖ae1±. This was nevertheless somewhat better than the game continuation.

18.♘d4 ♗g6

19.♘e6!
A pseudo-sacrifice which exploits the weak b3-g8 diagonal.

19...fxe6 20.dxe6
On account of the threatened discovered check, White recovers the piece he sacrificed. The black king position is weakened as a result of the exchange of the f7-pawn for White's IQP. The

e6-pawn even makes it to the seventh rank. The time required by Black to render the dangerous passed pawn harmless will be used by White to bring his attacking pieces into position: ♕g4 and ♘e4.

20...♔h7 21.♕xd7 ♕b6

After 21...♕xd7 22.exd7 ♖cd8 23.♖ad1 ♗f5 24.♗e6 ♗xe6 25.♖xe6 ♖f7 26.♖ed6+− the passed pawn will prove too strong in the long run. So all White has to do is find a way for his knight to get to b7, c6 or e6, from where it can attack d8.

22.e7 ♖fe8

22...♕xf2+ 23.♔h1 ♖fe8 24.♘e4 ♗xe4 25.♖xe4+−.

23.♕g4 ♕c5 24.♘e4 ♕xe7 25.♗c2

Black to move

How do things continue?

White has a beautiful position, but there are no points in chess for 'beautiful'! Specifics are important.

Did you spot that f4 is threatened? Agreed, so Black played:

25...♖f8

But 25...♖cd8 would be bad on account of 26.f4. But what now? The problem lies in the weakness of the light squares on the kingside. A white pawn on h5 would definitely be unpleasant. But to get there we need to cross h4, so:

26.g3+− ♕d8 27.♖ad1 ♕a5 28.h4 ♗e7 29.♘c3 ♗xc2 30.♖xe7 ♖g8 31.♖dd7 ♗f5 32.♖xg7+ ♔h8 33.♕d4 1-0

Kasparov was able to obtain the exchange of the IQP for the f7-pawn by means of a tactical trick on the b3-g8 diagonal. That was followed by a decisive attack against the weakened kingside.

26 Four Knights Game
Yury Averbakh
Paul Keres
Moscow 1950 (17)

1.e4 e5 2.♘f3 ♘c6 3.♘c3 ♘f6 4.♗b5 ♗b4 5.0-0 0-0 6.d3 d6 7.♘e2 ♘e7 8.c3 ♗a5 9.♘g3 c6 10.♗a4 ♘g6 11.d4 ♗e6 12.♗c2 ♖e8 13.♖e1?

A better move was 13.♗e3.

13...♗g4 14.♘f5 d5 15.h3 ♗xf3 16.♕xf3 ♘xe4 17.♗xe4 exd4! 18.♘xd4 ♗b6!

With this move Black ensures that the bishop will be exchanged for the knight on d4 and White will be left with the isolated queen pawn.

19.♗d2 dxe4 20.♖xe4 ♖xe4 21.♕xe4 ♗xd4 22.cxd4

In addition to the weak pawn White is also left with the bad dark-squared bishop. A lot of material has already been exchanged, so that there is hardly any hope of an initiative for Averbakh. Keres has a small, lasting advantage.

22...♕e7 23.♕g4

He avoids the exchange. Only the queen would perhaps allow White to develop some activity.

23...♕d6 24.♖e1 ♕d5

25.b3

GM Yury Averbakh is known to generations of chess players as an endgame expert and author of an endgame monograph which has been influential for decades. With the move in the game he positions his pawns on light squares, to complement his dark-squared bishop. 25.a3?, on the other hand, would allow the creation of a whole complex of weak light squares: c4, b3 and a2. Welcome entry squares for the black queen or the knight, which would then be able to attack the weakness on b2.

25...h5

This forces the exchange of queens. The weakness of the bad bishop gains in significance.

26.♕e4 ♕xe4 27.♖xe4 f6

Once again a pattern we already know. The pawn is placed on a square of the same colour as the opposing bishop and thus deprives the white pieces of the

e5- and g5-squares. The white queen's bishop can achieve nothing in this position, except to fight with the black pieces for one square or another or to threaten an exchange for the knight. Of course Keres will never permit this!

28.♔f1 ♔f7 29.♗a5

Black now has to play ...b7-b6 in order to get his rook to d8. The pawns on b6 and a7 become potential targets for the white bishop. But what is important is that Averbakh will not manage to fix these weaknesses. Keres can later play ...b6-b5 if he wants and if it is necessary.

29...b6 30.♗c3 ♖d8 31.♗b2 ♖d6 32.g4

This prevents ...f6-f5, which would drive away the rook and gain space on the kingside.

32...hxg4 33.hxg4 ♖e6?!

A better way was 33...♖d5 34.♗c3 ♘f8 and then ...♘e6.

34.f3

A typical method in all IQP positions: White positions a piece actively in the centre – the rook on e4 – and protects the latter with f2-f3. Should Black exchange, this clearly improves White's pawn structure. He would suddenly have the central pawn duo e4/d4. The endgame after the alternative 34.♖xe6 ♔xe6 would, on the other hand, be very hard to defend for White.

34...♘e7 35.♗c1 ♘d5 36.♗d2 ♖d6 37.♔e2 ♖d8 38.♔f2 ♘c7 39.a4 ♘e6

This set-up with knight and rook is a very effective attack on the IQP. We will meet it again in the third section of this chapter.

40.♗e3 ♖d5 41.♔g3 ♔e7

42.g5?

The understandable desire to simplify the position. But he would have done better to wait, e.g. with 42.♗f2 ♔d7 43.♗e3, even if there is no gainsaying Black's advantage. Waiting, however, is an art which is rarely in harmony with the nature of the chess player.

42...f5!

Averbakh had been aiming for simplifications with 42.g5. As a result of Keres' reply, however, a further weakness appears in the white camp: the g-pawn. After 42...fxg5 43.♔g4, on the other hand, the material is of less value than the activity of his king which is conceded to the opponent.

43.♖e5 ♔d6

43...♖xe5? 44.dxe5 g6 was very tempting: this exchange would see two white pawns fixed on the same colour of squares as the bishop and the blockading knight ideally placed on e6. At this point 45.a5? would be insufficient: 45...bxa5 46.♗xa7 c5 47.♗b6 c4 48.bxc4

a4 with a probably decisive advantage to Black, as would 45.b4? c5 46.bxc5 f4+! 47.♗xf4 ♘xc5 48.a5 bxa5 49.♗e3 ♘b3 50.♗xa7 ♔e6 51.♗b8 ♘d4–+. After 45.f4, the protected passed pawn, however, guarantees White the draw: 45...c5 46.♔f3 ♔d7 47.♔e2 ♔c6 48.♔d3 ♔d5 49.♔c3 a6 50.b4=.

44.♖xd5+ ♔xd5 45.g6!

White still has very good practical chances of a draw. These are based on the fact that the bishop is superior to the knight when the struggle is on both sides of the board.

45...a5!

Paul Keres (1916-1975) was often described as 'the eternal runner-up', because in a total of five appearances in Candidates' tournaments for the World Championship he took second place three times and thus only just missed out on a match for the highest crown. For more than four decades he belonged to the elite of world chess. Even today with the help of chess programs it is hard to surpass his analytical skill. Keres analyses the immediate win of a pawn: 45...♘xd4? 46.♗xd4 ♔xd4.

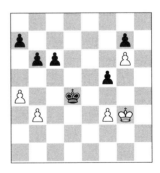

analysis diagram: position after 46...♔xd4

We experience here just how complicated pure pawn endings can be. At first glance it looks like a win for Black: 47.♔f4 b5 48.axb5 cxb5

49.b4 ♚c4 50.♚xf5 ♚xb4 51.♚e6 a5 52.♚f7 a4 53.♚xg7 a3 54.♚f7 a2 55.g7 a1♕ 56.g8♕ ♕a2+ 57.♚f8 ♕xg8+ 58.♚xg8.

analysis diagram: position after 58.♚xg8

There still seems no doubt that Black will win. The black king wins the last remaining white pawn, whilst the white king is far outside of the queening square of the b5-pawn king. The finish of Keres' analysis is, however, study-like. With a little 'Schadenfreude' (= joy in the misfortunes of others) we can point out that here the engines are helplessly showing '-9' (i.e. '–+'): 58...♚c4 59.f4 ♚d5 60.♚f7 b4 (60...♚e4 61.♚e6 ♚xf4 62.♚d5=) 61.f5 b3 62.f6 b2 63.♚g7 b1♕ 64.f7= (analysis by Paul Keres, 1964). Chess is a very deep game. Computers will still need some time before they are able to find such a subtle variation!

46.♚h4 ♘xd4 47.♗h6 ♘e6 48.♗e3 c5 49.♚h5 ♚e5 50.♗c1 ♘d4 51.♗h6 ♚f6 52.♗g5+ ♚e6 53.♗h6?

He could put up more resistance with 53.♗d8 ♚d7 54.♗f6 ♘e6 55.♗e5 ♚c6 56.♗xg7 ♘xg7+ 57.♚g5 ♘e8 58.♚xf5 ♚d6–+ (Keres).

53...gxh6 54.♚xh6 ♘c6 55.g7 ♘e7 56.♚h7 ♚f7 57.♚h6 ♚g8 58.f4 ♚f7 0-1

Model games
Steinitz-Von Bardeleben (Hastings 1895)
Karpov-Jussupow (Moscow 1988)
Adams-Jussupow (France tt 2005)

If you want to see amusing games, you are better off looking in an open tournament. I prefer to see a football match between France and Italy, even if it finishes 0:0, rather than a second division game that ends 7:6.
Vladimir Kramnik

IQP (III)
The third important structure with an isolated queen pawn comes about whenever in the struggle against the IQP the king's bishop is fianchettoed. The opposing queen's pawn immediately comes under pressure.

1.d4 d5 2.c4 e6 3.♘c3 c5 The so-called 'Tarrasch Defence' to the Queen's Gambit. Black is literally begging for the right to play with an IQP. **4.cxd5 exd5 5.♘f3 ♘c6 6.g3 ♘f6 7.♗g2 ♗e7 8. 0–0 0–0 9.♗g5 cxd4 10.♘xd4**

Specific characteristics
White's set-up was made popular by Akiba Rubinstein at the start of the 20th

century and even today it is still the most feared weapon against the 'Tarrasch Defence'. Siegbert Tarrasch (1862-1934), the 'Praeceptor Germaniae' ('Germany's schoolmaster'), was a great proponent of the IQP and considered the opening which was named after him to be the 'only correct' defence against the Queen's Gambit. In Rubinstein's set-up, the bishop on g2 attacks the IQP directly. In addition, the queen's bishop attacks the knight on f6, which further increases the pressure on d5. On the other hand, the latter's advance is not restricted by a white pawn on e3, so that it can often be moved. This somewhat restricts the white position.

Plans for White

As well as the plans which have already been discussed in the struggle against the IQP, the aggressive placement of the minor pieces gives White the opportunity to attack the black position straight away. In doing so, the transposition to a structure with the isolated pawn pair is often chosen with ♘d4xc6 b7xc6 (see the chapter 'Backward pawns'). With the lever e2-e4 White can open the position without freeing Black from all his weaknesses. Thereafter, whatever the exchange – exd5 or ...dxe4 –, an isolated pawn will be the result.

Plans for Black

Black is aiming for the advance ...d5-d4, gaining space and fixing the pawn on e2.

Another plan is the attack on the kingside with ...♗e6, ...♕d7, ...♗h3, ideally accompanied by major piece pressure on the e-file and also, where appropriate, ...h7-h5-h4xg3.

The advance of the IQP

27 Caro-Kann Defence
John Nunn	2600
Yasser Seirawan	2525

London 1984 (10)

1.e4 c6 2.d4 d5 3.exd5 cxd5 4.c4 ♘f6 5.♘c3 g6 6.cxd5 ♘xd5 7.♘f3 ♗g7 8.♗c4 ♘b6 9.♗b3 ♘c6 10.0-0 0-0

Here we have a similar position with reversed colours: the fianchettoed king's bishop attacks the IQP immediately.

11.d5

The latter advances thoughtlessly, which superficially does not look particularly worrying. On the contrary: it cannot advance any further and is still susceptible to attacks. Nor does it disturb the development of the black minor pieces – all of them have good squares.

Nevertheless, the pawn cramps the black position: the weakness on e7 is marked out. In addition, for the moment the black queen has no suitable square to which it can be developed.

11...♘a5 12.♗g5 ♗g4 13.h3 ♗xf3 14.♕xf3 ♘xb3?!

Once more the motif of the premature exchange crops up. Of course one would hardly be expecting to get White's king's bishop in return for the knight on the edge on a5. But there was no hurry. After the text move the a-file is opened and the enforced defence of the a7-pawn soon provokes the weakening ...a7-a6. So Seirawan would have done better to hold back this exchange until the rook on a1 had moved away, e.g. 14...♕d7 15.♖fe1 ♖fe8 16.♖ad1 ♘xb3 17.axb3=.

15.axb3 ♕d7 16.♖fd1

The f-rook goes to d1, Black having already, as it were, developed the other one for White.

16...♘c8

The knight was attacking d5, but for the moment that is really not achieving anything. For that reason Seirawan redeploys it, intending to occupy the blockading square d6. This, however, puts Black further behind in his development. 16...♖fe8 was more natural. 16...a6 17.♕e3 ♘c8 is similar to the game.

17.♕e3 ♖e8 18.♗f4 a6 19.♘a4

This is starting to look very appealing. Nevertheless, Black has everything covered and his structure is simply better. White must now single-mindedly exploit his greater activity.

19...♕f5?!

A better way was 19...♕b5 20.♗c7 (20.♖ac1 ♘d6) 20...♕d7 (20...♘d6? 21.♘b6 ♘f5 22.♕d3 ♕xd3 23.♖xd3 ♖a7 24.♖e1 ♔f8 25.d6+−) 21.♕c5±.

20.♖ac1 b5?!

Up till here Black was simply slightly cramped, but now he runs out of space. 20...♘d6 21.g4 ♕f6 22.♖c7± was preferable.

21.g4 ♕f6 22.♖c6 e6

The queen has no more squares. The text turns the IQP into a strong passed pawn.

After 22...♗d6 23.♗b6 ♖ad8 24.♖d2± Black is practically paralysed.

23.d6 ♘e7

23...bxa4 24.d7 ♖f8 25.♗g5 ♕xb2 26.d8♕ loses on the spot.

24.♗g5 ♘d5 25.♖xd5 exd5 26.♗xf6 ♖xe3 27.fxe3 ♗xf6 28.d7 ♖d8 29.♘c5+−

The d-pawn is ideally supported by the rook and knight. Seirawan will have to give up the bishop for it.

29...♗xb2 30.♖c8 ♗f6 31.♘b7 ♖f8 32.b4

As long as Black cannot move, White strengthens his position – just, no hurry!

32...♔g7 33.♔f2 ♗e7 34.♖e8 ♗h4+ 35.♔f3 h6 36.♖xf8 ♔xf8 37.d8♕+ ♗xd8 38.♘xd8 ♔e7 39.♘b7

Black resigned.

Nunn was able to restrict his opponent to such an extent with the advance d4-d5 that Seirawan was unable to find adequate squares for his pieces.

Attacking the IQP

28 Queen's Gambit Declined

Anatoly Karpov   2705
Garry Kasparov   2715

Moscow 1984 (9)

1.d4 d5 2.c4 e6 3.♘f3 c5 4.cxd5
exd5 5.g3 ♘f6 6.♗g2 ♗e7 7.0-0 0-0
8.♘c3 ♘c6 9.♗g5 cxd4 10.♘xd4
h6 11.♗e3 ♖e8 12.♕b3

This move highlights the strength of a fianchettoed king's bishop. If it had been developed by e2-e3, White would still need some time in order to attack the IQP.

12...♘a5 13.♕c2 ♗g4 14.♘f5 ♖c8
15.♗d4 ♗c5 16.♗xc5 ♖xc5 17.♘e3
Once more very effective play. The IQP is attacked one more time! In the event of the advance ...d5-d4 White is planning the pin ♖ad1.

> *You do not have to first restrict and blockade the IQP. You must take it!*
>
> Bent Larsen

17...♗e6
17...d4 18.♖ad1 ♕d7 19.♘xg4 ♕xg4
20.h3 ♕e6 (20...♕d7 21.e3 ♖c4
22.exd4 ♖xd4 23.♘d5±) 21.♖xd4
♕xa2 22.♖fd1±.

18.♖ad1 ♕c8 19.♕a4 ♖d8 20.♖d3

In game 26 we got to know the set-up ♘e3/♖d3 (with reversed colours). Here Karpov makes this formation even better with ♘c3, ♖d3 and ♘e3. Moreover, we had mentioned the rule that the player with the IQP – so on this occasion Black – normally avoids exchanging the minor pieces because he is hoping to develop more activity than his opponent.

But in this case it is all three remaining white minor pieces which are radiating the maximum of effective power. The only way for White to top this would be to triple his major pieces on the d-file by following up with ♖f1-d1-d2 and ♕a4-d1.

20...a6 21.♖fd1 ♘c4 22.♘xc4 ♖xc4
23.♕a5
23.♕b3 was more energetic. The advance of the IQP 23...d4? is again prevented by model tactical measures: 24.♕b6 ♘d7 25.♖xd4! (Karpov). Black must probably surrender a pawn, e.g. 23...♕c5 24.♕xb7 ♘g4 25.e3 ♖b4 26.♕xa6 ♖xb2 27.♘a4 ♕c2 28.♘xb2 ♕xf2+ 29.♔h1 ♕xb2 30.♖3d2 ♕c3 31.♕b6±.

23...♖c5 24.♕b6 ♖d7 25.♖d4 ♕c7
26.♕xc7 ♖dxc7
The position has been simplified, Kasparov has not managed to develop an initiative – on the contrary: he had

difficulty beating off the first wave of attacks.

Karpov now has everything under control and has a small advantage.

27.h3

The rash win of a pawn 27.♘xd5 ♘xd5 28.♗xd5 ♗xd5 29.♖xd5 ♖xd5 30.♖xd5 ♖c2 31.♖d8+ ♚h7 32.♖d7 ♖xb2 33.♖xf7 ♖xe2 gives Black sufficient counterplay and leads to 'drawish looking positions' (Karpov).

27...h5 28.a3 g6 29.e3

White's advantage consists not only of the hope of winning the IQP, but also of (for the long term) the difference in quality between the two bishops.

The white one works very harmoniously with the pawn structure. Black, on the other hand, must take care that all his pawns will not be fixed on light squares.

29...♚g7 30.♚h2 ♖c4 31.♗f3

31...b5

Although this game leads into one of the most famous of endgames, this pawn move, which is of such significance, is passed over without comment in many analyses. Kasparov places another pawn on a square of the same colour as that of his bishop. Naturally he had his reasons for this. On the one hand, this raises the possibility of activating a rook with ...b5-b4. On the other, on b7 the pawn was tending to become a weakness, which would have had negative consequences in variations with ♖xc4 and ...dxc4. Nevertheless, the move 31...b5 is open to question. In the further course of the game it leads to both the a- and the b-pawns being badly placed.

32.♚g2 ♖7c5 33.♖xc4 ♖xc4 34.♖d4 ♚f8 35.♗e2 ♖xd4 36.exd4 ♚e7 37.♘a2 ♗c8 38.♘b4 ♚d6 39.f3 ♘g8 40.h4 ♘h6 41.♚f2 ♘f5 42.♘c2 f6?!

This prepares the 'freeing' by means of ...g6-g5. Karpov refutes this plan, however. Kasparov would have done better to wait: 42...♗e6.

43.♗d3 g5 44.♗xf5 ♗xf5 45.♘e3

We have now reached a classic situation with a good knight against a bad bishop. Too many black pawns (a6, b5, d5 and h5) are fixed on squares of the same colour as that of the bishop. The decisive question is: in this closed position can White force a way into the opposing camp?

45...♗b1 46.b4 gxh4?

A very rare case: Kasparov makes a clear mistake, even after extensive analysis of a game which was adjourned on move 42. Of course he was counting on the 'automatic' 47.gxh4. A waiting move such as 46...♗g6 or 46...♚e6 was called for.

47.♘g2!!

This is the move which made this game famous! With his pawn sacrifice White obtains the necessary squares (especially h4) for his king to invade the opposing position. The remainder is still very complicated tactically. An important and constantly recurring motif is the helplessness of the bishop: there is nothing it can attack and all it can do is set up obstacles to the advance of the white pieces. The knight, on the other hand, in conjunction with its king, keeps forcing the opposing monarch further back, and thus White will finally win the isolated black pawns.

47...hxg3+ 48.♔xg3 ♔e6 49.♘f4+ ♔f5 50.♘xh5 ♔e6 51.♘f4+ ♔d6 52.♔g4 ♗c2 53.♔h5 ♗d1 54.♔g6 ♔e7

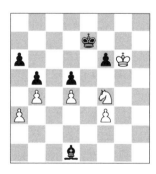

55.♘xd5+?

But this is rash. The pawn was – from Black's point of view – pretty much a block. Its disappearance frees the way for the king, which thus pushes via c4 towards the (now!) vulnerable white queenside pawns. In endgames of this type – pawns blocked on the same colour of squares as their bishop against a knight – the side with the knight can often decide the game without having to fear any counterplay.

Grandmaster Marin, a leading contemporary endgame expert, gives the following analysis in his book *Learn from the Legends*: 55.♘h5 ♗c2+ 56.♔g7 ♔e6 57.♘xf6 ♗b1 (57...♔f5 58.♔f7 ♔f4 59.♔e6 ♔e3 60.♔e5+−) 58.♘g4 ♔f5 59.♔f7 ♔f4 60.♔e6 ♔xf3 61.♘f6 ♔e3 62.♔xd5+−. Dvoretsky has shown that after 55...♗xf3 White also wins in a similar way.

55...♔e6 56.♘c7+ ♔d7 57.♘xa6 ♗xf3 58.♔xf6 ♔d6 59.♔f5 ♔d5 60.♔f4 ♗h1 61.♔e3 ♔c4 62.♘c5 ♗c6 63.♘d3 ♗g2 64.♘e5+ ♔c3 65.♘g6 ♔c4 66.♘e7

66...♗b7?

As a consequence of the over-hasty pawn grab on move 55, a very unstable situation has arisen, in which even two extra pawns do not guarantee that White will win the game. The reason for this is the activity of the black king as well as the disruptive effect of the bishop on the a8-h1 diagonal. After 66... ♗h1! endgame theoreticians have not been able to find a win for White!

   67.♘f5 ♗g2 68.♘d6+ ♔b3 69.♘xb5 ♔a4 70.♘d6   **1-0**

Model games
Nikolac-Nunn (Dortmund 1979)
Karpov-Chandler (London 1984)
Karpov-Illescas Cordoba (Leon 1993)
Sargissian-Akobian (Yerevan 1999)

Conclusion IQP

In the structures with an IQP which we have considered, the course of the games has been to a large extent marked by piece play. Apart from the pawn breakthrough d4-d5, questions of how to use the pawns lie in the background. Important preliminary decisions often occur in the early middlegame, when the question has to be answered as to whether the initiative of the side with the IQP will develop or whether the opponent can neutralise it – to his long-term positional advantage.

The IQP has weaknesses and strengths. You need to know them and to know how to exploit them.

Chapter 6
Backward pawns

Good players are always lucky.
José Raul Capablanca

A pawn whose neighbours have moved past it is described as 'backward'. It and the square in front of it cannot be protected by its fellow pawns. Thus the backward pawn on a semi-open file – charmingly described by Hans Kmoch in his classic *Pawn Power in Chess* as a 'straggler' – constitutes a static weakness, which can make itself felt in various ways. If the pawn is attacked it has to be protected by pieces. Also, opposing pieces can find a long-lasting outpost just in front of it, which can be unpleasant.

Of course, backward pawns cannot always be avoided. They occur frequently in practice and in various openings they are consciously accepted. One often gets another sort of positional advantage as compensation.

From the plethora of typical structures we will investigate more closely two representative examples:

The pawn pair c3/d4 and:

The pawn pair d6/e5

Many of the rules and motifs which we encounter in what follows can be applied to other positions with backward pawns.

The pawn pair c3/d4

The pawn pair c3/d4 is closely related to the IQP structure, from which it frequently arises as a result of an exchange on c3, as well as to hanging pawns. These arise when the c-pawn takes a step forward.

Specific characteristics

From the static point of view Black's structure is clearly preferable. It displays no weaknesses and has fewer pawn islands. As well as the a-pawn, the c3-pawn especially cannot be protected by a colleague and being in a semi-open file it can easily be subjected to a frontal attack.

A major role is played here by c4 as a blockading or stopping square. If Black can control it or occupy it with pieces, the weakness on c3 will be fixed.

Plans for White

Similar to IQP (I) White has a preponderance in space and mostly a slight lead in development, since the activation of the black queen's bishop requires several moves. White often controls the central squares e4 and e5.

The attacking options demonstrated in the games in the IQP chapter exist here in comparable form.

If play moves over to the queenside, White absolutely must anticipate the blockade of the backward pawn and advance it should the situation arise. The subsequent hanging pawns are often more valuable in the middlegame than in the endgame and should be deployed actively and aggressively (see also the chapter 'Hanging pawns').

Plans for Black

The first priority is, similarly to the IQP, the neutralising of any white initiative on the kingside.

Furthermore, Black tries to restrict the advance of the white c-pawn and to blockade it. This conveys particular significance to the outpost on c4. In order to obtain lasting control, the defenders of c4 should be exchanged. In general, the blockade takes preference over the direct attack. If Black is successful in this, the weak c-pawn can become a deciding factor.

Conclusion

The pawn pair c3/d4 is a static weakness, but offers White attacking chances since he is safe in the centre.

The restriction and blockading of the backward pawn can lead not only to the later win of the weak pawn, but it can also condemn the white pieces to permanent inactivity.

29 Nimzo-Indian Defence
Mark Taimanov 2585
Anatoly Karpov 2660
Moscow 1973 (1)
1.d4 ♘f6 2.c4 e6 3.♘c3 ♗b4 4.e3 c5 5.♗d3 0-0 6.♘f3 d5 7.0-0 dxc4 8.♗xc4 cxd4 9.exd4 b6 10.♕e2 ♗b7

11.罝d1

This contributes little to the improvement of the position. The d4-pawn did not have to be defended and the rook move does not set up a threat of the breakthrough d4-d5. It made more sense to first develop the queen's bishop: 11.盒g5.

11...公bd7 12.盒d2

Now the bishop is permanently passive. 12.盒g5 盒xc3 13.bxc3 嶜c7 14.盒d3 (14.公d2) 14...嶜xc3 15.公e5 would, however, be an unclear pawn sacrifice.

12...罝c8 13.盒a6

Taimanov tries to exploit the weakness of the light squares on the queenside. But in this game the plan does not work. 13.盒d3=.

13...盒xa6 14.嶜xa6 盒xc3 15.bxc3 罝c7 16.罝ac1 嶜c8 17.嶜a4

Now all that is missing is c3-c4. White could then take the passive 盒d2 off the defence of the c-pawn and entrust it with other tasks.

Black to move

How did Karpov meet the threatened advance c3-c4?

17...罝c4!

He sacrifices a pawn but obtains in return a permanent blockade of the white central pawns. Karpov transforms material into a positional advantage.

18.嶜xa7 嶜c6 19.嶜a3 罝c8 20.h3 h6

Black clearly has the better structure here. The pawn pair c3/d4 is blockaded and his pieces are active. The weakness c3 is already under siege and also the isolated a2-pawn can soon become a target. It is worth noting the clear domination on the light squares: a consequence of the exchange of the light-squared bishops. White, on the other hand, can neither attack anything nor threaten anything, but nevertheless is a pawn up. All in all the chances are approximately level.

21.罝b1 罝a4 22.嶜b3 公d5 23.罝dc1 罝c4 24.罝b2 f6 25.罝e1 曳f7 26.嶜d1

'"I cannot be worse here!" Taimanov stated definitely', I. Zaitsev reports in *The Complete Games of Anatoly Karpov*. He was probably correct, even if this game is often represented as a 'one-way street' in which Karpov wins more or less automatically.

Now and in what follows, however, the position does not decisively depart from equality.

26...♘f8

26...♘xc3 27.♗xc3 ♖xc3 28.♖be2 ♖c1 29.♕b3 ♖xe1+ 30.♘xe1 ♕c4 31.♕e3 ♖a8 32.♖c2 ♕d5 33.a3 e5 34.dxe5 with equality.

In this variation the recovery of the pawn in conjunction with the simplifications bring Black's positional superiority to an end. With two weaknesses in each camp the chances are level for both sides.

27.♖b3 ♘g6 28.♕b1 ♖a8 29.♖e4

29.♕d3 ♖xa2 30.♖xe6 ♔xe6 31.♕xg6 is an interesting alternative pointed out by Zaitsev, Karpov's trainer of many years standing.

29...♖ca4 30.♖b2 ♘f8 31.♕d3 ♖c4 32.♖e1 ♖a3 33.♕b1 ♘g6

34.♖c1?

The dilemma of a passive position. Extra pawn or not, at some point one has to go on to the counter-attack – especially if the board is still somewhat full. Eternal passivity leads to ruin, at least that is what one imagines.

But when is the correct moment? Apparently this was a good point to act. After the text move, White relinquishes the pressure on e6, which represented an important motif for counterplay. There were several alternatives:

A) 34.h4! h5 35.♖b3 ♖a6 36.♕c2 ♖ca4 37.♕e4 ♖xa2 38.c4 ♘de7 39.♕d3=;

B) 34.♔h1 ♘ge7 35.h4 ♘f5 36.h5 ♔g8 37.♖b3 ♖a6 38.♕e4 b5 39.♔g1 ♕d7 40.♖eb1 ♘d6 41.♕d3 ♖xa2 42.♖xb5=;

C) 34.♕d3 ♘xc3? (34...♘df4=) 35.♖b3+− (Zaitsev).

34...♘xc3 35.♕d3

There is also the interesting 35.♖xb6.

35...♘e2+ 36.♕xe2 ♖xc1+ 37.♗xc1 ♕xc1+ 38.♔h2 ♖xf3 39.gxf3 ♘h4

And Taimanov over-stepped the time limit.

Now 40.♖b3? is bad: 40...♕g5 41.♕f1 ♕f4+ 42.♔g1 ♘xf3+ 43.♔g2 ♘d2−+ (Zaitsev).

After 40.d5, however, the outcome of the game was not yet decided. White can still put up a defence: 40...♕f4+ 41.♔h1 exd5 42.♕e3 ♕f5 43.f4 with considerable resistance.

Attacking on the kingside

30 Nimzo-Indian Defence
Tiger Hillarp Persson 2548
Stellan Brynell 2493
Reykjavik 2006 (4)

1.d4 e6 2.c4 ♘f6 3.♘c3 ♗b4 4.e3 c5 5.♗d3 0-0 6.♘f3 d5 7.0-0 cxd4 8.exd4 dxc4 9.♗xc4 b6 10.♗g5 ♗b7 11.♘e5 ♗xc3 12.bxc3 ♘bd7 13.♕e2 ♕c7 14.♘xd7 ♘xd7

15.♖ac1

Unfortunately necessary, even if the passive protection of a pawn does not constitute much of a challenge for a rook. The backward pawn needs protection, but would we not be better to use the bishop on g5 for this unpleasant task, i.e. ♗g5-d2 ? This sort of move has often been played in similar situations. It would be an example of a 'bad' piece (♗d2) protecting the critical point in a position (c3). Thus on one hand the pressure of one or more opposing major pieces is neutralised and on the other it allows all one's own remaining pieces to be deployed actively.

Nevertheless ♗d2 is not the best move here, since Black can then comfortably get in the pawn lever ...e6-e5: 15.♗d2?! e5 16.♖fe1 (16.♖ac1 ♕d6) 16...exd4 17.cxd4 ♘f6=. In the game, Tiger Hillarp Persson finds a better way to distribute the tasks within his small army. The ♗g5 will, together with the ♕e2 and a future ♖fe1, suppress the opposing central thrust ...e6-e5. After some preparation he can play ♖e1-e3, deploying the rook actively and at the same time protecting the weak backward pawn. But instead of a probably permanently bad ♗d2 the Swedish grandmaster prefers to accept a passive rook. The bishop, on the other

hand, will be effectively posted on the kingside.

15...♖ac8

Actually structurally desirable, the central lever 15...e5 leads after ...e5xd4 to an opening of the c-file, on which a white rook is already waiting: 16.♗b5 ♗c6 17.♗d3±.

15...♕c6 16.f3 reminds us of the training exercise in the chapter 'The bishop'.

15...h6 is perhaps the best move. As an example of this we have the next game, which follows an entirely different course.

16.♗d3 ♖fe8 17.♖fe1

17...♘f8?!

This is a little passive. Perhaps Brynell thought that White had no other plan than the stereotypical c3-c4, transposing to a position with hanging pawns. But the 'Tiger' takes his time about that and with his next moves creates the conditions for a future attack on the king.

18.♕g4 ♕c6 19.h4 ♔h8 20.h5! h6

Practically forced. Otherwise after h5-h6 all the dark squares in the king position would be vulnerable, which would constitute a major disadvantage in view of the lack of a bishop to defend them. Now the g7-point has been fixed as the next target for Hillarp Persson.

21.♗f4 ♘h7

But 21...♘d7?? does not work on account of 22.♗e4+−.

22.♗e5±

Active, well centralised opposing pieces must be driven away or exchanged!

Right in our next section with the pawn formation d6/e5, we shall see a typical exception to this rule. But here Brynell has hardly any choice, since the bishop on e5 is too dominant. So, exchange or drive away? The move ...f7-f6 would further weaken Black's king position. So the Swedish grandmaster prefers the exchange.

22...♖g8

22...f6 23.♗f4 f5 24.♕g3 ♘f6 25.♕g6±. As is so often the case, the first weakening has brought about a second one: 25...♘xh5?! 26.♗e5 ♖f8 27.♕xh6+ ♔g8 28.♕g5 with a strong attack. After ♖e3-h3 White can also make use of the h-file which Black has so obligingly opened.

23.♖e3?!

At the wrong moment. 23.♕g3 ♘f6 24.c4± would have kept the advantage White had. Now, after Black has posted two pieces (♖g8 and ♘h7) for the defence of his kingside, it was time to bring about the transformation to hanging pawns.

23...♘f6 24.♕h3?!

24.♕g3 ♘d5 25.♖ee1±.

24...♕a4

This prepares 25...♘d7.

25.c4 ♘d7=

At last Black gets rid of the monster on e5.

26.♖ce1

26...b5

He prevents White from recapturing with the rook after ...♘xe5. Now the d4-pawn would do so. The alternative lay in 26...♘xe5 27.♖xe5. The classic breakthrough d4-d5 will then ensure that all the white pieces are taking part in the attack. The rooks are perfectly placed on the e-file, whilst the bishop and queen are working effectively against the h7-point. The white attack is strong, but Black can mount a defence. Here are some sample variations:

A) 27...♕xa2 28.d5 ♖cd8 29.♕f3 ♗c8 30.♗b1 (30.♕xf7 ♖gf8) 30...♕d2 31.♖5e2 ♕g5 32.♕xf7 and now 32...exd5? 33.♖e8;

B) 27...♗a6 28.d5 ♗xc4 (28...exd5? 29.♕f5+−) 29.♗xc4 ♖xc4 30.dxe6 fxe6 31.♕xe6 ♕xa2 32.♕f7 ♖a4 (the only move against the deadly threat of ♖e8 – if 32...♖c2 33.♖e6! ♖d2 (33...♕a4 34.♖e8) 34.♖xh6++−) 33.♖e6 ♖a5 34.♖1e4 with very exciting and unclear play. The white attack is worth the pawn he has sacrificed.

27.cxb5 ♕xa2 28.♕h4 ♖c3?

28...♘xe5 29.dxe5 ♖gd8=.

29.♕f4?

29.♕e7 ♘xe5 30.dxe5 ♕d5 31.♗f1 gave White a clear advantage.

29...♘xe5 30.dxe5 ♕d5?!

After this Black again has difficulties. 30...♕d2 31.♕xf7 ♖xd3 32.♕xb7 ♖xe3 33.♖xe3 ♕d1+ 34.♔h2 ♕xh5+ with a draw.

31.♗f1

The bishop on f1 looks weak, but is very useful in the middlegame. It is protecting g2 and the b5-pawn, which in turn fixes a7 as a weakness. The weak pawns on a7 and f7 have no appropriate defender. So one of them will soon be cast overboard.

31...♖xe3?!

31...♖c7 32.♖a3 ♕c5 33.♖ea1 ♗d5 34.♕e3 ♕xe3 35.fxe3±.

32.♕xe3 ♔h7

33.♖c1!+−

Once again, the patience of the grandmaster! The a7-pawn is going

nowhere. The opportunity to activate the rook, on the other hand, was only there for a moment: after the precise text move there is no longer any defence. An important pawn is lost and the attack on the king, which White prepared long ago and then delayed, finally happens.

33...g6

After 33...♖c8 34.♖xc8 ♗xc8 35.♕xa7 ♗b7 36.♕b8 ♕e4 37.♕c7 the f7-pawn also falls.

34.♖c7 gxh5 35.♖xf7+ ♖g7 36.♖xg7+ ♔xg7 37.♕xa7 ♔g6 38.♕e3 h4 39.♔h2 ♕d1 40.♕d3+ ♕xd3 41.♗xd3+ ♔g5 42.f3 1-0

The transformation to hanging pawns

31 Nimzo-Indian Defence
Leif Erlend Johannessen 2559
Michael Adams 2720
Birmingham 2006 (9)

1.d4 ♘f6 2.c4 e6 3.♘c3 ♗b4 4.e3 0-0 5.♗d3 d5 6.♘f3 c5 7.0-0 dxc4 8.♗xc4 ♘bd7 9.♕e2 cxd4 10.exd4 ♗xc3 11.bxc3 ♕c7 12.♗g5 b6 13.♘e5 ♗b7 14.♘xd7 ♘xd7 15.♖ac1 h6

The bishop is forced into a decision. If it moves back to e3 or d2 it will be very passively posted.

16.♗h4

Black to move

How did Adams nip in the bud his opponent's efforts to mount an attack?

16...♛f4! 17.♗g3 ♛e4!

With the exchange of queens Adams clearly simplifies the game. There can no longer be any question of chances worth mentioning for a white initiative on the kingside. The game now revolves principally around the backward pawn.

18.f3 ♛xe2 19.♗xe2 ♜ac8 20.♖fd1 ♞f6

White cannot be stopped from a transformation to hanging pawns with c3-c4. Johannessen will also have to make use of this possibility, since otherwise Adams will after some preparation lay siege to the weakness on c3. As we saw in Chapter 4, the strengths of the hanging pawns tend to lie in the middlegame, whereas in the endgame they tend to become a weakness.

Do you remember game 13, Hickl-Johannessen? Here too we want to emphasise once more the value of the white queen's bishop: it has no counterpart and so it can very much hamper the black pieces, especially the rooks. Let us imagine the position without the ♗g3 and ♞f6; by doubling the rooks on the c-file Black could work up a lot of pressure against the white c-pawn. However, the dark-squared bishop prevents this. The game is roughly level, with chances for both sides.

21.♗f2

When should the c-pawn advance? A difficult question. The following variation makes it clear that play can turn out to be very complicated even in this apparently simple position. The answer to the question as to whether hanging pawns or possibly a passed pawn which arises are strong or weak often depends on a tactical detail.

21.c4 ♗a6 (21...♞h5 22.♗d6 ♜fd8 23.c5 ♞f6 24.♖b1 ♞d5 25.♖b3±;) 22.♗e5 ♜c6 23.♖c2 ♜fc8 24.♖dc1 ♞e8 25.♗d3 f6 26.♗f4 (26.♗g3 ♞d6 27.♗g6 ♞f5) 26...g5 27.♗g3 ♔f7= 28.d5!? exd5 29.cxd5 ♜xc2 30.♖xc2 ♜xc2 31.♗xc2 ♗c4 32.♗b8 a6 33.d6 ♞g7 34.♗c7 ♔e6 35.♗e4 ♔d7 36.♗xb6 ♗xa2 37.♗d4 ♞e8 38.♗d3 ♔xd6 39.♗xa6=. This sample variation is far too long to be forced. Nevertheless, it clarifies in exemplary fashion the options available to both sides. A general piece of advice: *Use the bishop pair actively!*

The text move does not make White's situation any worse, but is somewhat passive. Johannessen again pursues the idea of using a piece, the queen's bishop, to secure his position: he is now protecting d4. Thus, after c3-c4, which will not be long in coming, he can double the rooks on the c-file.

21...♜fd8 22.♗f1 ♜d7 23.c4 ♗a6 24.♖c2 ♜c6 25.♖dc1 ♜dc7 26.a4 ♜c8 27.♗d3

27.a5 b5 28.c5 ♞d5 29.♖b2 b4 30.♗e1=.

27...♔f8=

The chances are still approximately level, perhaps even slightly better for White. It is easier for him to activate his king, e.g. on e3. In view of the bishop pair, on the other hand, it would be dangerous for the black monarch to approach the centre of the board. The pressure on c4 hampers White at the moment from advancing in the centre. However, it is also not so easy for Black to crank up this pressure. Perhaps the Norwegian grandmaster became impatient and wanted to finally 'do something'. But perhaps he was also running out of time. As the remaining thinking time decreases, almost all chess players tend to want to force matters, whether that is appropriate in the position or not.

Make good use of your thinking time, but avoid severe time trouble!

28.a5?!

28.♗e1 ♖d8 29.♗c3 ♘e8=.

28...bxa5 29.♗f1?!

29.♗e1 was better.

Black to move

Activate your worst piece!

29...♘d5!

After 29... ♘d7 30.c5 ♗xf1 31.♔xf1= Adams would have obtained nothing special.

30.c5

30.cxd5? ♖xc2 31.♖xc2 ♖xc2 32.♗xa6 ♖c1+ 33.♗f1 exd5−+. The a-pawn costs a piece.

30...♘b4∓

The knight is ideally placed here! It is attacking something, preventing ♖a2, being protected by the a5-pawn, and

can later also be transferred to the lovely blockading square c6, with pressure against the d4-pawn.

31.♖d2   ♗xf1   32.♔xf1   ♖6c7 33.♗g3 ♖b7 34.♖b2 ♖d7 35.♖c4 ♔e7 36.c6?!

He is presumably hoping for an exchange and chances for a draw a pawn down. It was however more tenacious to leave the protected passed pawn where it was. It was not so simple for Black to be able to manoeuvre around it. As a general rule, in bad positions it is better to aim for complications rather than to simplify.

36...♖d5

36...♖xc6? 37.♖bxb4.

37.c7 ♔d7

Black is left a pawn up, White's chances of a draw are marginal.

38.♖b3   ♘c6   39.♖b7   ♖xd4 40.♖xd4+   ♘xd4   41.♖xa7   ♘c6 42.♖a6 e5 43.♗e1 ♔xc7 44.♗xa5+ ♔d6

Of course Adams does not exchange the knight, which is superior to the bishop when the struggle is on a single wing.

45.♗c3 f6

The method we have already met several times of leaving the bishop 'biting on granite'.

46.♖a4 ♔d5 47.♔e2 ♖c7 48.♔d3 ♘e7 49.♗d2 ♖b7 50.♖a5+ ♔e6

51.♖a4 ♘f5 52.f4 ♖d7+ 53.♔e2 ♘d4+ 54.♔f2 ♔f5 55.fxe5 fxe5 56.♔e3 ♖b7 57.♗c3 ♖b3 58.♔d2 ♔e4 59.♖a6

59.♖a7?? allows a knight fork: 59...♖xc3!.
59...♖b7 60.♖g6 ♔f5 61.♖a6 ♘b3+ 62.♔c2 ♘c5 63.♖c6 ♘e4 64.♗b2 ♖d7!

This shuts out the white king.
65.♗c1 ♘f6 66.♖c5 ♘d5 67.♗d2 h5 68.♖c8 ♘f4 69.♖f8+ ♔e4 70.♖h8 g6 71.♖g8 ♖d6
White resigned.

Model games
Furman-Kholmov (Kiev 1954), laying siege to the backward pawn
Portisch-Pinter (Budapest 1981)
Jussupow-Hracek (Germany Bundesliga 2002/03)
Kasparov-Tal (Brussels 1987), black pawn on d5 instead of e6; attack on the kingside

You may perhaps get the impression that the very top players are really not so strong. But that is wrong. It is an illusion. With a computer by your side it is very easy to sit in judgement, but when you are sitting alone at the board, things look quite different.
Vladimir Kramnik

The pawn pair d6/e5

This structure arises from various variations of the Sicilian Defence, but also occurs frequently in the Ruy Lopez or the Philidor Defence.

Specific characteristics
The backward pawn is weak. Unlike in the case of the pawn duo c3/d4, however, there is no second weakness in the black camp. There the white a-pawn was also vulnerable, whilst here there is one pawn island less.
The pawns e4 and e5 divide the board into two halves. Whereas White's pieces can usually easily swing over from the queenside to the kingside, the d6-pawn breaks the contact on Black's side between the left and right sides of the board. The standard square for Black's king's bishop is e7. But it is passively placed there, and difficult to activate.
White has the freer game, though Black does have one more central pawn, which allows certain plans.

Plans for White
The main goal consists of permanent control and later occupation of the ideal blockading square d5. Not only a knight but even a bishop would be very effective if posted there.
Furthermore, White can aim for the pawn advance f2-f4-f5. After it the

black position would be cramped on the kingside too. If Black exchanges on f4, then each side has a pawn weakness – Black the d6-pawn, White the one on e4. Here it very much depends on the specific positioning of the pieces whether White can make anything of his very minimal advantage in space.

Plans for Black

The permanent installation of a white outpost on d5 should be prevented. If there is an opportunity to take a white piece on that square at a moment when White is obliged to recapture with the e-pawn, Black has no need to fear the transformation of the structure. After exd5 he may have less space at his disposal, but the reduced number of pieces makes this bearable. Moreover, there then arises the possibility of space-grabbing counterplay with ...f7-f5. The pawn weakness d6 is now clearly harder to attack, since the d-file is blocked.

Before the opponent's attack on the left of the board, beginning with ♘d5, Black now and then gets the set-up a6, b5, ♗b7 and ♖c8. This exerts strong pressure on the centre, on the one hand with the threat of ...b5-b4, which drives off the knight on c3, on the other with the typical Sicilian exchange sacrifice on c3. In the chapter 'Weak squares' we shall see an example of this, in which the terrible white pawn structure a2, c2, c3 can on its own represent sufficient compensation for an exchange sacrifice on c3.

Another important plan consists of the lever ...d6-d5. If this can be played without incurring other disadvantages, Black usually obtains a level game.

Also worth considering is the attack on the centre from the flank: ...f7-f5 by Black opens the f-file, down which pressure can be exerted on the white pawn on f2. There will possibly be the option of ...f5-f4 in order to attack the cramped white kingside.

Conclusion

The structure characterised by the pawn duo d6/e5 promises double-edged play. White tries to steer the game into calm waters, whilst Black aims for dynamic counterplay.

32 Sicilian Defence
Efim Geller
Miguel Najdorf
Zurich 1953 (13)

1.e4 c5 2.♘f3 d6 3.d4 cxd4 4.♘xd4 ♘f6 5.♘c3 a6

Najdorf of course plays the variation of the Sicilian Defence which is named after him.

6.♗e2 e5 7.♘b3

With his last move Black has driven away the ideally posted central white knight and gained space in the centre, but the price he has accepted to pay for this is the backward pawn on d6. What if White manages to get permanent control of the outpost on d5? The course of the game will provide a clear answer to this question.

7...♗e6

Actually logical. Black immediately over-protects the central square which has just been weakened, so that for the moment d5 cannot be occupied with pieces. Najdorf would, as outlined above, react to ♘d5 with ...♗xd5 or (preferably) ...♘xd5. After exd5 White would admittedly have an advantage in space, but not an 'eternal' central outpost. That is something he can aim for with ♗c1-g5 and the subsequent exchange against the black king's knight, so as to only then follow up with ♘d5. Najdorf has taken measures against specifically that case with his 7...♗e6. On 8.♗g5 he plays 8...♘bd7, which maintains the control over d5.

All quite logical? According to the ideas of the day, yes. The Najdorf Variation, however, was still, as it were, in short pants. Over the next five decades White tried out many ideas, and nowadays 'Najdorf players' prefer instead of 7...♗e6 the move 7...♗e7. The reason is the susceptibility of the ♗e6 to attacks by the white f-pawn, which also occur in this game.

8.0-0

8.f4 ♕c7 9.g4 exf4 10.g5 ♘fd7 11.♗xf4± followed up by ♕d2 and queenside castling is a modern plan.

8...♘bd7 9.f4 ♕c7 10.f5 ♗c4

The advance of the f-pawn is having an effect. The gain of space on the kingside could, after kingside castling, lead to a pawn storm by means of g2-g4-g5. But what is more important is that as a result of the exchange of the light-squared bishop White's control of d5 is strengthened.

11.a4 ♖c8 12.♗e3 ♗e7

In view of the sobering way the game continued, the suggestion of the tournament winner David Bronstein in his book on the Candidates' tournament in Zurich 1953 is worth considering: 12...d5 13.exd5 (13.♘xd5 ♘xd5 14.exd5 ♗xb3 15.cxb3 ♗c5) 13...♗b4.

13.a5 h5

Perhaps Najdorf feared that after castling kingside he would come under violent attack there. He was wrong! 13...0-0 14.g4?! (14.♗xc4) 14...h6 15.h4 d5!. 'An attack on the flank should be met with a central counter-thrust', wrote Nimzowitsch. This is of course only a rule of thumb which does not absolve one from concrete calculation at the board. But in positions of this type it fits exactly. The situation is no less dangerous for the white king than for the black one.

14.♗xc4 ♕xc4 15.♖a4 ♕c7 16.h3 h4 17.♖f2

Geller protects the c2-pawn, so that after ♗e3-g5xf6 the knight on c3 can go to its dream square d5.

17...b5

In the tournament Bronstein describes Najdorf as having a 'temperament which is not made for passive defence without active counterplay'. But the position is unsuitable for that: 17... 0−0 18.♗g5±, e.g. 18...♘c5 19.♗xf6 ♗xf6 20.♘d5 ♕d8 21.♖b4±.

18.axb6 ♘xb6

White to move

Which of the following possibilities is preferable: take the a6-pawn, move the rook away or exchange minor pieces on b6?

19.♗xb6!

When exchanging it is not what disappears from the board which is important, but what is left on it.

Just now we were still prepared to give up the lovely dark-squared bishop, the best-looking piece on the board, for the knight on f6 – 'only' in order to be able to occupy the d5-square on a permanent basis. Now it is easy to exchange it for the other knight, which is not only guarding d5 but could also become unpleasant from c4.

With the text move Geller achieves complete control over the position. Black is forced into passive defence of the weak a6-pawn. That gives White the time he needs to send his miserably placed b3-knight on the long journey to d5. The resulting dark-squared weaknesses can be neglected so long as the bishop on e7 cannot become active, which is at present not foreseeable.

The alternatives did not promise White much: 19.♖xa6 ♘c4 20.♕f3 (20.♗c1 ♕b7) 20...♘xb2 (winning back the sacrificed pawn) 21.♗d2 ♕b7 22.♖a2

♘c4 23.♗g5 and the d5-square is still significant, but Black has withstood the worst (±).

19...♕xb6 20.♕e2 ♖a8 21.♔h2 0-0 22.♖f1 ♖a7 23.♖fa1 ♖fa8 24.♖1a2

This protects b2, so that the knight on b3 can set off on its journey.

24...♗d8 25.♘a5 ♖c8 26.♘c4 ♕c6 27.♘e3 a5 28.♖c4 ♕a6 29.b3 ♗b6

Najdorf allows Geller to realise the plan he was aiming for. Was it perhaps worth trying to prevent ♘e3-d5 ? After 29...♖xc4 30.♘xc4 the knight is diverted from its route, but after 30...♖d7 31.♕d3 ♕c6 (31...♗b6 32.♘d5) 32.♘d5 ♘xd5 33.♕xd5± the knight is no less effective on c4 than it would be on d5.

30.♖xc8+ ♕xc8 31.♘ed5 ♘xd5 32.♘xd5±

White has obtained the ideal position he was aiming for. His knight is dominating the board. Now the bishop is suddenly helping the black queen to threaten mate. After Geller has parried the danger, however, the bad bishop more and more falls prey to insignificance.

32...♕c5 33.♖a1 ♕f2

Geller could prevent this exchange on the next move with ♖f1, after which Najdorf would also have to reckon with an attack on the kingside by White, beginning with ♕g4.

34.♕xf2 ♗xf2 35.♖f1 ♗d4

35...♗g3+? 36.♔g1. The bishop on g3 is out of the play and will not be able to keep the white king away from the queenside in the long term: 36...a4 37.♖a1 a3 38.♔f1.

36.c3 ♗c5 37.g4

Geller certainly would not have wanted to exchange the weak h4-pawn. But otherwise the king cannot get out of the corner.

37...hxg3+ 38.♔xg3 ♖b7 39.♖b1

Alternatively White could have created a passed pawn with 39.b4 axb4 40.cxb4, since 40...♗xb4 fails to 41.♖b1. But this would be against the spirit of the position.

The key to understanding this is 'control'. Black has no chances of becoming active, the bishop has no targets and the rook does not have an open file along which to invade the white camp. And

he will also not get one by exchanging pawns on the queenside. White has everything under control and has all the time in the world to bring his king to c4 or c2 and then set about the weaknesses in the black position with the rook: the pawns on a5 and g7.

Such situations require to be evaluated (in advance!). Then all that is required is, as has been stated so often, the patience to strengthen one's own position to the maximum before engaging in active operations.

That sounds very simple, but how can YOU more easily recognise these situations in the future? The evaluation of a position is considerably easier if you are aware of relevant patterns. Study your own games and also as many games by other players as possible.

39...f6

Najdorf accepts a further weakness in his position on g6. But in return he gets the f7-square for the king, so that his rook can occupy the h-file.

40.♔f3 ♔f7 41.♔e2 ♖b8 42.b4

In view of the counterplay now threatened by Black, White is now forced to become active.

42...g6?!

This makes the win easier. But even with tenacious defence the game cannot be saved. The difference in the activity of the kings and minor pieces is too great: 42...axb4 43.cxb4 ♗d4 44.b5 ♔e8 45.h4 ♔d7 46.h5 ♖h8 47.♖h1 ♖b8 48.♖h4 ♖b7 (48...♖xb5 49.♖g4+−) 49.♔d3+−.

43.♔d3

Geller now wins without major problems. In the further course of the game too, the black bishop remains ineffective.

43.♖f1 was the simplest. It could be followed by 43...axb4 44.cxb4 ♗xb4 45.♖b1 gxf5 46.exf5 ♖b5 47.♘xb4 d5 48.♔d3+−.

Another way to win consisted of 43.fxg6+ ♔xg6 44.bxc5 ♖xb1 45.c6 ♖b8 46.c7 ♖a8 47.♘b6 ♖h8 48.c8♕ and ♘xc8. Why did Geller not play that? Because he was not looking for it! A positional victory is no longer in doubt, so an intensive search for alternatives is unnecessary. In clearly won positions there are often several ways to win which present themselves. If we have calculated a simple and clear way right to the end, then we should play it. There are no prizes for finding the 'shortest' or the 'most beautiful' win. But a lot of points have already been given away because the laborious search brought confusion or time trouble into the equation!

Never play for the 'gallery'!

43...gxf5 44.exf5 axb4 45.cxb4 ♗d4 46.♖c1

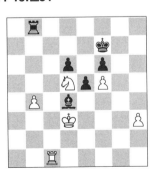

46...♔g7

White dominates the middle of the board, so that the black king can only move to the edge. But there it will turn into a target.

After 46...♖b7 47.♖c7+ the passed pawns would decide matters.

47.♖c7+ ♔h6 48.♔e4 ♔g5 49.♖h7 ♗f2 50.♖g7+ ♔h4 51.♔f3 ♗e1 52.♔g2

Threatening 53.♖g4+ ♔h5 54.♘xf6+ ♔h6 55.♖g6#. You should remember this mating pattern. It frequently appears in endgames with rook and knight.

52...♖f8 53.b5 ♗a5 54.b6 ♗xb6 55.♘xb6 ♖b8 56.♖g4+ ♔h5 57.♘d5   **1−0**

33 Sicilian Defence
Vassily Smyslov
Iosif Rudakovsky
Moscow 1945

1.e4 c5 2.♘f3 e6 3.d4 cxd4 4.♘xd4 ♘f6 5.♘c3 d6 6.♗e2 ♗e7 7.0-0 0-0 8.♗e3 ♘c6 9.f4 ♕c7 10.♕e1 ♘xd4 11.♗xd4 e5 12.♗e3 ♗e6?!

12...b6.

13.f5 ♗c4?

13...♗d7 14.♗g5 ♗c6.

14.♗xc4 ♕xc4

White to move

What would you suggest?

15.♗g5!±

You definitely found this move quickly! If not, please go back through game 32, Geller-Najdorf.

Here it is, as usual, interesting to see the evaluation of the position by our electronic assistants. Tactically they are already superior to even the top GMs, but positionally they hardly have a clue! After the move in the game, Black's situation can only be ranked as 'strategically critical'. That does not mean that White has a forced win, but the position is very difficult to defend in a practical game. Komodo 9 evaluates the position as only '±'.

15...♖fe8 16.♗xf6 ♗xf6 17.♘d5 ♗d8 18.c3 b5 19.b3 ♕c5+ 20.♔h1 ♖c8 21.♖f3

Watch out for the kingside! With his next move Rudakovsky allows the destruction of his pawn structure. Otherwise things would have become too cramped around the black king.

How do the engines evaluate the position? In the meantime they consider White to have almost a pawn of an advantage, White stands better. That is progress, but still not correct. Black's position is probably untenable.

21...♔h8?!

21...f6 was the more resilient defence. However, this is not the sort of move one makes in practice since the black position loses all flexibility. The light squares have been too greatly weakened. But it is not easy to provide 'proof' of a win for White, and for that reason we again need our computer. Here is simply one sample variation:

22.♖h3 ♔h8 23.♕h4 h6 (after White has forced this move, he can open the kingside with the pawn storm g2-g4, h2-h4 and g4-g5) 24.♕e1 a5 25.g4 a4 (Black tries to open a file so as to exchange major pieces. There is clearly nothing else he can do) 26.b4 ♕c4 27.♖g3 ♖f8 28.♕e3 ♖f7 29.♖g2 (now there should be no defence left against the advance of the pawns on the kingside. But White will first place his queen's rook on the h-file) 29...♖b7 30.h4 ♔g8 31.♔h2 ♔f7 32.♖h1 ♕c6 33.♔g3 ♕c4 34.♕f3 ♖bb8 35.♖h3 ♖b7 36.♔h2 ♔g8 37.g5 fxg5 38.hxg5 ♗xg5 39.f6 ♖f8 40.♖xg5 hxg5 41.♕h5+−.

Of course this variation is not forced. But it is a good illustration of how much the knight on d5 cramps Black's game and makes a defence against the attack on the king difficult.

22.f6+−

With this White forces the decisive weakening of the black castled position.

22...gxf6 23.♕h4 ♖g8 24.♘xf6 ♖g7 25.♖g3 ♗xf6 26.♕xf6 ♖g8 27.♖d1 d5 28.♖xg7

Black resigned.

Attacking with a touch of bluff, as happened previously, does not work any more nowadays. Under the influence of the computer we are defending much more precisely. Even Kasparov has adapted his style to this.

Vladimir Kramnik

34 Sicilian Defence
Oleg Korneev 2657
Alexander Moiseenko 2632
Fügen 2006 (4)

1.e4 c5 2.♘f3 ♘c6 3.d4 cxd4 4.♘xd4 ♘f6 5.♘c3 e5 6.♘db5 d6 7.♗g5 a6 8.♘a3 b5 9.♘d5 ♗e7 10.♗xf6 ♗xf6 11.c3

After the previous examples it is amazing that nowadays even leading grand-masters voluntarily concede complete control over d5 to their opponents. What is Black hoping to gain from this plan? The really typical course of this game makes that clear.

If you do not agree with this severe neglect of the central d5-square by Black, then you find yourself in good company. In the early 70s of the last century, there was little respect for the dynamic possibilities of this then very new opening. Evgeny Sveshnikov, after whom this system was named, explains in Kasparov's *Revolution in the 70s* how after a game Karpov recommended him to play a different variation. Petrosian was astonished that nobody had yet found a refutation and threatened to change his opening repertoire and himself turn to 1.e4 in order to find one.

The d5-square will again be an issue later. For the moment we hold on to the fact that in return for his central outpost White had to pay the price of a clear lag in development: the knight on a3 will move a few more times before being properly developed.

11...♗g5

A clear difference is appearing between this and the previous games. In those White could cramp the black kingside with f2-f4-f5. Here, on the other hand, Black cannot be prevented, after he has castled, from attacking the centre with ...f7-f5, opening the f-file for his rook and making space for his pieces.

12.♘c2 ♘e7 13.♘cb4 0-0 14.a4

With this White obtains the c4-square for his bishop. An isolated black pawn on b5 would be weak, so the exchange is practically forced.

14...bxa4 15.♕xa4 ♘xd5 16.♘xd5 ♗d7 17.♕d1 a5 18.♗c4 ♔h8 19.0-0 f5

The reason for Black's set-up becomes clearer. The knight on d5 looks nice, but does not represent a threat. Moreover, it is blocking the d-file, so that it is difficult to attack the weak backward pawn on d6. On the other hand, the pawn lever ...f7-f5 forces White into concessions in the centre. The exchange may not surrender control of the central squares e4 and d5, but it opens the f-file, down which Black can exert pressure in the direction of f2. Should White support the centre with f2-f3, then ...f5-f4 could follow, with attacking chances against the white king.

20.exf5 ♗xf5 21.♕e2

21.♗d3 is an attempt to manage without the weakening move f2-f3 which follows in the game. Since the dark-squared bishop no longer has a counterpart, the pawns on the kingside should, as far as possible, protect the dark squares and also keep the a7-g1 diagonal closed: 21...♗d7 (21... e4 22.♗c2±; the e4-pawn is being attacked) 22.♗e4=. Here White has achieved a king position which has not been weakened and a perfect blockade of the black central pawns. We prefer this to the game continuation; but it is not easy to cash in on it.

21...♕b8 22.♖fd1 ♗e6 23.♔h1 ♖a7 24.f3

As we said: we would gladly have avoided this move.

24...♗d7 25.♗d3 g6 26.♗e4 ♗e6 27.g3?!

It will become clear that this is not an improvement of the position. But in a practical game we always want to have an airhole for our king.

27...♗d8

Nimzowitsch would still have been satisfied. The blockade of the central pawn duo d6 and e5 with pieces is

perfect and apparently unbreakable. We will meet this subject in a different form in the chapter 'Pawn chains'. Nevertheless, everything is fine for Black too. The weaknesses are protected and with his bishop pair he can intervene on both sides of the board. The semi-open f-file is also important. The black rooks will be very effectively posted there, whereas the white ones have no prospect of activity any time soon.

28.h4

Who is attacking whom? It is not so clear whether White is dreaming of a future h4-h5 or whether he is wanting to anticipate ...g6-g5 by Black – probably the latter. Here we can see a typical scenario: the first softening of the structure (f2-f3) is quickly followed by another one (g2-g3) and this then gives rise to a third one (h2-h4). Happy are those who have a solid pawn rampart in front of their king!

28...♖af7 29.♔g2 ♗f5

30.♖f1

Instead of attacking d6, the rook defends passively. After 30.♗xf5 gxf5 the weakening provoked by g2-g3 and h2-h4 makes itself felt. White has no antidote to the threatened doubling of the rooks on the g-file.

30...♗b6 31.♖ad1

One way to equality was 31.♘xb6 ♕xb6 32.♗d5 ♖f6 33.f4! ♗e6 34.♗xe6 ♖xe6

35.fxe5= (both kings are 'equally badly placed' and for the rook on f1 the file is at last being opened) 35...♖b8 36.♖f2 ♖xe5 37.♕g4= (Moiseenko). But it is psychologically understandable that Korneev did not want to give up his centrally posted knight.

31...♗c5

A good sign for Black. The once passive bishop is on an important diagonal and in addition is still protecting the backward pawn.

32.♖d2 ♕c8 33.♔h2?!

White is now clearly forced on to the defensive. His central blockade is achieving nothing, Black is simply playing around it.

A better way was 33.♗xf5 ♕xf5 34.f4=.

33...a4 34.♖d3 ♕d8 35.♔g2 ♗d7∓

Moiseenko deploys the bishop pair cleverly. After taking permanent control of the a7-g1 diagonal with the dark-squared one, he now swiftly changes sides of the board with the other one.

36.♖dd1 g5!

Opening the g-file would make possible a strong attack for Black.

37.h5 ♕e8 38.g4

Intending to set up a sort of fortress on the light squares.

38...♕c8 39.♔g3?!

Not a good place.

39...♕b8 40.♕d2 ♗b5 41.♖h1 h6 42.♘e3?

42.♖he1 ♗c4 or 42.♔g2 ♗c4, in each case with a clear advantage for Black.

Black to move

How did Moiseenko transform his positional superiority into something tangible?

42...d5!−+

The typical way of 'jemmying open' this sort of position. As long as the blockade held, White could still protect everything, despite the loosening up of his king position. After the disappearance of the central pawns all the diagonals are opened up, as is the f-file. The black pieces are ideally placed for the attack on the exposed white king.

43.♕xd5

The emergency brake. However, a piece down, he will have no realistic chances of saving the game. Other moves also lose:

A) 43.♘xd5 ♖xf3+ 44.♗xf3 e4+ 45.♔g2 ♖xf3 (45...exf3+ 46.♔h3 f2 47.♔g2 ♕c8−+) 46.♖h3 ♕f8 47.♖xf3 ♕xf3+ 48.♔h2 ♗d6+ 49.♔g1 ♕xg4+ 50.♔h1 ♕h3+ 51.♔g1 ♗c5+;

B) 43.♗xd5 e4+;

C) 43.♗f5 d4 44.♘d5 e4+ 45.♔h3 e3 46.♕e1 ♖xf5 47.gxf5 ♕e5 (analysis by Moiseenko).

43...♗xe3 44.♕e6 ♖f6 45.♕e7 ♕a7 46.♕xa7 ♗xa7 47.♖he1 ♗b8 48.♔g2 ♗c6 49.♗xc6 ♖xc6 50.♖d3 ♖b6 51.♖d2 ♗d6 52.♖ee2 ♔g7 53.♖d5 ♔f6 54.♖a5 ♖fb8 55.♖xa4 ♖xb2 56.♖a2 ♖xe2+ 57.♖xe2 ♖b3 58.♖c2 ♗a3 59.♔f2 ♖b2 60.♖xb2 ♗xb2 61.c4 ♗d4+ 62.♔e2 e4 63.fxe4 ♔e5   **0–1**

The permanent control over d5 brought White nothing in this game. After ...f7-f5 Black was able to activate all his pieces and conduct operations on both sides of the board.

Model games

Adams-Salov (Dortmund 1992), attacking the backward pawn

Robatsch-Fischer (Havana 1965)

Marin-Narciso Dublan (Solsona 2004)

Karjakin-Shirov (Heraklion 2007)

Geller-Fischer (Willemstad 1962), transformation of the central structure with exd5, then creation of a passed pawn on the queenside

Shirov-Topalov (Morelia/Linares 2008), double rook endgame with the potential to become a classic.

Chapter 7

Passed pawns

In my opinion the passed pawn has a soul, just like a human being, desires which slumber in it unrecognised, and fears the existence of which he himself is scarcely aware.

Aaron Nimzowitsch

A pawn is described as a 'passed pawn' when it can no longer be prevented from being promoted by opposing pawns. Its lust to advance constitutes a danger which should not be under-estimated. The opponent's pieces must dedicate themselves to the task of keeping it in check.

Passed pawns appear in all areas of the board; mostly not until the endgame, but also frequently in the middlegame and even in the opening. As they advance, the danger of promotion grows – at the same time, however, they become more susceptible to attacks. The correct evaluation as to whether a passed pawn is strong or weak often depends on details and requires above all experience.

In this chapter we will treat as an example a typical structure with a central passed pawn.

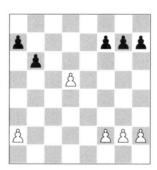

Characteristics

The white d-pawn has already crossed the centre line and secured an advantage in space: the 'rearspan' mentioned in the chapter 'The rook' consists of four ranks, compared to three available to Black. On a full board this can lead to the black pieces suffering from a shortage of space. Their possibilities of switching from the queenside to the kingside are limited.

On its way to the opposing back rank the pawn creates outposts. In any case it can also take on the characteristics of the IQP (see Chapter 5).

Since it cannot be protected by other pawns it is a target for attacks by opposing pieces. Should these be better coordinated than White's 'support troops', the pawn becomes a weakness in 'enemy territory' (Nimzowitsch). We shall take a closer look at this topic in the game Spassky-Karpov.

On the queenside Black has a sound majority, which for its part can create a distant – from the centre and the kingside – passed pawn. However, that requires five tempi (...b6-b5, ...b5-b4, ...a7-a5, ...a5-a4 and ...b4-b3). In the endgame the distant passed pawn almost always constitutes an advantage.

Plans for White

The passed pawn loses strength as fewer pieces are left on the board: as soon as the black king intervenes actively in the action, it can take over the job of supervision. White should retain as much material as possible. The extreme case, a pure pawn ending, e.g. with the white king on d4 and the black one on d6, would be totally lost. Black creates a distant passed pawn by advancing the queenside pawns; it decisively diverts the white king from the main arena, the kingside (we will deal with a similar example further on).

On a full board White will often try to attack on the kingside. The d-pawn restricts the black pieces and can prevent the latter from being manoeuvred over to the right side of the board to help in the defence.

The plan which is probably encountered most often consists of a well-supported advance. The emphasis is on well-'supported'. Many passed pawns are blockaded and later destroyed! But if it is reliably protected, White's advantage in space can assume oppressive forms. A good example is game 18, Smyslov-Karpov, in the chapter 'Isolated pawns'. With the appearance of the IQP on d6 Karpov's forces lost all coordination.

The passed pawn is particularly strong in endgames with queens. Here, as well as the threat of promotion, dangers for the opposing king frequently crop up. This was demonstrated in the final phase of game 22, Predojevic-Golubovic, also in the chapter 'Isolated pawns'. Moreover the queen is the only piece in a position to help the pawn to advance without the support of other pieces.

But White can also try to occupy the outpost on c6 with a piece. If Black exchanges the latter, the passed pawn is 'helped' forward from d5 to c6, where it is an important square closer to promotion. In the model game Karpov-Kasparov, on the other hand, White, with the help of the outpost on c6, seizes the important c-file, which turns out to be decisive in the game due to the lack of compensation for Black.

Plans for Black

The highest priority is the blockade of the pawn on the stopping square d6. In doing so, Black aims for simplifications so that at a later stage in the game he can also involve the king actively in the struggle. After a successful blockade the defending side devotes itself to its majority on the queenside and creates a distant passed pawn.

Black often meets White's plan of conquering the c-file by blocking it on c5 with a piece of his own well supported by the b6-pawn. If there remains enough time,

Black can push this outpost into the opposing half of the board with the advance of the b-pawn, i.e. to c4 (with the pawn on b5) or even c3 (pawn on b4).

Conclusion

In the position in the diagram the strengths of the passed pawn lie in the middlegame, where it cramps Black and disrupts the communication between queenside and kingside. In endgames with queens the pawn is also powerful. Black seeks his chance, on the other hand, in queenless endgames, where his candidate passed pawn on the b-file is often superior to White's d-pawn.

Whoever is in charge of the square in front of the pawn, controls it! A well blockaded passed pawn can constitute a considerable disadvantage.

The passed pawn in the middle-game

We were impressed by two games of the German grandmaster Artur Jussupow.

35 Catalan Opening

| **Artur Jussupow** | 2450 |
| **Sergey Dolmatov** | 2495 |

Graz 1978 (6)

1.c4 e6 2.g3 d5 3.♗g2 ♘f6 4.♘f3 ♗e7 5.0-0 0-0 6.d4 dxc4 7.♕c2 ♗d7 8.♘e5 ♗c6 9.♘xc6 ♘xc6 10.e3 ♘a5 11.♖d1 c6 12.♘d2 b5 13.b3 cxb3 14.axb3 ♕b6 15.♗a3 b4 16.♗b2 ♖ac8 17.e4 ♖fd8 18.♕b1 c5 19.♕a2 ♘c6 20.d5 exd5 21.exd5 ♘d4 22.♘c4 ♕c7 23.♗xd4 cxd4 24.♖xd4 ♗c5 25.♖d2

Up until this point the game has not been particularly exciting. A slight white advantage from the opening has been evaporating more and more.

Black to move

How should he continue?

The opponent has a passed pawn, which has to be stopped. The ideal blockading piece is the knight. If we bring together both parts of the puzzle we will quickly find the most important candidate move:

25...♘e8

We already came across this topic in the chapter on knights in game 4, Atalik-Hickl. Since it is extremely important, here are some basics again:

analysis diagram: the ideal square for a knight

This structure could have arisen from the King's Indian Defence. White played f2-f4, went on to exchange on e5 and Black recaptured with the d-pawn. Let us first familiarise ourselves with White's plans. On which flank will he become active? Which pawn lever should be aimed for?

It is probably not easy for you to construct a plan. Perhaps play down the semi-open f-file? Probably not, since even tripling the major pieces does not produce a threat worth the mention. The centre is locked, so we are left with the queenside. The possible lever b2-b4 could be met with ...b7-b6, after which the change in the structure is insignificant.

And now Black. The knight is exerting pressure on the two pawns c4 and e4, protecting f7 and supporting the levers ...b7-b5 and ...f7-f5. Of these, ...f7-f5 is the less pleasant for White. A capture leads to the powerful pawn pair e5/f5; not doing so can under certain circumstances be met with ...f5-f4 and the activation of the kingside majority. In all these considerations the white

109

passed pawn has no role to play! Black is better.

Back to the game:

   26.♖e1   ♘d6   27.♘xd6   ♕xd6
   28.♕b1   ♖e8   29.♖de2   ♖xe2
   30.♖xe2 g6 31.♕e4 ♗b6

At this point the two players agreed on a draw.

White to move

Evaluate the position!

Choose between the following evaluations:

1) The white passed pawn is harmless and the king is badly placed. Black has a clear advantage.

2) Bishops of opposite colours increase the tendency towards a draw, the passed pawn has no great part to play. The position is level.

3) White has a passed pawn which cannot be attacked and the better king position. The black majority on the queenside can achieve nothing because of the b3-pawn. Enough for a slight plus!

That bishops of opposite colours increase the likelihood of a draw is a widely held misconception! This statement only holds true for bishop endings (also in combination with knights). If rooks are still present, the bishops increase for the most part the imbalance on the board and favour the attacking side.

In our example they are the reason for Black's clear advantage. Answer 1 is correct! The passed pawn is under control and is making the bishop on g2 the worst piece on the board. Its counterpart, on the other hand, has a clear target to attack – the f2-point. In addition the rook is threatening to invade on the c-file and attack b3 or f2. Over and above that, the pawn majority on the queenside also represents a serious danger. With ...a5-a4 Black can at any time create his own passed pawn. We should always bear in mind that a passed pawn is not an extra pawn. The opponent is frequently better placed on another part of the board.

The draw which followed has several possible causes. The most probable, in addition to securing a good position in the tournament, is quite simply psychology. Up until then Dolmatov had to defend a worse position. After the apparent improvement in his situation, he took advantage of the first opportunity to offer a draw, without realising that he already had a better position.

36 Queen's Gambit Declined
Artur Jussupow   2490
Vladimir Tukmakov   2575
Frunze 1979 (10)

   **1.c4 ♘f6 2.♘c3 c5 3.g3 ♘c6 4.♗g2
e6 5.♘f3 d5 6.cxd5 ♘xd5 7.0-0
♗e7 8.d4 0-0 9.e4 ♘xc3 10.bxc3
cxd4 11.cxd4 b6 12.d5 exd5
13.exd5 ♘b4 14.♘e5 ♗f6 15.♖e1
♗b7 16.♗a3 ♖e8 17.♗xb4 ♖xe5
18.♖c1 ♖xe1+ 19.♕xe1 a5 20.♗c3
♗xc3 21.♖xc3 ♕d6 22.♖e3**

The position which has arisen is very much like the previous game, in which Black had the advantage. The only difference consists of the black bishop, which is on this occasion present on the light squares.

Black to move

Is the evaluation different from the previous game?

Quite clearly so! Of course the bishop on b7 cannot be described as bad according to our definition, but it is making no contribution to the defence of the kingside. Much more important, however, is the lack of counterplay. There is no black pressure on f2 and there is at present no sign of the creation of a passed pawn on the queenside. The d5-pawn can be sufficiently well protected. White is slightly better.

22...g6

According to our rule, the airhole is on the opposite colour of square from that of the opposing bishop. The fact that it makes his own bishop somewhat worse is of lesser importance since it will not be able to become active on the other half of the board in the foreseeable future.

23.h4

A typical attacking set-up on the king-side.

23...h5

If the white pawn gets to h5, the capture ...gxh5 weakens the structure and after a possible recovery of the weak pawn on h5 opportunities arise to attack the black king. There is no way the coffin nail h5-h6 can be allowed. Immediately mating patterns spring to the eye on the weakened back rank or on the g7-square.

24.♕b1 ♗a6

An inaccuracy which allows the rook on to c6. A better way was the immediate 24...♖c8, because the intended 25.♖b3 is not a threat since now d5 is hanging: 25...♗xd5! 26.♗xd5 (26.♖d3? ♗xa2∓, that did not work with the rook on a8; 26.♕d3 ♖c5; 26.♕d1 ♖c5 27.♖d3 ♕c7 with the threat of ♖c1, which is of course easy to overlook) 26...♕xd5 27.♖xb6=.

25.♔h2

But Jussupow also misses his chance: 25.♖c3 (threatening 26.♖c6 with an advantage) 25...♗b7 26.♖b3± ♗xd5? 27.♖d3+− ♗xa2 28.♖xd6 and at the end the rook is left hanging on a8.

25...♖d8 26.f4 ♗c8 27.♖b3 ♗f5 28.♕b2 ♖b8 29.♕d4 b5=

Black activates his majority. The position is completely level.

30.♖c3

30...♗d7?!

It is understandable that Tukmakov did not want to let the rook on to c6, but now the seventh rank becomes an issue. After 30...♖e8, intending 31...♖e2 – this move gains in strength as a consequence of 26.f4 –, Black activates his last piece.

There is no sign of any advantage for White.

Always think about having all your pieces take part in the struggle!

31.♕a7

This occupies the important seventh rank and attacks the a-pawn, which provokes the subsequent reaction.

31...a4

Now the queenside majority is clearly devalued. It is no longer so easy for Black to create a passed pawn.

32.♖c7 ♖d8 33.a3

33.♖b7±.

33...♗e8

34.f5

The only possibility to breathe some life into a position which was heading for a draw. White sharpens the play a little. The destruction of the black structure is good value for the pawn sacrificed, but also no more than that.

34...gxf5 35.♖c3 ♗d7 36.♕d4 ♖e8 37.♗f3

37...♕e5?

Why? As long as the passed pawn is effectively blockaded, Black has little to fear. Both 37...♖b8 and 37...♖c8 were worth considering, with equality. Now the passed pawn gets going and the picture changes abruptly.

38.♕xe5 ♖xe5 39.♖c7 ♗e8 40.d6 ♖e3 41.♗d5?!

Jussupow could force the creation of a dangerous passed pawn: 41.♗xh5+− ♖d3 42.♖c8 ♔f8 43.♗e2 ♖d2 44.d7! ♖xd7 45.♖xe8+ ♔xe8 46.♗xb5 ♔e7 47.♗xd7 ♔xd7 48.♔g2 with a winning pawn ending.

41...♔g7 42.d7 ♗xd7 43.♖xd7 ♖d3 44.♗c6 ♖xa3 45.♗xb5 f4 46.gxf4 ♖f3 47.♖d4 a3 48.♖a4 a2 49.♖xa2 ♖xf4

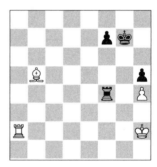

We have in front of us a laborious, though relatively easily won endgame. The only thing to avoid if possible is an exchange of rooks. After that we would reach an endgame with the wrong colour of corner square.

If the bishop does not control the promotion square of the rook pawn, apart from very few exceptions the position is drawn!

50.♔g3 ♖g4+ 51.♔h3 ♖e4 52.♗e2 ♖e3+ 53.♔g2 ♖e5 54.♔g3 ♖d5 55.♗f3 ♖b5 56.♔f4 f6 57.♖a7+ ♔g8 58.♗e4 ♔f8 59.♗g6 ♔g8 60.♗f7+ ♔h8 61.♗e6 ♖c5 62.♖d7

♖e5 63.♗d5 ♖e1 64.♔g3 ♖e5 65.♗f3 ♔g8 66.♔f4 ♔f8 67.♖a7 ♔g8 68.♗e4 ♖c5 69.♗g6 ♖b5 70.♗f7+ ♔h8 71.♗e6 ♖c5 72.♖f7 ♖a5 73.♖xf6 ♔g7 74.♖f7+ ♔g6 75.♖c7 ♔f6 76.♗b3 ♖f5+ 77.♔g3 ♖e5 78.♗d1 ♔g6 79.♖c6+ ♔g7 80.♗f3 ♖a5 81.♔f4 ♖b5 82.♗e4 ♖a5 83.♖g6+ ♔h8 84.♖g5 ♖a7 85.♖xh5+

If it was acceptable to ask White to show his plan for the endgame up till here, resigning would now be appropriate. *Accepting the superiority of one's opponent is part of the game, even if it sometimes hurts.*

85...♔g8 86.♖c5 ♔g7 87.♔g5 ♖e7 88.♗f5 ♖a7 89.♖c8 ♖a6 90.h5 ♖g6+ 91.♔h4 ♖f6 92.♗g6 ♖a6 93.♖c7+ ♔g8 94.♔g5 ♖a5+ 95.♔h6 ♖a8

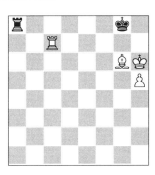

96.♖g7+ ♔f8 97.♖h7
Black resigned.

The following game was not chosen on account of its beauty or brilliance, but more as an example of the workaday experience of the chess player. Games seldom take such a rectilinear course as the numerous model games in the books make you think. We all know the ups and downs, the internal arguments during the game and also for days after it. Things are no different at a higher level!

Even today's widespread bondage to opening theory is not appropriate. Naturally, for those above Elo 2700 other requirements are in force.

Club players, however, should devote to work on opening theory only a small part of the training time at their disposal.

Hardly any games are decided in the opening. There is almost always a second chance, sometimes even a third or a fourth. The understanding of chess must take pride of place!

37 King's Indian Attack

Jörg Hickl	2600
Ralf Lau	2510

Vienna 1996 (7)

1.g3 d5 2.♗g2 c6 3.♘f3 ♘d7 4.0-0 e5 5.d3 ♘gf6 6.♘bd2 ♗d6 7.e4 0-0 8.b3 ♖e8 9.♗b2 ♘f8 10.♖e1 ♘g6 11.a3 a5 12.c3 h6 13.♕c2 ♗d7 14.♖ac1 b6 15.b4 ♖a7 16.♘f1 ♗e6 17.♘e3 ♕d7 18.♘d2 ♘e7 19.♘ef1 ♘g6 20.♘e3 ♘e7 21.♖e2 axb4 22.cxb4 ♖c8 23.d4 exd4 24.♗xd4 ♘e8 25.exd5 cxd5 26.♕b2 ♖xc1+ 27.♕xc1 ♗c7 28.♘b3 ♘d6 29.♗b2 ♘b5 30.♘c2 ♘f5 31.♘bd4 ♘bxd4 32.♘xd4 ♘xd4 33.♗xd4 ♗d8 34.h4 ♖b7

Fortunately the introductory moves are not relevant to our topic. When looking back over our own games years later, we involuntarily ask 'Did I play that? Was I the one who played such bad chess?'

Chess players develop as they gain experience, and that is precisely what must be the aim of their training: opening horizons! Considering some candidate move or other which was previously hidden to them, or recognising the tactical nuance which changes the evaluation of the position.

White to move

The opponent has a passed pawn.
Assess Black's advantage.

An important ability for a student is the ability from time to time to check and question the trainer's judgement. You have certainly noticed that there can be no question of Black having an advantage. Quite the contrary, the IQP is well blockaded, the effectiveness of the minor pieces is quite different. White himself is aiming to create a (distant) passed pawn on the queenside. My only worry was the outpost on c4.

35.♕c3 f6 36.a4?!

It was more important to first exert maximal pressure on the d-pawn: 36.♕d3 ♗f7 (36...♗f5? 37.♕b3! loses the d5-pawn) 37.♖d2 with a clear advantage.

36...♗f7 37.b5 ♖c7 38.♕e3 ♕d6 39.♔h2 ♖c4

The rook has arrived, as was feared. In spite of the bad bishop on d8 the position is more or less level.

40.♖a2 ♔f8?

This loses time and places the king on a bad square. The prime aim must of course be the elimination of the blockading piece on d4. There is a simple way of doing that: 40...♕b4, and after 41.♗xb6 (41...d4? 42.♕f4 ♗xb6 43.♕b8+) 41...♖c3 42.♕d4 ♖c4 43.♕e3 ♖c3 the game ends in a repetition of moves. Move 40, however, is frequently heavily influenced by time trouble and seldom a high quality one!

41.♗f1 ♖c8 42.a5

White can implement the plan sketched out at the start and after the creation of the passed pawn his advantage is obvious.

42...bxa5 43.b6 ♔g8

There was the possible threat of a pin from c5, but it is already too late to correct the unfortunate move 40.

44.♖xa5 ♖b8 45.♖b5 ♕c6 46.♖b2 ♕b7 47.♕a3

With the simple idea of 48.♕a7, followed by 49.♗a6. On account of the far advanced pawn it is irrelevant that after the capture on a7 the rook on b2 is en prise. White gets a new queen on a8. All that is left is:

47...♖a8

to battle with White for the a-file. But positional superiority almost always leads to tactical possibilities. As is the case here.

White to move

Find several solutions.

48.♕a7

The alternative consisted of 48.♕xa8 ♕xa8 49.b7 ♕b8 50.♗a7 ♕xa7 51.b8♕ ♕d7 52.♕a8 ♔h7 53.♗d3+ ♗g6 54.♖b8 ♗xd3 55.♖xd8 ♕f7 56.♖f8 ♕e7 57.h5+−.

'How complicated. I could never have found that', might be the thought going through your mind. Although I had seen as far as 52.♕a8 and though this variation is the favourite of the computer − with a lead of 5.5 pawns over all others − all this seems to me too much and, above all, unnecessary calculation. My solution was the more human.

48...♕xa7 49.bxa7 ♗c7 50.♗a6

This only wins a piece. After the beautiful 50.♖b7 ♗d6 51.♗c5 it is also all over. But one of the important basic tenets of chess is 'We give nothing away' or even 'To take is more blessed than to give'.

50...♗e5 51.♗xe5 ♖xa7 52.♗d3 ♖a8 53.♗d4 ♖d8 54.♖b7 ♔f8 55.g4

Black resigned.

Modern chess involves enormous strain. It is too much for a normal human being to sustain.

Viktor Kortchnoi

The passed pawn in the endgame

Many basic pawn structures lose in significance in the later phase of the game, which is why the focal point of this book is dealing with middlegame positions. The passed pawn, on the other hand, often does not display its power until the endgame. The number of pieces which are restricting its urge to move forward is then less. The topic of promotion is of central importance. So let us briefly refer to the most important elements.

The distant passed pawn

Typically in endgames with a distant passed pawn, matters are decided on the other flank. In our diagram, the white rook's pawn diverts the black king, after which the white one can help itself on the kingside.

1.a5 f6 2.a6 ♔c6 3.a7 ♔b7 4.♔c5 ♔xa7 5.♔d6 e5 6.fxe5 fxe5 7.♔xe5 ♔b6 8.♔f6 ♔c6 9.♔g7

Basically this advantage is also relevant in endgames with pieces, see the model game Vaganian-Smyslov.

The protected passed pawn

Of course Black has the opportunity to create a distant passed pawn after ...b6-b5. But since the king cannot intervene to provide support, that is of no importance. On account of the threat that the h5-pawn will promote, he cannot go to the d-file. An attack on the g4-pawn is also excluded for the same reason.

The white king, on the other hand, has greater freedom of movement, which it uses to mop up the queenside majority. After that it can turn to the promotion of its own pawn.

1.♔d4 ♔f6 2.♔d5 ♔f7 3.♔c6 b5 4.axb5 axb5 5.♔xb5 ♔f6 6.♔c5 ♔f7 7.♔d5 ♔f6 8.♔d6 ♔f7 9.♔e5 ♔g7 10.♔f5 ♔h6 11.♔f6

And White wins.

Connected passed pawns

Passed pawns gain in value if they are connected, if they cannot be effectively blockaded!

38 Irregular Opening

| Jörg Hickl | 2571 |
| Jonny Hector | 2520 |

Germany Bundesliga B 2007/08

1.g3 e5 2.♗g2 d5 3.c4 dxc4 4.♕a4+ c6 5.♕xc4 ♘a6 6.d3 ♘b4

7.a3 ♗e6 8.♕c3 ♘a2 9.♕c2 ♘xc1 10.♕xc1 g6 11.♘f3 ♗h6 12.♕c2 f6 13.♘c3 ♘e7 14.♘e4 0-0 15.♘c5 ♗c8 16.0-0 b6 17.♘a4 ♗e6 18.♖fd1 c5 19.b4 ♖c8 20.bxc5 b5 21.♘b2 ♘f5 22.d4 ♘xd4 23.♘xd4 exd4 24.e3 ♕e7 25.exd4 ♖fd8 26.♕c3 ♕f7 27.♘d3 ♗b3 28.♖db1 ♗c4 29.♘b4 ♕d7 30.♘c2 a6 31.a4 f5 32.axb5 axb5 33.♗f1 ♗xf1 34.♖xf1 f4 35.♖ab1 ♔h8 36.♖fd1 ♗g7 37.♖d3 h5 38.♖bd1 ♖f8 39.♔g2 h4 40.gxh4 f3+ 41.♔h1 ♕h3 42.♖g1 ♖f4 43.♘e3 ♖xh4 44.♘f1 b4 45.♕b3 ♖f8 46.♕d1 b3 47.♖g3 ♕e6 48.♕xb3 ♕e2 49.♕d1 ♕xf2

Up till here the game had followed a peculiar course. I had only been able to guess a few moves by my opponent. Possibly it had been the same for him with my moves. Nothing is left of the great advantage White had at the start. It is actually time to head towards a draw, e.g. with 50.♖dxf3 ♖xf3 51.♖xf3 ♕xd4 52.♕xd4 ♖xd4. Actually, had it not been for the fact that my team needed at least one full point for promotion... A further ten minutes went past and my search for a solution to keep the game alive was apparently successful:

50.d5??

It is unbelievable what chess players are capable of!

Before playing a move the following questions have to be answered:

'How does the move improve my position?' and (even more important) 'What does it ruin?'

Here it is easier to answer the second question than the first one: it surrenders the e5-square!

50...♗e5

And after this simple, obvious reply the game should soon be over.

51.♖d2 ♖xh2+ 52.♘xh2 ♕xg3 53.♕g1 ♕xg1+?

The simple 53...♕h4 with the threat of ...f3-f2 would have decided the game, but in the sixth hour of play all sorts of things are possible: 54.♕f2 ♗g3 55.♕d4+ ♕xd4 56.♖xd4 ♗xh2–+.

54.♔xg1 f2+ 55.♔f1 ♗xh2

56.d6

But not 56.♖xf2? ♖xf2+ 57.♔xf2 ♔g7–+ 58.♔f3 ♗g1! (a typical manoeuvre: the pawns are forced to advance, so that the bishop can easily stop them) 59.c6 ♗h2 and Black wins. After the move in the game the connected passed pawns show themselves to be equal to the bishop. Stupidly, mulling over the task after the brilliant 50th move had cost me almost all my thinking time. I had two minutes left. But who would have thought that things would go on for so long?

56...♗g3?! 57.♖d3 ♗e5

Not, however, the originally planned 57...♗h4, since after 58.♖h3 Black even loses. The two connected passed pawns on the sixth rank win against the rook: 58...g5 59.c6.

58.c6 ♔g7 59.c7

So that it does not come to a blockade, the pawns move on to squares of the same colour as that of the bishop. The position is totally balanced and Black should have taken a draw, e.g. by 59...♗xd6 and 60...♖c8. In his efforts to win the game, however, Hector goes too far. As he later explained, he had not seen White's next four moves.

59...♖a8

He clears the f-file, to bring the king closer. 59...♔f6?? 60.♖f3++–.

60.♖a3!

The threat of promotion for the pawns makes the rook untouchable.

60...♖h8 61.♖h3!

And again.

61...♖g8

The only hiding place.

62.♖c3! ♖c8?

And suddenly one of the pawns becomes a queen... 62...♗xd6=.

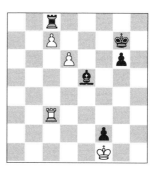

63.d7 ♖xc7 64.d8♕ ♖xc3 65.♕e7+ ♔h6 66.♕xe5

Despite the material superiority, the position is still clearly drawn. The next move is completely unbelievable.

66...♖c4??

And the computer shows mate in 42 moves. The correct move was 66...♖f3 followed by 67...♖f5.

67.♔xf2

Now the black rook can no longer make it to f- or h5, after which the game would be a draw, since the rook moves to and fro on the outposts provided by the pawn, which prevents the approach of the opposing king – a classic fortress in the struggle of rook and pawn against queen.

But a winning position is of no use when there are only a few seconds left. Here I had approximately 15 left, missed a mate on one with 9 left and with 5 left decided to call the arbiter to claim a draw. You can understand that the remaining moves could not be reconstructed. Hardly error-free, but an exciting performance for the onlookers.

As already pointed out in the previous game, two passed pawns can often take on a rook. If they reach the sixth rank they are even superior to it. To make this clear, here is a typical example:

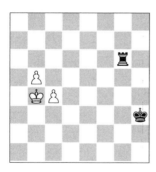

Leko-Carlsen: Miskolc rapid m(5) 2008

The black king is not in the equation, so White can easily advance the pawns to the sixth rank. Carlsen has his hands full getting a draw.

52.c5 ♖g4+ 53.♔a5 ♖c4 54.♔b6 ♔g4 55.♔c6 55.c6 ♔f5 56.♔c7 ♔e6 57.b6 ♔d5 58.b7 ♖xc6+ also only leads to a draw. **55...♔f5 56.♔d5 ♖c1 57.b6 ♖d1+ 58.♔c6 ♔e6 59.b7 ♖b1** The rook belongs behind the furthest advanced of the passed pawns, the king must attack the one which has remained behind. **60 ♔c7 ♔d5 61.c6 ♖b2 62.♔d7 ♖b6 63.c7 ♖xb7 64.♔d8 ♖xc7 65.♔xc7**

½–½

The end of the following game is curious:

Ortueta-Sanz, Madrid 1934, Black to move

Everything seems to be okay. White's minor piece looks better and he has a pawn majority on the kingside. However, the black rook can create trouble on the second rank: **1...♖d2** Ortueta probably did not have the slightest idea of what was awaiting him – otherwise he would have hit on the other candidate move 2.a4. Then the capture 2...♖xb2 leads after 3.a5 ♖b3 4.axb6 ♖xc3 (or even 4...axb6 5.♘d5 c3 6.♘xc3 ♖xc3 7.♖xb6=) 5.bxa7 ♖a3 to a draw. **2.♘a4? ♖xb2! 3.♘xb2 c3 4. ♖xb6** 4.♘d3 c4+ (even bad bishops can be good) 5.♖xb6 cxd3 and the connected passed pawns reach the sixth rank – the rook is powerless. **4...c4! 5.♖b4 a5! 6.♘xc4 c2**

0–1

The power of the (passed) pawns!

39 Caro-Kann Defence
Boris Spassky
Anatoly Karpov
Leningrad 1974 (6)

**1.e4 c6 2.d4 d5 3.♘c3 dxe4
4.♘xe4 ♗f5 5.♘g3 ♗g6 6.♘f3 ♘d7
7.♗d3 e6 8.0-0 ♘gf6 9.c4 ♗d6
10.b3 0-0 11.♗b2 ♕c7 12.♗xg6
hxg6 13.♕e2 ♖fe8 14.♘e4 ♘xe4
15.♕xe4 ♗e7 16.♖ad1 ♖ad8
17.♖fe1 ♕a5 18.a3 ♕f5 19.♕e2
g5 20.h3 g4 21.hxg4 ♕xg4 22.d5
cxd5 23.cxd5 e5 24.d6 ♗f6 25.♘d2
♕xe2 26.♖xe2 ♖c8 27.♘e4 ♗d8**

White to move

Evaluate the position.

After the American Bobby Fischer had two years previously broken the Russian hegemony in 'the Match of the Century', another challenger had to be found. The Candidates' match in Leningrad in 1974 heralded the change in the power structure. The recently dethroned World Champion Boris Spassky (*1937, World Champion 1969-72) met the new Russian hope, Anatoly Karpov. After a weakish start, the young Karpov finally won through. If at that time there were any doubts about his playing strength, he would prove in the subsequent decades that his lofty place in the list of the best chess players of all time was fully justified.

White has reached an apparently promising position. His passed pawn on the sixth rank is so close to the promotion square – and yet so far. How does he now proceed? And how can the blockading knight be eliminated? Questions which Spassky cannot answer in what follows. The black position, on the other hand, is very easy to play. The king is brought to e6 as the strongest piece, and after that Karpov worries about the activation of the pieces. Each exchange weakens the passed pawn, which will be gobbled up sooner or later.

White cannot be worse off, but there is no cause for euphoria because of the 'advantage of the passed pawn'. Quite the contrary! Spassky is obliged to justify the change in the pawn structure instigated on move 22.

28.g4

The knight has to be supported.

28...f6 29.♔g2 ♔f7 30.♖c1!?!

This move puts Spassky on the slippery slope. Tal pointed out that White should keep all four rooks on the board. Then the black king would not be able to close in on the passed pawn without danger. A better way was 30.a4.

**30...♗b6 31.♖ec2 ♖xc2 32.♖xc2
♔e6 33.a4 a5! 34.♗a3 ♖b8! 35.♖c4
♗d4**

With 33...a5! and 34...♖b8! Karpov prepared the advance ...b7-b5. By doing so he opened a file for his rook, which will be active when placed on b3. What is significant is that the passed pawn, despite apparently being well supported by the knight and bishop, does not offer White any serious play. Even the possession of the c-file achieves nothing for him, since penetration to c7 is ineffective: the well-centralised black king is protecting d7. Kasparov, who analysed this game in detail in his series *My Great Predecessors*, Volume V, gives Spassky's next move an exclamation mark. However, another interesting try would be to defend the white position with 36.♞d2, which would cover the entry squares b1 and b3.

36.f4 g6 37.♞g3?!

According to Kasparov White should continue here with 37.fxe5 ♗xe5 38.♖c7 b6! 39.g5! f5 40.♞d2, after which Black retains winning chances with 40...♗f4.

37...exf4 38.♖xd4 fxg3 39.♔xg3 ♖c8 40.♖d3

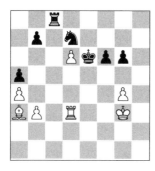

40...g5!

What is valid for normal mortal grandmasters, does not have to be so for the very great ones: Karpov makes an excellent 40th move. It is a momentous decision to allow a permanent blockade

of all the pawns on squares of the colour of the opposing bishop with the final move before the time control. But it does fix the weakness g4.

41.♗b2

Things gradually go backwards. The pawn on d6 will fall.

41...b6 42.♗d4

In view of the numerous targets for the bishop one might think that a pure minor piece endgame should end in a draw: **42.♖c3 ♖xc3+ 43.♗xc3 ♔xd6 44.b4**. Kasparov, however, proves in his detailed analysis that Black can force the win. Even if it takes us far beyond our subject, we cannot let you miss out on his exciting main variation.

analysis diagram: position after 44.b4

44...b5!! With this move Black creates a distant passed pawn on the a-file. **45.bxa5 bxa4 46.♗b4+ ♔c6 47.♔f3 ♞e5+ 48.♔g3 ♞c4 49.♗e7 a3 50.a6 a2 51.♗xf6** Here it can be seen that the extra weakening by 40...g5 does not play any part. The bishop must guard a1. **51...♔b6 52.♔f3 ♔xa6 53.♔e2** The counter-attack with 53.♔e4 arrives that infamous 'one tempo too late': 53...♔a5 54.♔f5 ♔a4 55.♔xg5 ♔b3 56.♗a1 ♔c2 57.♔f4 ♔b1 58.g5 ♔xa1 59.g6 ♞e5! 60.g7 ♞g6+ 61.♔g5 ♞e7 62.♔f6 ♞g8+ 63.♔f7 ♔b2 64.♔xg8 a1♕—+. **53...♔b5 54.♔d3 ♞a3!!** Decisively preventing the approach of the white king. **55.♔d2** 55.♔e4 ♔c4 56.♔f5 ♔d3 57.♔xg5 ♘c4 58.♔h6 ♔c2 59.♗a1 ♔b1−+. **55...♔c4 56.♔c1 ♔b3 57.♗g7 ♘c4 58.♗f6 ♘e3−+**

Chess artistry!

42...♖c6 43.♗c3 ♖c5?

He had to transpose with 43...♖xd6 44.♖xd6+ ♔xd6 45.b4 b5! to the minor piece ending mentioned above.

44.♔g2 ♖c8 45.♔g3 ♘e5 46.♗xe5 fxe5 47.b4?

Spassky returns the compliment (for Karpov's mistake on move 43). According to Kasparov he could have held the position after 47.♔f2! ♖d8 48.♖f3.

47...e4 48.♖d4 ♔e5 49.♖d1 axb4 50.♖b1 ♖c3+ 51.♔f2 ♖d3 52.d7 ♖xd7 53.♖xb4 ♖d6 54.♔e3 ♖d3+ 55.♔e2 ♖a3

White resigned.

The passed pawn shows itself to be much stronger in the next example:

40 Grünfeld Indian Defence

Vladimir Kramnik	2715
Jan Timman	2635

Novgorod 1995 (2)

1.♘f3 g6 2.d4 ♘f6 3.c4 ♗g7 4.♘c3 d5 5.cxd5 ♘xd5 6.e4 ♘xc3 7.bxc3 c5 8.♖b1 0-0 9.♗e2 cxd4 10.cxd4 ♕a5+ 11.♗d2 ♕xa2 12.0-0 ♗g4 13.♗g5 h6 14.♗e3 ♘c6 15.d5 ♘a5 16.♗c5 ♗f6 17.e5 ♗xe5 18.♖b4 ♗xf3 19.♗xf3 ♗f6?

A better way was 19...♖ae8 20.♗e3 b6. Kramnik now liquidates into an endgame. In doing so he takes advantage of the unprotected situation of the knight on a5 to create for himself a far advanced passed pawn.

20.♖a4 ♕b3 21.♖xa5 ♕xd1 22.♖xd1 b6

Even for a world-class player such as Jan Timman it is from time to time hard to foresee how play will develop in a few moves. The mistake on move 19 leads by force to a position in which he is at a disadvantage.

23.d6! ♖ac8

Nor is he any better off after 23...exd6 24.♗xb6+− or 23...bxa5 24.dxe7 ♖fc8 25.♗xa8 ♖xa8 26.♖d7+− and Black is paralysed.

24.d7!

This was hard to calculate five moves previously.

24...♖cd8

The most tenacious defence went 24...bxa5 25.dxc8♕ ♖xc8 26.♗e3 (26.♗xa7?! a4 27.♗e4 a3 28.♗b1 ♔g7 is not clear) 26...a4 27.♖d5 and then ♖a5 with a clear advantage, but still with some hard work to do before winning.

25.♗xe7 ♗xe7 26.♖xa7 ♖b8

26...♗c5 27.♗c6 and with his well secured passed pawn White wins in similar fashion to the game.

27.♖e1 ♗d8

27...♗f6 28.♗c6 (or 28.♗d5 b5 29.♖e8 ♖bxe8? 30.dxe8♕ ♖xe8 31.♗xf7+) 28...b5 29.♖c7 b4 30.♖e8 ♖d8 31.♖b7 is winning for White.

28.♖e8 b5 29.♖a8 ♖xa8 30.♗xa8 b4 31.♗d5 ♔g7 32.♔f1   1-0

The king heads off towards c8. A nice performance by the future World Champion Vladimir Kramnik (*1975, World Champion 2000-2007).

Model games

Karpov-Kasparov (Lyon/New York m 1990), c-file

Vaganian-Smyslov (Lvov 1978), distant passed pawn

Keres-Taimanov (Moscow 1951)

Chapter 8

Doubled pawns

Every chess champion was once a beginner.

Irving Chernev

The exchange of a piece can lead to a serious change in the structure – to doubled pawns. Weak squares are created – the formation is devalued. The widespread opinion with which everyone was probably confronted at the start of his life as a chess player, namely 'doubled pawns are bad', must however absolutely be contested. Structures involving doubled pawns, described by Nimzowitsch as 'doubled pawn complexes' or in brief 'double complexes', sometimes also have advantages.

We shall go on to look into 'static' and 'dynamic' weaknesses. Thereafter more light will be cast on two double complexes, the Nimzo-Indian (pawns on c3/c4/d4) and the Sicilian (f7/f6/e6/d6).

Static weak squares

Specific characteristics

The doubled pawns f2/f3 protect important central squares. The semi-open g-file can be made active use of by the major pieces. On the other hand, the h-pawn is isolated. The h3- and h4-squares are open to opposing pieces as outposts. Control by the white pawns is clearly insufficient in this part of the board.

Plans for White

'The strength of doubled pawns lies in holding firm', says Nimzowitsch. In the ideal case White should not move the pawns. The move f3-f4 gives up the control of the e4- and g4-squares, but the structure remains firm and intact. And e3-e4, on the other hand, should really not be envisaged: f4 and, depending on circumstances, e5 too, become possible outposts for the opponent and in this case the pawns can only be evaluated as weak. The less material remaining on the board, the clearer the loss of importance of the semi-open g-file and better control of the central squares. So White should avoid excessive exchanging.

Plans for Black

Simplifications are absolutely to his advantage. In the endgame the greater number of pawn islands can make itself felt negatively. Above all the isolated h-pawn constitutes a notable weakness when attacked from in front (by the rook or the king).

Conclusion

Doubled pawns offer control of squares, but decrease the dynamic possibilities. On account of the reduced number of pawn levers, play with the pieces is prevalent. Evaluation of the situation here always depends on the individual case.

41 Queen's Gambit Accepted
Erich Cohn
Akiba Rubinstein
St Petersburg 1909

1.d4 d5 2.♘f3 c5 3.c4 dxc4 4.dxc5 ♛xd1+ 5.♔xd1 ♘c6 6.e3 ♗g4 7.♗xc4 e6 8.a3 ♗xc5 9.b4 ♗d6 10.♗b2 ♘f6 11.♘d2 ♔e7 12.♔e2 ♗e5 13.♗xe5 ♘xe5 14.♖hc1 ♖ac8 15.♗b3 ♖hd8 16.♘c4 ♘xc4 17.♖xc4 ♖xc4 18.♗xc4 ♘e4 19.♔e1 ♗xf3 20.gxf3 ♘d6 21.♗e2 ♖c8 22.♔d2 ♘c4+ 23.♗xc4 ♖xc4

The white structure is weakened by the doubled f-pawns. This affects above all the isolated h2-pawn.

Rubinstein, an accomplished master of rook endings, is already threatening 24...♖h4, which would either win a pawn or force a white piece into passive defence.

White to move

The choice is: 24.♖c1 or 24.f4.

24.♖c1?

White would have to do without the exchange of rooks. The general rule is: 'You should only allow the transition to a pawn ending whenever the consequences can be evaluated exactly.' And that is much easier said than done! As well as the usual endgame topics, there are in addition in pawn endings motifs such as 'zugzwang', 'the opposition' and 'corresponding squares'. Precise calculation over the board is mostly difficult if not impossible. But the difference of a single tempo frequently decides between victory and defeat. Therefore: 'If in doubt, never!'. It could be done if you are lacking in alternatives or are in a lost position and want to overwhelm the opponent with more calculations.

Here, however, Cohn had a good continuation in 24.f4. After it Black has a tiny advantage, but White can hold the position.

24...♖xc1–+ 25.♔xc1 ♔f6 26.♔d2 ♔g5 27.♔e2 ♔h4 28.♔f1 ♔h3 29.♔g1

Possibly Cohn had this position in his mind's eye when he boldly exchanged the rooks.

The invasion of the black king led to the attack on the h-pawn, which, however, is reliably defended by its white counterpart. Since it has at its disposal the g1- and h1-squares, it can apparently not be put into zugzwang. But by forcing the exchange of the weak doubled pawns and the h-pawn, Rubinstein gains the opposition and finally the e-pawn. This is the direct consequence of the superior activity of his king.

29...e5 30.♔h1 b5 31.♔g1 f5 32.♔h1 g5 33.♔g1 h5 34.♔h1 g4 35.e4

The pawn will soon be easily snapped up on e4. 35.fxg4 fxg4 36.♔g1 e4 37.♔h1 h4 38.♔g1 g3 would also turn out similar to the game continuation, nor would it even be safe on e3.

35...fxe4 36.fxe4 h4 37.♔g1 g3 38.hxg3 hxg3

White resigned.

In the pawn ending the actually tiny weakening of the h3- and h4-squares turned out to be decisive.

Dynamic weakness

The diagram in the next column shows a typical structure such as occurs in the Exchange Variation of the Ruy Lopez after the moves **1.e4 e5 2.♘f3 ♘c6**

3.♗b5 a6 4.♗xc6 dxc6 5.d4 exd4 6.♕xd4.

Whereas White has a sound pawn majority on the kingside, Black has doubled pawns on the queenside.

A pure pawn ending would probably be lost for Black, since there is no way of cashing in on the majority on the queenside. White will create a passed pawn on the kingside and win. That is of course easy to say and is what is stated in every book on the Exchange Variation of the Ruy Lopez. We do not want to reproduce here the analyses of the best of endgame experts such as Euwe, Averbakh and Speelman. It is sufficient for us to establish that White's advantage in the pawn ending is probably decisive.

So, should we, where possible, avoid doubled pawns if they are to be described as weak both in their 'dynamic' and 'static' aspects?

No, do not be afraid! Similar to the cases of the IQP and hanging pawns there are basic advantages.

Even in the Ruy Lopez Exchange Variation Black gets compensation in the form of the bishop pair, an additional semi-open file and also control of the central squares.

Central control and semi-open files

In the next example, Mikhail Tal (1936-1992, World Champion 1960-1961), one of the most brilliant attacking players of all time, falls victim to – at first sight – very bad-looking doubled pawns.

42 Sicilian Defence
Mikhail Tal
Yury Balashov
Moscow 1973 (3)

1.e4 c5 2.♘f3 ♘c6 3.d4 cxd4 4.♘xd4 e6 5.♘c3 d6 6.♗e3 ♘f6 7.f4 ♗e7 8.♕f3 e5 9.fxe5 dxe5 10.♘xc6 bxc6 11.♗c4 0-0 12.h3

White delayed castling to be able to get all his pieces into active positions. Black, on the other hand, does not have a good square for his queen's bishop. And there is no sign of any compensation for the weakened queenside.

12...♗e6!?

Balashov allows Tal to completely ruin the black pawn structure. What does he get in return? On one hand, the semi-open f-file. With the imminent retreat of the queen he gains the time required to set up some threats. On the other, after ♗xe6 fxe6 the admittedly ugly doubled e-pawns will control the important central squares d5 and d4.

At first that appears somewhat vague. However, it relieves the c-pawn from the duty of guarding the d5-square, so that it can be set in motion if needed.

13.♗b3

Another possible continuation would be 13.♗xe6 fxe6 14.♕e2 ♖b8 15.b3. The attack on b2 provokes the weakening of the c3-square. If White had already castled, everything would be okay. Now, however, his problems grow with every move: 15...♕a5 16.♗d2 ♗b4 17.♘b1 (17.♕c4? ♖bd8−+) 17...♖bd8 with an attack on the white king which has been stuck in the middle.

13...c5 14.♕e2 ♖b8 15.♗xe6 fxe6 Black may well have four isolated pawns, but as compensation he also has *three* open or semi-open files. Thanks to his lead in development he manages as the game continues to extend his initiative move by move.

16.b3

Balashov employs the c-pawn to further open up the position:

16...c4! 17.♕xc4

After 17.0-0 ♕c7 18.♗d2 ♗b4 or 18...♖fd8 the black pieces become active. The only really obvious weakness on the board is the white e-pawn, the defenders of which are coming more and more under pressure.

17...♕c8∓ 18.0-0 ♕xc4 19.bxc4

Ironically, the white queenside now consists of four isolated pawns, which are harvested one by one by the black rooks. Tal does not manage to defend effectively. Moreover, as the game continues the coordination between the white pieces is made difficult thanks to the central control exerted by Black's doubled e-pawns.

19...♖b4 20.♗xa7 ♖a8 21.♗e3 ♖xc4 22.♘b5 ♖a5 23.a4 ♖xe4 24.♗d2 ♖axa4 25.♘c3 ♖xa1 26.♖xa1 ♖c4 27.♖a8+ ♔f7 28.♖a7 h6 29.♘b5 ♘e4 30.♗a5 ♔f6 31.♖c7 ♗c5+ 32.♔h2 ♔g6 33.♗e1 ♖xc2 34.♘c3 ♗d4 35.♘b5 ♖b2 36.♘a3 ♖a2 37.♗b4 ♖a1 38.g4 ♖f1 39.♖c2 ♖f3 40.♘c4 ♘g5 41.♗d6 ♖xh3+ 42.♔g2 ♖c3 43.♖xc3 ♗xc3 44.♘xe5+ ♗xe5 45.♗xe5 ♘f7 46.♗c3 e5 47.♗b4 ♔f6 48.♔f2 ♘g5 49.♔e3 ♘h7 50.♔f3 ♔e6 51.♗a3 ♘f6 52.♗f8 ♔f7 53.♗c5 ♘d7 0-1

Doubled pawns can therefore also display strength purely statically, their control of the central squares showing itself to be very valuable. In this game, however, what was decisive was that Balashov was able to make use of the semi-open files, for which he had the bad pawn structure to thank, with a gradually increasing initiative.

In the sections which follow we will present the strengths and weaknesses of the doubled pawns through two typical structures. The first one, with the doubled pawn complex c3/c4/d4, often arises in games which were opened with 1.d4. In the second, 'Sicilian' one, Black has the pawns f7/f6/e6/d6. In both structures the side with the doubled pawns has at its disposal similar strengths:

- bishop pair
- better central control
- semi-open file

The doubled pawn complex c3/c4/d4

This sort of position is the result of the exchange of the black king's bishop for the white queen's knight on c3. Until the 20s of the last century the exchange ...♗b4xc3 in queen's pawn openings was considered dubious, as it conceded to the opponent the bishop pair and strengthened the white centre. Nimzowitsch, however, then demonstrated in the opening which bears his name, the 'Nimzo-Indian

Defence', 1.d4 ♘f6 2.c4 e6 3.♘c3 ♗b4, that after the exchange Black retains sufficient influence in the centre of the board with his remaining pieces and can sometimes exploit the weakness of the doubled pawns.

Specific characteristics

The well supported central pawn on d4 creates for White an advantage in space in the centre and on the kingside. This advantage can then be extended even further by e2-e4.

On the other hand, the a3- and c4-pawns tend to be weak.

Plans for White

There is a chance to employ the advantage in space for an attack on the kingside. The pawn thrusts e2-e4 and f2-f4 are the order of the day. There is a specific imbalance inherent in the presence of the white queen's bishop, which no longer has a counterpart. If it manages to pin the black knight on f6 against the queen on d8, it is an uphill struggle to shake off this pressure.

If Black blocks the centre with ...e6-e5, then d5 becomes a potential central outpost for white pieces. We shall see in the game Botvinnik-Chekhover how White occupies d5 with pieces. If he does not manage to do so, ...e6-e5 is often met with d4-d5, which fixes the advantage in space in the middle of the board. There is then the opportunity to open the f-file with f2-f4, as in game 45, Petrosian-Benko.

Plans for Black

The c4-pawn or square is the main target of Black's operations. After it has been fixed with ...c7-c5, the pressure can be increased with ...♘c6-a5, ...♗a6 and ...♖c8. A classical plan of attack intends to transfer the king's knight via e8 to d6 so that it too attacks c4.

The opponent will not be a mere onlooker. Black should therefore pay careful attention to the opponent's efforts to attack on the kingside. The thrust f2-f4 must be immediately met with ...f7-f5. If the white pawn does make it to f5, then it must be stopped at the latest by ...f7-f6, though the defensive position will already be somewhat cramped.

Conclusion

Though at first sight there is not a dramatic worsening of White's pawn position as a result of the exchange ...♗b4xc3, bxc3, it does lead to major imbalances: the bishop pair, an advantage in space and chances for an attack on the king offer White compensation.

43 Nimzo-Indian Defence

Artur Jussupow	2645
Anatoly Karpov	2725

Linares 1993 (11)

1.d4 ♘f6 2.c4 e6 3.♘c3 ♗b4 4.e3 c5 5.♗d3 ♘c6 6.a3 ♗xc3+ 7.bxc3 0-0 8.♘e2 b6 9.e4 ♘e8 10.0-0 ♗a6 11.f4

11...f5!

Necessary! The careless 11...d6? 12.f5 e5 13.f6! led in the model game Bronstein-Najdorf to a decisive attack on the king.

12.♘g3 g6 13.♗e3 cxd4!

With this and the next move Karpov voluntarily frees his opponent from his doubled pawns. In any case there was no alternative: after 13...d6? 14.d5± Jussupow would have cracked open the light-squared chain e6-f5. Karpov is playing for control of c4! He simplifies the position and obtains a permanent outpost for his knight. In the long term the latter will be superior to the remaining dark-squared bishop.

14.cxd4 d5 15.cxd5 ♗xd3 16.♕xd3 fxe4 17.♕xe4 ♕xd5 18.♕xd5 exd5=

An exchange of queens was hardly on Jussupow's wish list. Without the strongest piece and the light-squared bishop nothing will come of the attack on the king he was aiming for. The subsequent breakthrough f4-f5, which activates the queen's bishop, however, still leaves the game more or less level.

19.♖ac1 ♖c8 20.f5 ♘d6 21.fxg6 hxg6 22.♖xf8+ ♔xf8

23.h4?!

He is going in for a race. Black will create a passed pawn on the queenside, White one on the kingside. It was, nevertheless, better to activate the king: 23.♔f2 ♘c4

24.♖c3 ♔g7 (or ♔e7) 25.♘e2 and the white king gets involved in the struggle on the other side of the board.

23...♘c4∓

24.♗g5 ♘xd4 25.h5?! 25.♖d1?! ♘e6 26.♖xd5 ♘xa3 is similar to the game continuation. Karpov recommended 25.♖f1+ ♔e8 26.♖e1+ ♔d7 27.♖e7+ ♔c6 28.♖g7∓.

24.♗g5 ♘xd4 25.h5 gxh5 26.♖f1+ ♔e8 27.♘xh5 ♘xa3∓ 28.♘g7+ ♔d7 29.♖f7+ ♔c6 30.♖xa7 ♘ac2 31.♗f6 b5 32.g4?!

32.♖a2 ♖g8 (32...b4 33.♘f5 ♘xf5 34.♖xc2+ ♔b7 35.♖xc8 ♔xc8 36.♔f2∓) 33.♖b2 ♔c5 34.♘e6+ ♘xe6 35.♗e7+ ♔b6 36.♖xc2 ♖g7 37.♗f6 ♖g6 38.♗e7 d4 was a tougher defence.

32...b4 33.♖a2 b3 34.♖b2 ♔c5 35.♘f5 ♖g8 36.♘xd4 ♖xg4+ 37.♔f2 ♘xd4 38.♗xd4+ ♔xd4 39.♖xb3 ♖e4 40.♖a3 ♖e8

Cutting off the opposing king. Since White cannot prevent the advance of the d-pawn, he resigned.

With the resolution of the central tension (and of the doubled pawns), in this game Karpov reached an ending in which the knight on c4 revealed itself to be the dominating minor piece.

44 Nimzo-Indian Defence
Mikhail Botvinnik
Vitaly Chekhover
Leningrad ch-URS sf 1938

1.d4 ♘f6 2.c4 e6 3.♘c3 ♗b4 4.♘f3 0-0

The subsequent pin on the f6-knight does not lead to any immediate consequences, but it is not so easy to shake it off: ...♗e7 would now be illogical on account of the loss of tempo and moreover would concede to White great superiority in the centre without

a struggle; ...h7-h6 followed by ...g7-g5 is out of the question after kingside castling. Today's theory prefers 4...b6 or 4...c5.

5.♗g5

White takes the first step towards developing pressure on the kingside.

5...d6 6.e3 ♕e7 7.♗e2 e5 8.♕c2 ♖e8 9.0-0 ♗xc3 10.bxc3 h6 11.♗h4

11...c5?!

Chekhover would like to first clarify the position in the centre. For the moment there is no sign of any white piece which could occupy the weakened d5-square, but pawns cannot move backwards! A more prudent move was 11...♘c6 or 11...♘bd7, in each case with a slightly passive position, though without any weaknesses.

12.♖fe1 ♗g4 13.♗xf6 ♕xf6 14.♕e4 ♗xf3 15.♗xf3 ♘c6 16.dxc5 dxc5 17.♖ad1 ♖ad8 18.♖d5

Here and subsequently White makes massive use of his central outpost. Chekhover turns down the exchange of rooks since that would free White of his doubled pawns: 18...♖xd5 19.cxd5 ♞e7 20.d6! (this is important since Black was planning ...♞c8-d6 with the ideal blockading knight) 20...♕xd6 21.♕xb7 and 'the superiority of the bishop over the knight has increased' (Botvinnik). The black minor piece requires some moves before it can sensibly intervene in the struggle.

18...b6 19.♖ed1

White dominates in the centre and on the single open file. It is difficult to coordinate the black pieces, on the other hand. There may be some squares for the knight, for example d6, but for the moment these are out of its reach.

19...♞a5 20.h3 ♖xd5 21.♖xd5

'Repairing' the pawn position with 21.cxd5 is clearly weaker. The passed pawn on d5 gets in the way of all three white pieces (there is more on this formation in Chapter 7, 'Passed pawns'). After the text move, on the other hand, White's forces are active and centrally posted, with the result that the weakness of the doubled pawns is not noticeable.

21...♕e7 22.♗g4 ♕b7 23.♗f5!

23...♕b8?

The decisive mistake! After 23...♔f8 he could still have hopes of a successful defence.

**24.♖d7   ♖d8   25.♕xe5   ♞xc4
26.♕xb8   ♖xb8   27.♗e4   ♞a3
28.♗d5 ♖f8 29.e4 a5 30.c4**

Botvinnik kept up his domination into the endgame. Black cannot improve his position on account of the weak f-pawn, whereas White simply activates his king.

**30...b5 31.cxb5 ♞xb5 32.e5 a4
33.f4 ♞d4 34.♔f2 g5 35.g3 gxf4
36.gxf4 ♞e6 37.♔e3 c4 38.f5 ♞c5
39.♖c7 ♞d3 40.e6 fxe6 41.fxe6**

Black resigned.

The game serves as a good example of the power of a central outpost.

45 Nimzo-Indian Defence
Tigran Petrosian
Pal Benko
Budapest 1955 (7)

**1.d4 ♞f6 2.c4 e6 3.♞c3 ♗b4 4.e3
c5 5.a3 ♗xc3+ 6.bxc3 ♞c6 7.♗d3
b6**

Benko immediately prepares the attack on the white c-pawn. But it is going nowhere. So it was advisable to first bolster his centre with 7...d6.

8.e4 e5 9.d5

9...♘a5

9...♘e7 10.f4 would not have stemmed the white initiative on the kingside either.

10.♘f3

This is somewhat half-hearted. White should attack the centre directly with 10.f4, with a slight initiative.

10...♕e7

10...d6 11.h3 ♕e7 is similar to the game continuation.

11.0-0

The pin 11.♗g5 achieves nothing before Black has castled: 11...h6 12.♗e3 (12.♗h4 g5 13.♗g3 ♘h5 14.♘d2 ♘f4 15.♗xf4 gxf4∓) 12...♘g4=.

11...♗a6 12.♘h4! g6 13.f4

13...0-0-0?!

In view of his unstable centre Benko had to resort to tactical tricks so as to obtain at least some counterplay. 13...♘xd5 14.cxd5 ♗xd3 15.♕xd3 ♕xh4 16.fxe5 is evaluated by Keene and Simpole as 'hopeless', but would have probably been a good practical chance: 16...♘b3 17.e6 0-0 with unclear play.

But after 13...♗xc4 14.fxe5 ♕xe5 15.♗h6 too, he could create complications which are hard to evaluate.

After the text move Petrosian conquers the centre.

14.♘f3 d6?!

14...exf4 was the last opportunity to put up some resistance: 15.♗xf4 ♘h5 16.♗h6 (16.d6? ♕e6 17.♘g5 ♕e8 18.e5 h6 19.♘e4 ♘xf4 20.♖xf4 ♖f8∓) 16...♗xc4 17.♗xc4 ♘xc4 18.♕e2 ♘d6 19.g4 ♕xe4 20.♕xe4 ♘xe4 21.gxh5±.

15.fxe5 dxe5 16.♗g5 h6 17.♗h4 ♖d6

But 17...g5? 18.♘xg5+− leads to a loss on account of the pin after 18...hxg5 19.♗xg5.

The knight on f6 is badly rather than well protected. Petrosian now took advantage of this shaky position to play a *'petite combinaison'*.

White to move

18.♘xe5! ♕xe5 19.♗g3 ♕e7

19...♕xc3 20.♗xd6 ♗xc4 21.♗xc4 ♘xc4 22.♕a4! ♘a5 23.♖ae1+−.

20.e5 ♖d7 21.♖xf6 h5 22.h4 ♗b7 23.♕a4 ♖g8 24.♖af1 ♖g7 25.d6 ♕d8 26.e6 ♖xd6 27.♗xd6 **1-0**

Benko was incapable of waiting before attacking the weak c-pawn and in doing so neglected the centre. And it was precisely there that his opponent played f2-f4 to occupy the key e5-square.

Model games

Spassky-Fischer (Reykjavik 1972), Black accepts doubled pawns on g6 so as to open the f-file

Bronstein-Najdorf (Budapest 1950)

Geller-Euwe (Zurich 1953)

Johner-Nimzowitsch (Dresden 1926), a classic on the topic of staunching White's attack

Nimzowitsch-Johner (Bern 1931), copy-book besieging of the doubled pawn complex

Zude-Haba (Nuremberg 2008), opening the f-file

The doubled pawn complex f7/ f6/e6/d6

This structure often appears in the Sicilian Defence after the exchange ♗g5x♘f6.

Specific characteristics

Unlike with the Nimzo-Indian formation, here the side with the doubled pawns does not have an advantage in space. The pawns on f6, e6 and d6, however, control the fifth rank from c5 to g5, whereas in addition the pawn on f7 supports e6. Here too the doubled

pawn complex provides a good grip on the centre.

The d6-pawn needs to be protected by black pieces.

Analogous to the game Cohn-Rubinstein, the isolated h-pawn is vulnerable to attacks by the white pieces.

Plans for White

The most effective method to shatter the solid black pawn block is the advance f4-f5, accompanied by ♗c4 and ♘d4 with an attack on e6. If the black e-pawn moves forward, the d5-square becomes an ideal outpost for a minor piece.

Alternatively, White can also open the centre with e4-e5 and sound the attack on the black king. Kasparov provides us with an impressive example of that in the model game against Hracek.

One motif consists of the blockade of the weak black h-pawn. ♕h5 or ♗h5 are common threats which Black should not allow, since otherwise he runs the danger of being paralysed in this area of the board.

In general White has the better protected king position, and so he tries to force a decision in the middlegame. The exchange of queens should be avoided; in the endgame it becomes harder to conquer one of the black weaknesses.

Plans for Black

Where should he go with the king? This central question has a considerable influence on Black's plan for the game. The kingside is weakened. But since White no longer has his dark-squared bishop, sometimes castling kingside comes into consideration, depending on whether the black king will find shelter on h8. Of course this option is no longer open if ...h7-h5 has been played.

Queenside castling is met with more frequently. It has the disadvantage, however, that the typical Sicilian counterplay with ...b7-b5 would strip bare the king position. In this scenario Black has to manoeuvre more patiently, e.g. ...0-0-0, ...♔b8, then ...♗c8 or even ...♖c8, if counterplay on the c-file is being aimed for.

Since both castled positions have their disadvantages, it comes as no surprise that the black king often remains in the middle, where it can seek shelter behind the central pawn block. On e7 it helps with the protection of d6, so that the dark-squared bishop can be activated via h6 – usually after the move ...h7-h5. The at first inconspicuous h6-c1 diagonal reminds White of his lack of a queen's bishop. Coordination of the pieces is considerably disrupted by the black bishop. With the king on e7 Black can also move to rapid counterplay by means of ...b7-b5-b4. He will meet White's attempts to open the centre by f4-f5 with ...e6-e5. What is important is that White does not obtain minor piece control over d5, thus developing the light-squared bishop via ♗f1-c4(-b3) is prevented, and the queen's bishop gets to b7 in time to achieve sufficient control over the central square.

Conclusion

The doubled pawn complex leads to lively play. Whereas in the Nimzo-Indian structure c3/c4/d4 the side fighting against the doubled pawns often seeks its chances in the endgame, it is exactly the opposite here. White is aiming to open up the position with the advance f2-f4-f5, before the queens have been exchanged, whilst Black often goes in for simplifications.

46 Sicilian Defence
Alexey Suetin
Mikhail Botvinnik
Moscow 1952 (19)

1.e4 c5 2.♘f3 ♘c6 3.d4 cxd4 4.♘xd4 ♘f6 5.♘c3 d6 6.♗g5 e6 7.♕d2 h6 8.♗xf6 gxf6 9.0-0-0 a6 10.f4 ♗d7 11.♗c4 h5 12.♔b1 ♕b6

Everything is prepared for the f4-f5 advance and for laying siege to the doubled pawn complex, however Black's queen sortie disrupts that.

White to move

13.♖hf1?!

Not the best choice. The exchange of queens relieves Black of all his worries concerning the safety of his king. A better way was 13.♘xc6 bxc6 14.♗b3 with the plan f4-f5, ♖hf1, possibly followed by ♘e2-d4 and pressure on e6.

13...♕xd4 14.♕xd4 ♘xd4 15.♖xd4 ♖c8 16.♗b3 ♖g8 17.♖d2 h4 18.f5 ♔e7 19.♖df2

White's play looks really appealing. If Black now plays 19...♗g7 to protect the pawn which is under attack, he will be relatively passive. Suetin could calmly continue the siege, e.g. with 20.♖f4. Botvinnik, however, gladly gives up the pawn in order to manoeuvre his bishop on to the dream square e5.

19...♗h6! 20.fxe6 fxe6 21.♖xf6 ♖cf8

First sacrifice a pawn and then simplify? That is not so simple psychologically. No matter the number of pawns on either side, the white rook on f6 was much more active than the rook on c8. *Swap off your opponent's actively posted pieces!*

22.♖xf8 ♗xf8

But just one of them, please. Of the remaining pair of rooks the one on g8 is now the more active, since the potential entry squares for the white rook are protected by the king.

23.♖f2 ♗h6!

With World Champions everything often fits together. The bishop wants to go to e5 and at the same time is keeping the opposing king away from the main battlefield.

24.♗c4 ♗e3 25.♖e2 ♗g1

26.g3

'Correct. After 26.h3 White risks losing both pawns on the kingside.' (Botvinnik)

26...hxg3 27.hxg3 ♖xg3

Black has recovered the sacrificed material and with it a clear advantage. The weak e4-pawn is a welcome target to attack. In addition, all the black pieces are active.

In the subsequent interesting endgame Botvinnik manages to wrest the full point from his opponent.

28.a3 ♗e8 29.♔a2 ♗h5 30.♖e1 ♗d4 31.♖h1 ♖g5 32.♔b3 ♗e5 33.♗d3 ♗g6 34.♖h4 ♖g3 35.a4 ♗f6 36.♖h1 ♖g4 37.♖e1 ♗e5 38.♘d1 ♖f4 39.♘c3 ♖f3 40.♘b1 ♗g3 41.♖g1?

41.♖e2 (Botvinnik).

41...♗xe4 42.♘d2 ♗d5+ 43.♔a3 ♖f2 44.♘e4 ♗h2 45.♖g6 ♗xe4 46.♗xe4 d5 47.♗d3 ♗e5 48.♖g8 ♔d7 49.b4 ♗f6 50.♖g1 ♖h2 51.♔b3 ♔d6 52.♖d1 ♔e7 53.c4 ♖b2+ 54.♔a3 dxc4 55.♗xc4 ♖c2 56.♗b3 ♗b2+ 57.♔a2 ♖f2 58.♗c4 a5 59.bxa5 ♗c3+ 60.♔b3 ♗xa5 61.♗b5 b6 62.♔c4 ♔f6 63.♔d4 ♖f4+ 64.♔e3 ♔e5 65.♖h1 ♖e4+ 66.♔d3 ♖g4 67.♖h5+ ♔d6 68.♖h8 ♔e5 69.♖h5+ ♔f4 70.♖h3 ♖g 71.♖h4+ ♔e5 72.♖h5+ ♔d6

73.♖h4?!

73.♖h3 (Botvinnik).

73...♖g3+ 74.♔e4 ♗d2 75.♗d3?

75.♔d4 or 75.♖h5 put up some resistance.

75...♗g5?

75...♔c5 76.♖h5+ ♗g5 was conclusive.

76.♖h5?

With 76.♖h1 ♗g4+ White could still delay the loss.

76...♔c5

White resigned.

The final position is worth a diagram.

White either loses the bishop, gets into a lost pawn ending, or – with much reduced material – is mated in the middle of the board.

After the transition to the endgame Black had nothing to worry about: as compensation for the pawn he sacrificed Botvinnik was able to force his opponent into permanent passivity.

> *All obvious moves look suspicious in the analysis after the game.*
> Viktor Kortchnoi

47 Sicilian Defence
Paul Keres
Mikhail Botvinnik

Moscow 1956

1.e4 c5 2.♘f3 ♘c6 3.d4 cxd4 4.♘xd4 ♘f6 5.♘c3 d6 6.♗g5 e6 7.♕d2 h6 8.♗xf6 gxf6 9.0-0-0 a6 10.f4 h5 11.♔b1 ♗d7 12.♗e2 ♕b6

Keres correctly does not allow the exchange of queens.

13.♘b3! 0-0-0 14.♖hf1

14...♘a5?!

This leaves Black too far behind in development.

14...♔b8 was preferable.

15.♖f3

Keres gives the following sample variation: 15.♘xa5 ♕xa5 16.♖f3 ♔b8 17.♕d4 ♗e7? (17...♖h6) 18.b4! ♕c7 19.♘d5! exd5 20.♖c3 ♗c6 21.exd5 and White is winning. This move order demonstrates the vulnerability of the black queenside.

15...♘xb3 16.axb3 ♔b8 17.♘a4! ♕a7?

Here the queen is out of the play. The only way to bring it back into the game is by means of ...b7-b5, which would once again weaken the position of the king.

A better way was 17...♕c7 18.♕d4 with advantage to White.

18.f5 ♗e7

With this passive defence Botvinnik admits that there is nothing active he can do against the white pressure on d6 and f6.

19.fxe6 fxe6

The ungainly position of the black queen could be the basis for a tactical motif.

White to move

Play like Keres.

20.♖xf6 ♖h7

On a7 the black queen is depriving its king of an important escape square. So there is no question of playing 20...♗xf6 in view of 21.♕xd6+ and then 22.♘b6+. With the queen and two pawns against a rook and bishop White is quite clearly winning. And 20...b5 21.♖f7 ♗e8 22.♖g7 is also clearly better for White. The knight cannot be taken: 22...bxa4? 23.♕b4+ ♔a8 24.e5+−. After 20...♗xa4 matters are decided by 21.♖xe6+−.

21.♖g6±

Keres has a sound extra pawn and the more active position.

After achieving a clearly advantageous position it is important to continue to act decisively. One of the most popular mistakes we all make in tournament games is: we win a pawn and have a good position and everything indicates that with normal play the game is won. Then, however, we fall into a routine, make 'natural moves' and thus give our opponent the opportunity to get back into the game. Keres wrote in the comments on one of his games: 'The hope that the position "wins itself" has already cost many a young player valuable points.'

As the game continues the Estonian demonstrates that he had learned from personal painful experience.

21...b5 22.♘c3 ♕c5 23.♘a2 ♔a7 24.♘b4 ♖f8 25.♗f3 h4 26.h3 ♗c8 27.♘d3 ♕c7 28.♘f4 ♖f6 29.♗g4 ♖xg6 30.♘xg6 ♗b7?

An oversight in a hopeless position. In time trouble he overlooked that the e4-pawn is taboo on account of ♕d4+.

31.♗xe6 ♗d8 32.♗d5 ♗xd5 33.♕xd5 ♖f7 34.e5

Black resigned.

48 Sicilian Defence

Erik Zude	2421
Tomas Likavsky	2498

Germany Bundesliga B 2006/07 (5)

1.e4 c5 2.♘f3 d6 3.d4 cxd4 4.♘xd4 ♘f6 5.♘c3 a6 6.♗g5 e6 7.f4 ♕c7 8.♗xf6 gxf6 9.♕d2 ♘c6 10.0-0-0 ♗d7

11.♗c4!?

White's set-up looks somewhat unstable. But the bishop is exerting maximum pressure down the b3-f7 diagonal. The alternatives 11.♔b1 and 11.♗e2 are, in contrast, less energetic.

11...b5

The Slovakian grandmaster plays as actively as the position allows. After the alternative 11...♘xd4 12.♕xd4 ♕c5 the white queen is forced into a retreat: 13.♕d3 b5 14.♗b3 b4 15.♘e2 ♗b5 16.♕f3 a5 17.♘d4 a4 18.♗xe6 fxe6 19.♘xe6 with a strong attack. Likavsky

137

could have steered into calmer waters with 11...0-0-0.

12.♗b3 ♘a5 13.f5

13.♔b1!? ♘xb3 14.cxb3 b4 15.♘ce2 was safer. However, he did not want to lose any time with the attack on the doubled pawn complex, which is in any case desirable.

13...b4 14.fxe6 ♘xb3+ 15.axb3 fxe6 16.♘a4

16.♘ce2!? was a possible alternative. The text move, however, prevents Black from sooner or later opening the a-file.

16...a5?

With 11...b5 Likavsky had set out his stall with the idea of meeting the attack on his king with a counter-attack on the queenside. When playing as sharply as this, however, the protection of a pawn is a luxury one cannot always afford! Perhaps he did not want to invest any thinking time in variations in which White takes the pawn now or later.

What was indicated was 16...♖c8 17.♔b1 ♗g7 18.g4 (18.♕xb4? e5∓) 18...0-0 19.h4 with attacking chances for both sides.

17.♕e2 ♗g7?!

In game 46, Suetin-Botvinnik, we saw how dominating the black king's bishop can be on e5. But here this square cannot be reached without problems:

17...♗h6+?! 18.♔b1 ♗f4? 19.♕g4 and White wins.

The best was probably 17...h5 18.♕f3 ♗g7 19.♔b1 (19.e5? d5 20.exf6 0-0 21.♕xh5 ♖xf6∓) 19...♖c8 20.♔a1 with better play for White.

18.♕h5+ ♔e7 19.♖d3± ♖ac8

What else can Black do but force the counter-attack? Defence with 19...♖ag8 appears too passive.

20.♖g3 ♗f8

20...♖cg8.

21.♖f1 e5?

The last chance consisted of 21...♕a7 22.♖d1 (22.♖d3±) 22...♕c7 23.♖d2, but also here, White is clearly better.

22.♖xf6+−

22.♕h4+−.

22...exd4?

After 22...♗e8 23.♕h4 exd4 24.♖xd6+ ♔xd6 25.♕f6+ ♔d7 26.♘b6+ ♕xb6 27.♕xb6 White is winning, but still has some work to do.

White to move

How does the attack continue?

23.♖g7+

The critical point is e7, so we must divert the dark-squared bishop or eliminate it: 23...♗xg7 (23...♔d8 24.♖xf8+; 23...♔xf6 24.♕g5+ ♔e6 25.♕f5#) 24.♖f7+ leads to mate. Therefore Black resigned.

49 Sicilian Defence

Vassily Ivanchuk	2720
Viswanathan Anand	2690

Linares 1992 (1)

1.e4 c5 2.♘f3 d6 3.d4 cxd4 4.♘xd4 ♘f6 5.♘c3 ♘c6 6.♗g5 e6 7.♕d2 a6 8.0-0-0 h6 9.♗e3 ♘xd4 10.♗xd4 b5 11.f3 ♕a5 12.a3 e5 13.♗e3 ♗e6 14.♔b1 ♗e7

White can hardly make progress in the centre without playing ♘d5, which, in any case, leads to an exchange of queens, with a roughly level game. After the following move, however, a weakening is created which the future World Champion will exploit with subtle play.

15.g4?!

15.h4 ♖b8 16.♘d5 ♕xd2 17.♘xf6+ gxf6 18.♖xd2 f5 is equal according to Anand.

15...♖b8

The playing style of Viswanathan Anand (*1969, FIDE World Champion 2000-2002, World Champion 2007-2013) is hard to characterise for normal mortal chess players. He unites the most subtle feeling for positional nuances and the greatest mastery of tactics. He is brilliant in attack and considered to be the best defensive player in the world – not least on account of his incredible calculating abilities. In his games, much appears

simple and clear which does not work for other players.

Here Anand analyses as follows: 15... b4 16.axb4 (16.♘d5 ♗xd5 17.exd5 ♖b8 or 16.♘a2 d5 17.axb4 ♕c7 with compensation) 16...♕xb4 17.♘d5 ♘xd5 18.exd5 ♕xd2 19.♖xd2 ♗d7=.

16.♘d5 ♕xd2 17.♘xf6+?

Another imperceptible mistake, which Anand refutes with an original plan. In any case, after 17.♖xd2 ♘xd5 18.exd5 ♗d7 he also prefers the black position. The lever ...f7-f5 will follow.

17...gxf6!

17...♗xf6 18.♖xd2 ♔e7 19.h4± was perhaps what Ivanchuk had calculated. With the text move Black voluntarily accepts a doubled pawn complex. What are his intentions? At first sight we notice only the doubled pawns and the apparently irreparably weakened squares f5 and d5. It looks like a perfect blockade. Anand has, however, spotted that he can mark off as weaknesses the pawns on h2 and g4. Their defence will create disruption in the white camp, which Black goes on to exploit.

18.♖xd2 h5! 19.♖g1 hxg4 20.fxg4

20...♗c4!

The keystone in Anand's plan: it is only this brilliant move, which liberates the h3-square and with it the h-file, which justifies his 17th move. It is in total opposition to all we have been thinking so far. Black exchanges his best for the weakest minor piece.

But: bad bishops protect good pawns. White's king's bishop could, after h2-h3 and ♗g2, be used to stabilise the kingside. After that the pressure of the black rooks down the semi-open g- and h-files would be neutralised.

21.b3

21.♗xc4 bxc4 22.♖d5 ♖b5∓ (Anand).

21...♗xf1 22.♖xf1 ♖h3

Anand is now intending, after ...♔d7 and ...♖g8 or ...♖bh8, to increase the pressure on the kingside. When the white rooks are tied to the protection of h2 and g4, he will play ...d6-d5 to exchange the d- for the e-pawn, and later with ...f6-f5 the f- for the g-pawn. The result he is aiming for is the passed pawn duo f5 and e5. Out of an apparently immovable doubled pawn complex he creates two connected passed pawns – supported by the king. Original and effective!

Ivanchuk himself employs the lever g4-g5, but cannot materially change the course of events.

23.♖e2 ♔d7 24.g5 ♔e6 25.gxf6 ♗xf6 26.♗d2 ♗e7 27.♗e1 f6 28.♗g3 d5 29.exd5+ ♔xd5 30.♖f5

30...♔c6

As long as his opponent still has two rooks and a minor piece, the open middle of the board is a dangerous place for the king. Black has some reefs to steer around here, so: 30...♔e6? 31.♗xe5 ♖e8 32.♖xf6+= or 30...♖b7? 31.♗xe5 ♔e6 (31...fxe5? 32.♖fxe5+ ♔d6 33.♖e6+ ♔d5 34.♖2e5+! ♔d4 35.♖xe7 ♖xe7 36.♖xe7 ♖xh2 37.♖e6±) 32.♗xf6+ ♔xf5 33.♗xe7=.

31.♖ef2?

The decisive mistake! After 31.♖f3 ♖h7 32.♖c3+ ♔b7 (Anand) White could still offer some resistance.

31...♖h6 32.♔b2 ♔d7 33.♖e2 ♗d6 34.♖f3 ♖c8 35.♗e1 ♔e6 36.♖d3 ♖h7 37.♖g3 ♗c5 38.♔a2 ♖d7 39.♖c3 ♖cc7 40.h4 ♖d1 41.♗f2 ♗d6 42.♖g3 e4 43.♖xe4+ ♗e5 44.♖xe5+ fxe5 45.♔b2 ♖d2 0-1

An impressive game with a long-term plan. Anand spotted that the 'bad' dark-squared bishop had a great future in front of it. The weakening of the light squares was unimportant because Black was able to actively deploy an extra piece, namely the king.

Once more it could be seen that the massive black pawn structure is hard to attack in the endgame. The central king position is more of an advantage here than a disadvantage.

Model games

Leko-Morozevich (Mexico City 2007), winning the black rook pawn

Shirov-Kozul (Sarajevo 2005 & Heraklion 2007)

Timman-Kasparov (Niksic 1983)

Ragozin-Botvinnik (Moscow 1951), activating the bishop pair

Kasparov-Hracek (Yerevan 1996), opening the centre with e4-e5

Jussupow-Gavrikov (Horgen 1994), attack on the king down the semi-open g-file.

Chapter 9

Weak squares

One ought to be contesting the false conception that every
move should have to achieve something immediately;
waiting moves and quiet moves also have a right to exist.
Aaron Nimzowitsch

A square is designated 'weak' whenever it can no longer be controlled by its own pawns. Opposing pieces obtain an outpost, from which they can no longer be driven. A single weakening of the pawn structure in isolation can decide a game. In this chapter we introduce four typical pawn constellations which frequently occur in practice:
- the 'fianchetto holes'
- the isolated doubled f-pawns
- a weakened queenside with pawns on a7 and c6
- the knight outpost on f5

Somehow everyone knows that these weak squares represent a disadvantage. But they cannot always be avoided. We will examine why such structures – including their effects – nevertheless occur in practice and how one can provoke and exploit them.

We will then look into a pawn formation in which the central d4-square is permanently weakened in the opening: the structure of the King's Indian Exchange Variation.

The 'fianchetto-holes'

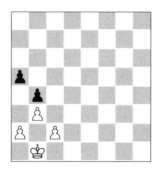

This formation can arise if after the fianchetto of the bishop the neighbouring central pawn (here d2) is swapped off.

Specific characteristics

The dark-square weaknesses on c3 and a3 are striking. They were fixed by the well-supported black b-pawn. If one imagines black minor pieces on a3 or c3 – or doubled major pieces on the c-file – dark clouds soon appear on the horizon.

Our tip: think things through before making an 'airhole' for your king. The rule of thumb: if in doubt, move the rook pawn!

The reason is simple: in a sound structure with pawns on a2, b2 and c2 the move a2-a3 does not create a weak square; b3 is after all protected by the c2-pawn.

If we play b2-b3, then two points lose their pawn protection, a3 and c3. Consequently they must be guarded by pieces or even by the king itself. Very often that is not something you want to do – sometimes it even constitutes a serious disadvantage.

Plans for White

White has problems with the safety of his king. How great these are depends on the remaining pieces. In each case he must bear in mind the opponent's plans: Black will be directing minor pieces towards a3 and c3 and doubling major pieces on the a-file in order to open the latter with the lever ...a5-a4. White has too little space to hold out against this. As long as the king is not too badly endangered, space for the defence can be created by c2-c3. The holes may remain, but nevertheless the rooks get opportunities for deployment on the c-file and if required can protect the a2-pawn along the second rank.

Plans for Black

In addition to the attacking ideas described above, Black has two other ways to take advantage of the unfortunate situation on the white queenside.

On one hand, the c-pawn is backward on a semi-open file and thus a welcome target for thorough siege by the major pieces.

On the other, White is often under threat of still suffering from the weaknesses even in the endgame. The pawn majority on the queenside needs the support of a piece to create a passed pawn. Sometimes Black will exploit this. See on this subject game 51, Kasparov-Andersson.

Conclusion

The weaknesses on c3 and a3 should be avoided for as long as the opponent still has available the means to exploit them.

50 French Defence
Judit Polgar
Alexey Shirov

Prague 1999 (2)

1.e4 e6 2.d4 d5 3.♘c3 ♘f6 4.e5 ♘fd7 5.f4 c5 6.♘f3 ♘c6 7.♗e3 cxd4 8.♘xd4 ♗c5 9.♕d2 0-0 10.0-0-0 a6 11.h4 ♘xd4 12.♗xd4

Judit Polgar (*1976), for decades by far the best woman chess player in the world, is known for her classical attacking chess and her powerful calculating abilities. She has inflicted defeats on almost all of the world's best grandmasters.

In the position in the diagram she has an advantage in space on the kingside, which gives her attacking chances. The central d4-square and the bad black queen's bishop also favour White. Shirov, however, has possibilities for an attack on the white king.

12...b5 13.♖h3

By default one would rather develop the king's bishop to d3. However, the exchange on c5 needed to achieve this would entice the black knight towards e4, which does not suit White. So Polgar first moves the rook, which can be employed in various positions along the third rank.

13...b4 14.♘e2

14.♘a4 ♗xd4 15.♕xd4 a5 16.♗b5 was a good alternative. The minor pieces stop the black pawn storm.

14...a5

15.♕e3

Finally forcing the exchange of pieces, but it invests a valuable tempo, which will be lacking in the attack on the kingside. 15.♗xc5 ♘xc5 16.h5 h6 17.♘d4 was preferable, with double-edged play.

15...♕c7 16.♗xc5 ♘xc5 17.♘d4 a4 18.♔b1?!

The most exciting moment in the game. Polgar was possibly reckoning on the file opening with 18...b3 and brings the king into safety. A better way, however, was 18.a3, stemming the black counter-play. If this is followed by 18...b3 19.cxb3, then Black achieves nothing concrete with the possible discovered check 19...♘xb3+.

18...a3!

Shirov now forces a tangible weakening of the king position. This may not lead to an immediate attack on the white king, since the a- and b-files remain closed, but right till the end of the game Polgar will not be able to get rid of the hole on c3.

19.b3 ♗a6

A pleasant side-effect of the pawn storm: the bad bishop can join in at last.

20.♗xa6?!

A better way was 20.♗d3 f6 with a tiny advantage for Black. White can then try to bring about simplifications with ♖c1 and a later c2-c3. She can defend against the direct attempt at an attack 20...♘xd3 with 21.cxd3 ♖fc8 and now not 22.♖c1?? ♗xd3++− but 22.♖hh1∓.

20...♖xa6 21.♕e1

21.c3 bxc3 22.♕xc3 ♕b6 23.♖c1 ♘e4 24.♖e3 h5∓.

21...♖b6 22.c3 ♕b7 23.♖c1 ♘e4 24.cxb4 ♖xb4 25.♖d3?

25.♘c6 ♖b6 26.♘d4 h6 27.h5 ♖c8∓.

With his next move Shirov forces a change in the position which speeds up his attack.

25...♖c4! 26.♖xc4

26.♖dd1 ♖fc8 27.♘e2 ♕b6 28.♕g1 ♖xc1+ 29.♖xc1 ♖xc1+ 30.♕xc1 h5 and the black queen invades, e.g. 31.♕xa3 ♕f2−+.

26...dxc4 27.♖d1 ♘c5 28.♕c3 ♕xg2−+ 29.b4

29.bxc4 offers greater resistance, but in no way changes the result: 29...♕e4+ 30.♘c2 h5 with a winning position for Black.

29...♘d3 30.♕xa3 ♖a8 31.♖xd3 cxd3 32.♕xd3 ♕xa2+ 33.♔c1 ♕a1+ 34.♔d2 ♖d8 35.♔e3 ♕e1+ 0-1

With his pawn storm ...b7-b5, ...a7-a5, ...b5-b4, ...a5-a4 and then ...a4-a3, Shirov provoked a weakening of the c3-square which left Polgar an arduous defensive task.

In chess there is no place for gallantry.
Irving Chernev

51 Queen's Gambit Declined

Garry Kasparov 2760
Ulf Andersson 2625

Reykjavik 1988 (2)

1.d4 ♘f6 2.c4 e6 3.♘c3 d5 4.cxd5 exd5 5.♗g5 c6 6.♕c2 ♗e7 7.e3 ♘bd7 8.♗d3

White has developed the 'bad' bishop outside of the pawn chain f2-e3-d4, where it is actively posted. The black queen's bishop, on the other hand, has (as yet) no rosy prospects.

8...♘h5 9.♗xe7 ♕xe7 10.♘ge2 g6

A totally inconspicuous, voluntary weakening with the idea of swapping off the bad bishop by means of ...♘g7 and later ...♗f5.

11.0-0-0 ♘b6 12.♘g3!

This forces Andersson to give up on his planned ...♗f5.

12...♘g7 13.♔b1 ♗d7 14.♖c1

Play on both wings! It is not yet clear where the black king is going. An over-hasty attack on the right-hand side of the board could be ineffective. So Kasparov prepares an attack on the queenside.

14...0-0-0

After 14...0-0 15.h4 h5 16.♘ce2 Andersson has to defend his kingside.

15.♘a4 ♘xa4 16.♕xa4 ♔b8 17.♖c3 b6

So as to meet 18.♖a3 with 18...♗e8. Now, on the other hand, the c-pawn becomes weak.

18.♗a6

An energetic move. The black king should be worried. In addition Kasparov prevents Andersson from bringing his rooks on to the c-file. Moreover, from now on he must always bear in mind the consequences of ...b6-b5, which shuts in the bishop.

18...♘e6 19.♖hc1 ♖he8 20.♕b3 ♕d6 21.♘f1 ♔a8 22.♘d2 ♘c7

Now and on the next move the capture of the h2-pawn was well worth considering. The confusing complications would hardly have worked out to the advantage of Black.

23.♗f1 ♘e6

The holes on f6 and h6 are still of no significance. Black has at his disposal a promising central lever in ...c6-c5 and all the major pieces are still on the board. Despite that, Kasparov finds a possibility to make something out of the weakened kingside.

24.g3 ♖c8 25.♗g2

The fianchetto exerts pressure on the d5-pawn and makes ...c6-c5 difficult.

25...♖c7 26.h4!

This looks like an absolutely everyday improvement in the white structure, preparing at the same time a future line opening h4-h5.

26...♖d8 27.♘f3

This move could also be wrongly interpreted by his opponent. The knight should certainly be centralised?!

27...♗c8?!

Andersson allows it. Perhaps his thoughts were too firmly fixed on the centre? After 27...f6 the game remains balanced.

28.♕a4 c5?!

A better way was 28...♗d7±.

29.♘g5!

This forces the exchange on g5, after which the holes on f6 and h6 are fixed. 29.♘e5?!, on the other hand, looks nice but achieves nothing tangible. Even when occupying attractive central squares we need to have a plan!

29...♘xg5

29...f6 30.♘xe6 ♗xe6 31.b4 ♖b8 (31...
c4 32.♖xc4) 32.bxc5 bxc5+ 33.♔a1±
would have lost a pawn.

30.hxg5

Unlike in game 50, Polgar-Shirov, the
holes on f6 and h6 have no consequences
for the safety of the king. Nevertheless,
they represent a permanent structural
problem. Without support from the
pieces, the black kingside is paralysed.
The troops are, moreover, needed for
the defence of c5 and d5. In addition,
the backward h-pawn constitutes a
palpable weakness.

Similarly to the variation after the
previous move Kasparov is now
threatening to win a pawn with 31.b4.
That gives him the tempo needed for
the following queen manoeuvre.

**30...♗b7 31.dxc5 bxc5 32.♕f4!?
♕xf4 33.gxf4± d4?**

After 33...c4 34.♖d3 ♖c5 (34...cxd3
35.♖xc7 ♔b8 36.♖c5 d4 37.♗xb7
dxe3 38.fxe3 ♔xb7 39.♔c1) 35.♖d4±
Andersson would have been faced with
a laborious defence. Now, on the other
hand, he loses by force.

**34.♖xc5 ♖xc5 35.♗xb7+ ♔xb7
36.♖xc5 dxe3 37.fxe3 ♖e8**

Possibly the threatened ♖e5 should be
prevented.

38.♖e5!

In the pawn ending one pawn (g5)
will stop three opposing ones (f7, g6
and h7). For that reason the white
majority on the queenside will be
decisive. You certainly still remember
the advice from the previous chapter,
only to aim for pawn endings when the
consequences can be clearly worked out.
We assume that Kasparov had properly
calculated the subsequent endgame. In
view of the long variations and some
possible transpositions of moves that is
absolutely no trivial matter!

38...♖xe5

38...♖f8 39.♖e7++−.

**39.fxe5 ♔c6 40.♔c2 ♔d5 41.b4
♔xe5 42.a4 f6 43.gxf6 ♔xf6 44.b5**

White now gets two widely separated
distant passed pawns a and e, against
which the black king is powerless. The
black passed g- and h-pawns will, on
the other hand, be stopped by the white
king, so Andersson resigned.

In this game Kasparov showed why for
more than two decades he dominated
the peak of world chess. In addition to
all the rest, he was able to convert an
inconspicuous weakness into the full
point against a fine positional player
such as Andersson.

There is no genius without passion.

Theodor Momsen

Study by Alekhine 1924, White to play and win

1.g5 After 1.♔e5 ♔c8 2. g5 ♔d8 it takes a bit longer. **1...♔c8 2.♔c5 ♔d7 3.♔d5 ♔d8 4.♔c6 ♔c8 5.d7+ ♔d8 6. ♔d6+−** and Black must move the f- or h-pawn.

Model games

Beliavsky-Portisch (Reggio Emilia 1986), the black queen's bishop which is actually bad becomes very strong in view of the holes on f3 and h3

Cheparinov-Ivanchuk (Sofia 2008), an entertaining mutual attack on the king, in which Ivanchuk's minor pieces bring about the decision on c3.

Isolated doubled f-pawns

White has no e-pawn

Things are getting worse. What do you think of the white pawn structure? Not a particularly intelligent question. The concept of 'structure' is elastic, but hardly still applicable here.

Specific characteristics

The kingside resembles a ruin. If we had previously brought into being two weaknesses (f3 and h3) with one pawn move (g2-g3), now here after g2xf3 there are four! The squares f3, f4, h3 and h4 can no longer be protected by pawns and are inviting black pieces to take permanent possession of them, so very close to the white king. But there is no use weeping and wailing: in the heat of battle this sort of 'constellation' can come about, usually as a result of desperate defence or when tempted by material gains. But from time to time even experienced grandmasters accept them willingly – just to get an exchange of queens and the advantage of the bishop pair. Take a look at game 52, Van Wely-Short.

Plans for White

Not much planning is possible. The watchword is: survive, somehow or other. If things go well, White has in return for his ruptured kingside compensation in some other part of the board.

Plans for Black

According to the means available, the white king can be got to grips with. Minor pieces aim for f3, f4, h3 or h4, major pieces are frequently doubled on the h-file. In many cases, all it takes is a knight permanently posted on f4 to make White's life difficult on the kingside.

Conclusion

This destruction of the kingside with isolated doubled f-pawns should be feared even more than the fianchetto holes. The more pieces there are on the board, the more endangered is the position of the white king.

52 Queen's Gambit Declined

Loek van Wely	2679
Nigel Short	2674

Wijk aan Zee 2005 (13)

1.d4 ♘f6 2.c4 e6 3.♘c3 d5 4.cxd5 exd5 5.♗g5 c6 6.e3 ♗f5?!

A wayward treatment of the opening from Nigel Short, a positionally very solid grandmaster. But if you think that it was just that the world-class English player wanted to try something different, you are well off the mark! Short regularly plays this variation.

Our advice: just don't imitate him! Even if the bishop pair and the majority on the queenside represent a certain amount of compensation, continually having to look for sufficient dynamic counterplay all through a long game is a major undertaking. Why should we put ourselves under pressure? That is a task for our opponents.

6...♗e7 and 6...♘bd7 are the usual continuations.

7.♕f3 ♗g6 8.♗xf6 ♕xf6 9.♕xf6 gxf6

Since the queens have already been exchanged, the situation does not look quite so dramatic for the black king. Black is planning to push forward with his pawn majority on the queenside. The bishop pair is very well placed for that. White will, on the other hand, try to occupy either the f5- or the h5-square.

10.♘f3 ♘d7 11.♘h4!

Van Wely plays the next phase of the game with impressive clarity. In doing so he exploits the fact that Black's best plan with his pawns on the kingside should be to keep still.

11...♗e7 12.g3 ♘b6

12...f5?! would only make the situation on the right-hand side of the board worse.

13.f3 a5 14.♔f2 a4 15.♖c1 ♘c8

After 15...♘c4?! 16.♗xc4 dxc4 the move 17.a3! deprives Black of any hope of active play. In the closed position the knights are very flexible and can easily attack the numerous weaknesses.

16.♗e2 ♘d6 17.♖hd1 0-0?

As we shall see, he is castling straight into disaster. The king is better placed in the middle or on the queenside.

18.♗d3 ♖fe8 19.g4!

Up till here Short had been able to hold the status quo on the important f5-square. With the text move, however, Van Wely prepares the transfer ♘e2-g3-f5. There is nothing which can be done against that.

19...♗f8 20.♘e2 ♗h6 21.f4 ♗xd3 22.♖xd3 ♗f8

22...♘e4+ cannot prevent the occupation of f5 either: 23.♔g2 ♘d6 24.♘g3.

23.♘g3 ♖a5 24.♖c2 ♖b5 25.♘hf5

Van Wely's manoeuvres are crowned with complete success. Short has no counterplay and has to put up with the sight of the powerful knight. If at least the king were not squeezed in on g8!

25...♘c4 26.b3 axb3 27.♖xb3 ♖xb3?!

The most tenacious defence was 27...♗b4.

28.axb3 ♘a5!?

28...♘d6 29.♖a2 puts up longer resistance, but is equally hopeless in the long run.

29.♘h5 ♖e6 30.♖a2 b6 31.♖a4 1-0

In the game Short did not manage to deploy his bishop pair actively. He had to just look on as his opponent manoeuvred a knight to f5 – with an overwhelming position.

53 English Opening

Vassily Smyslov	2620
Jonathan Mestel	2200

Hastings 1972 (15)

1.c4 ♘f6 2.♘c3 e5 3.♘f3 ♘c6 4.g3 ♗b4 5.♗g2 0-0 6.0-0 ♖e8 7.♘d5 e4 8.♘e1 d6 9.d3 ♗xe1?!

A better way was 9...h6.

10.♖xe1 exd3

Here we get to know a further motif which leads to a ruined pawn structure: greed! In the heat of battle, so much can be accepted for the gain of a pawn. After 10...h6, however, White has a permanent advantage. So Mestel prefers the complicated continuation.

11.♗g5

Smyslov could also hope for a slight advantage after simply 11.exd3. Nevertheless, he gladly sacrifices the pawn because the risk is negligible.

11...dxe2 12.♖xe2 ♖xe2 13.♕xe2 ♗e6 14.♘xf6+ gxf6 15.♗h4

With the subsequent centralisation Black gets the opportunity to swap off the annoying bishop on h4 by ...♘g6.

15...♘e5 16.♗xb7 ♗xc4 17.♕h5

An important tempo for the attack.

17...♖b8 18.♗e4 ♘g6 19.b3 ♗a6?!

So as to attack the white queen with ♖b5. But 19...♗e6 is better, since

149

after it the whole attack is not so easy to conduct. That is fighting chess: a kingside in shreds in return for an extra pawn. Why not, if you can defend? But in the game Mestel did not manage to do so.

20.♖e1 ♖b5 21.♗d5!

The queen does not move from the spot, and at the same time the motif ♗xf7+ makes an appearance.

21...♔g7

With accurate play Black could reach a level endgame: 21...c6 22.♕h6 (22.♗xf7+? ♔g7−+) 22...♕f8 (here Smyslov analyses only 22...♘xh4 23.♗xf7+ ♔xf7 24.♕xh7+ ♔f8 25.♕h8+ ♔f7 26.♕xd8 ♘f3+ 27.♔h1 ♘xe1 28.♕d7+ ♔g6 29.♕e8++− and 22...♖xd5 23.♗xf6 ♕f8 24.♖e8 ♖d1+ 25.♔g2 ♗f1+ 26.♔f3 ♖d3+ 27.♔g4 ♗e2+ 28.f3 ♗xf3+ 29.♔h3+−) 23.♕xf8+ ♔xf8 24.♗xc6 ♖c5 25.♗f3 ♘xh4 26.gxh4=. A sign that Mestel's risky plan was not wrong. But he had to calculate very accurately!

22.a4 ♖b4?!

Only now does the defence become shaky. After 22...♖c5 23.b4 ♖c3 24.♗xf7 ♗c4! the chances are roughly level.

23.♗xf7 ♕d7?

The decisive mistake. 23...♘e5 24.♗d5 ♖d4 25.♗e4 ♘g6± held the position

together. After the move in the game Smyslov's attack drives home.

24.♗xg6 hxg6 25.♗xf6+ ♔xf6 26.♕h8+ ♔g5 27.f4+ ♔g4 28.♖e3 g5 29.♕h6 ♖xf4 30.gxf4 ♔xf4 31.♔f2 ♕c6 32.♕f6+ ♔g4 33.♖g3+ ♔h4 34.♕xg5#

From the objective point of view it was justifiable for Black to snap up the extra pawn, even if it meant that the safety of his king suffered. In practical play, however, it is very dangerous. Mestel played with fire and got his fingers badly burned. Well, on the other hand he might have been sitting there with an extra pawn 20 moves later – and then we would perhaps have been praising him for his artistry. A fine line!

After seeing in both the previous games what difficult defensive tasks are caused in the middlegame by the pawn structure f2/f3/h2, it is time for the exception to the rule, which, as everyone knows, always exists.

either side to move

In the frequently met ending with four against three pawns on one flank, the doubled f-pawns are an advantage and lead to a comfortable draw. On account of the reduced material, the weaknesses are sufficiently defensible. Of course, it is also possible to hold the 'standard endgame' with a white pawn on g3 rather than f3, but in it there is still some work to do. The most important plan for Black consists of the creation of a passed pawn on the e-file, which is however prevented by the doubled f-pawns here.

Model games
Movsesian-Kasparov (Sarejevo 2000)
Navara-Short (Prague 2007)

The tactician needs to know what he has
to do, if there is something to do; the
strategist needs to know what he has to do,
if there is nothing to do.
Savielly Tartakower

Queenside in shreds with pawns on a7 and c6

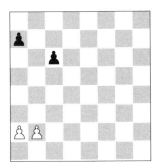

Specific characteristics
We immediately notice an isolated pawn on a semi-open c-file. Here too a pawn move, ...b7xc6, caused several weak squares: a6, a5 and c5. These are serious weaknesses, which should only be accepted in return for good compensation. In Tal-Najdorf, however, Black had no counterplay and had to defend passively. What is particularly instructive about the game is how

Tal exploited an inaccuracy by the Argentinian in order to bring about this structure.

Plans for White
White will lay siege to the isolated pawn on the c-file. The outpost c5 is the ideal blockading square, either for a knight or for a bishop.
The presence of major pieces is to White's advantage. He has chances to employ his own actively and to tie down the black ones to the defence of the pawns on c6 and a7. The b-pawn is safely protected on b3.

Plans for Black
Black can try after b2-b3 to get rid of his weak isolated pawn with the advance of the c-pawn, ...c6-c5-c4xb3.
It would be in his favour if he could exploit the outpost in the centre produced by his weakling and place a minor piece on the central d5-square. This would be the (only) advantage of the weak structure on the queenside: the c6-pawn protects d5.

Conclusion
The weakened black queenside is especially vulnerable if there are a lot of major pieces on the board. In any case Black must take active measures against the siege.

54 Sicilian Defence
Mikhail Tal
Miguel Najdorf
Belgrade 1970 (3)
1.e4 c5 2.♘f3 ♘c6 3.d4 cxd4 4.♘xd4 e6 5.♘c3 ♕c7 6.g3 a6 7.♗g2 ♘f6 8.0-0 d6 9.♖e1 ♗d7 10.♘xc6 bxc6

Tal has developed his pieces quicker than Najdorf. The latter has obtained in return a compact pawn mass in the centre, which will keep the white pieces at a distance.

White to move

Develop a plan for White. Which changes in the pawn structure should he aim for?

If you are an attacking player, you perhaps suggested 11.f4, intending to storm the black position with 12.e5. That is possible, but risky, since doing so opens up the white king position. Tal chose a positional way to treat the situation.

11.♘a4

Making space for c2-c4. After this, Black's pawn thrusts in the centre, ...e6-e5, ...d6-d5 and ...c6-c5, become less attractive.

11...e5?!

At the same time c2-c4 also set up the threat of c4-c5. Najdorf would have had to draw the teeth of it: 11...♖b8 12.c4 c5 (Tal) with approximately level chances.

12.c4± ♗e7

Here too he had to prevent 13.c5. The hole on d5 was the lesser evil, e.g. 12... c5 ('±' – Tal) 13.♗g5 ♗xa4 14.♕xa4+ ♕d7 with a tiny disadvantage.

13.c5

This weakens the black queenside.

13...0-0

13...d5?! 14.exd5 cxd5 15.♘b6±.

14.cxd6 ♗xd6

The change in the position from move 11 worked to the advantage of White. Black has no counterplay. Tal explains in his very personal and entertainingly written games collection that White should now unhurriedly lay siege to the queenside, beginning with 15.♗e3. As he frankly admits, in what followed he lost his focus and played without a plan.

15.♗g5 ♗e7 16.♕c2 h6 17.♗e3 ♖ab8 18.♖ac1 ♖fd8 19.h3?!

One of these 'semi-automatic' moves with which we deprive our opponent of certain possibilities, here ...♗g4 or ...♘g4, but in return weaken our position. The pawn becomes a target on h3. The correct move was 19.♗c5.

19...♘h7 20.♗c5 ♗e8 21.♖ed1 ♖xd1+ 22.♖xd1 ♘g5 23.♗xe7 ♕xe7 24.♘c5 ♘e6?!

This premature exchange really does not suit the counterplay for Black which he has just drummed up. Tal analyses the active defence 24...♖b5 25.♖c1 (25.♘xa6 ♖a5 26.♕c4 c5 27.b4 cxb4 28.♘xb4±, or 28.♕xb4 ♕xb4 29.♘xb4 ♘e6±) 25...♘e6 26.♘xe6 ♕xe6 27.b3 ♖b4 28.♗f1 ♖d4± and White still has to bear in mind the weakness on h3.

25.♘xe6 ♕xe6 26.b3 ♕e7 27.♕c3 ♖b4 28.h4

Protects the pawn and at the same time opens the h3-c8 diagonal for the bishop.

28...f6?

Actually this is the correct structure for a bishop ending, which still, however, lies in the far distance. In the middlegame the move of the f-pawn is a palpable weakening. The bishop may be covering the light squares, but should (and will), however, be employed for active tasks. A better way was 28...a5, to protect the rook, linked with the idea of 29...♗d7.

29.♖d3 ♔h7 30.♗h3 ♗g6?!

Najdorf would like with his counter-attack to divert attention from the weaknesses of the black position. But 30...c5 31.♖d5 c4 32.bxc4 ♗c6± offered greater resistance. The 'magician from Riga' does not need a second invitation to an attack on the light squares.

31.♖d7 ♕f8 32.♕xc6 ♖xe4 33.♕xa6 ♖e1+ 34.♔h2 f5 35.♖d6 ♗h5 36.♕d3 e4 37.♕d5

37...♗g4?

The decisive mistake. 37...♗f3 38.♕xf5+ (38.♗xf5+ ♔h8 39.g4 ♖h1+ 40.♔g3 ♖g1+ 41.♔f4 ♖d1 (41...♖xg4+? 42.♔e3+− Tal)) 38...♔g8! 39.♕xf8+ ♔xf8 40.♗g2 ♖e2 41.♗xf3 exf3 42.a4 ♖xf2+ 43.♔h3± leads to a rook ending with winning chances for White.

38.♖d8 ♕f6 39.♕g8+?

Shortly before the time control even the greatest players do not pass by the chance for a check. There was an immediate win with 39.h5!.

39...♔g6 40.♕e8+ ♔h7 41.♗xg4 fxg4 42.♕g8+ ♔g6 43.♖f8

If the queen moves, 44.♖e8 decides matters. Najdorf resigned.

With the advance of the c-pawn, c4-c5, Tal left the solid black pawn structure in tatters and then laid siege to the weaknesses on Najdorf's queenside.

Model games
Kasparov-Karpov (Seville m 1987)
Sasikiran-Hansen (Copenhagen/ Malmö 2005)

The outpost on f5
We already noticed a similar beautiful knight in game 2, Wolff-Bronstein:

That is where we want it, that is where it belongs! There is no question but that something has gone wrong for Black if a white piece can establish itself permanently on f5, whilst the 'fianchettoed' black king's bishop is controlling the shortest possible 'long diagonal'. Let us not describe and analyse this misery for long. We are principally interested in the question: how could it come to that?

In the next games, ex-World Champion Max Euwe (1901-1981, World Champion 1935-1937) and Alexander Onischuk, two strong grandmasters, are reduced to a comparable situation.
Whereas Euwe did play ...g7-g5 of his own accord, Onischuk was simply guilty of a few inaccuracies which English grandmaster Michael Adams punished with fine positional play. His methodical way of going about it is extremely instructive.

55 Ruy Lopez
Vassily Smyslov
Machgielis Euwe
Groningen 1946 (8)
1.e4 e5 2.♘f3 ♘c6 3.♗b5 a6 4.♗a4 ♘f6 5.d3 d6 6.c3 g6 7.0-0 ♗g7 8.♖e1 b5 9.♗c2 0-0 10.♗g5 h6 11.♗h4 ♕e8 12.♘bd2 ♘h5 13.♘f1

With his next move Euwe closes the h4-d8 diagonal.
13...g5?!
Nevertheless that was not necessary. Possibly he was fed up with the provocative bishop. In the further course of the game Black will suffer from the weakness of f5. Nevertheless, ...g6-g5 also deprives him in the long term of an opportunity to become active on the kingside.
An important idea behind the white set-up is by means of d3-d4 to obtain the central pawn duo d4/e4. Black can no longer prevent that and should try to exert pressure on the white pawn duo. If his opponent at some point plays d4-d5, he may have a great advantage in space, but Black can then get counterplay with ...f7-f5. We will come across dealing with pawn chains in the next chapter. In any case, after Euwe has moved his g-pawn forward, a future ...f7-f5 will be less attractive for Black.
14.♗g3 ♘e7
To set free the c-pawn. According to how things turn out he can now play ...c7-c6 or even ...c7-c5.
15.a4! ♘xg3
Now the hanging ♘h5 made itself felt: 15...♗d7? 16.♘xe5±. After 15...♘f4 it is beautifully placed, but ineffective. White can play 16.d4 to increase the pressure in the centre.

16.hxg3 ♗e6 17.d4 f6

This weakens the light squares even more. The subsequent exchange of bishops was in any case on the cards, and Euwe would also like to get the queens off the board at once.

18.♗b3± ♗xb3 19.♕xb3+ ♕f7 20.♕xf7+ ♔xf7 21.♘e3 ♖fb8

21...c6 prevents first and foremost the closing of the centre. But White can continue with 22.g4 and then ♘f3-h2-f1-g3-f5. If Black plays the knight to f4, it will be driven away after White's knight journey by g2-g3.

22.axb5 axb5

23.d5!?

Smyslov thus secures the better structure in the long term. If Euwe now plays ...c7-c6, he will be left after dxc6 with two weak pawns, the backward pawn on d6 and the isolated one on b5. After 23.g4 Black continues with ...c7-c6, after which White must first prepare d4-d5.

23...h5 24.♔f1 g4

Just 'forcing' the knight to set out for f5. But in any case White will be playing with a strong knight against the bad bishop, e.g. 24...♔g6 25.g4 hxg4 26.♘xg4 f5 27.exf5+ ♘xf5 28.♘d2 and then ♘e4. There too he is looking good.

25.♘h4 ♗h6 26.♘ef5

The ideal position for White.

26...♘g8 27.♔e2 ♖a4 28.♖xa4 bxa4 29.♖b1 ♖b3

On 29...a3 follows 30.b4!.

30.♔d3 a3 31.♔c2 ♖xb2+ 32.♖xb2 axb2 33.♔xb2

33...♗d2

Black can probably not defend the endgame. What is decisive in the following variations is that the king will invade on c6. Thereafter White wins every pawn ending. Smyslov is considered one of the greatest endgame experts. Here is his analysis: 33...♗g5 34.♔b3 ♗xh4 35.gxh4 ♘e7 36.♘xe7 ♔xe7 37.♔c4 f5 38.f3 f4 39.♔b5 ♔d7 40.c4 ♔d8 41.♔c6 ♔c8 42.c5 dxc5 43.♔xc5 ♔d7 44.♔c4 ♔e7 45.♔b4 ♔d6 46.♔b5 (zugzwang) 46...g3 47.♔b4 ♔e7 (47...c6 48.dxc6 ♔xc6 49.♔c4) 48.♔c4 ♔d6 49.♔b5 ♔d7 50.♔c5 ♔c8 51.d6+− (Smyslov).

34.♔c2 ♗e1 35.f3 ♘e7 36.♘xe7 ♔xe7 37.fxg4 hxg4 38.♘f5+ ♔f7 39.c4 ♔g6 40.♔b3 ♔g5

The passive defence 40...♔f7 loses in a similar way, as shown in the analysis to move 33. Euwe tries a piece sacrifice. Knights are known to have great difficulties in the struggle against passed pawns. However, Smyslov keeps everything under control.

41.♔a4   ♗xg3   42.♘xg3   ♔f4
43.♘h5+   ♔xe4   44.♘xf6+   ♔f5
45.♘e8 e4 46.♘xc7 e3 47.♘b5 ♔f4
48.♘c3 ♔g3 49.c5

Black resigned.

In this game Euwe voluntarily accepted the hole on f5. However, after the former World Champion did not manage to create sufficient counterplay, Smyslov had his nose in front in the endgame.

56 Two Knights Defence

Michael Adams   2680
Alexander Onischuk   2625

Tilburg 1997 (1)

1.e4 e5 2.♘f3 ♘c6 3.♗c4 ♘f6 4.d3
♗e7 5.0-0 0-0 6.a4 d6 7.♘bd2 ♗e6
8.♖e1 ♗xc4

Possibly a premature exchange. The white king's bishop was going nowhere. It seems simpler to play 8...♕d7.

9.dxc4!?

For Adams the reliable control of d5 is more important than a beautiful pawn chain. 9.♘xc4 is the 'normal' continuation.

9...♖e8 10.♘f1 ♗f8 11.♗g5 h6?!

A very inconspicuous weakening on the kingside. Of course the pawn does not belong permanently on a square of the colour of its own bishop, but it is in no way fixed on h6 as yet. We shall see...

The structure f7-g6-h7 suits the bishop and keeps the game level: 11...g6 12.♘e3 ♗e7= and after 13.♗xf6 ♗xf6 Black

would have no problems. He can play ...♗g7 and, after good preparation, later ...f7-f5.

12.♗xf6 ♕xf6 13.♘e3 ♕e6 14.a5

With this White secures for the long term attacking chances on the queenside.

14...♘e7

If he stops the a-pawn with 14...a6?!, then a future ...c7-c6 will weaken the b6-square.

15.♖a3 g6 16.h4!

With this move, the 17th, 21st and 23rd moves, Adams systematically exposes the disadvantages of ...h7-h6. Each of these moves receives an exclamation mark because of the overall plan. It is interesting that from the start he left the third rank free, thus doing without the 'usual' b2-b3. Therefore both ♖d3 and ♖g3 are possible.

16...♗g7

The normal reply to the advance of the white rook pawn would be 16...h5. At this moment, however, the g5-square is vulnerable: 17.♘g5 ♕d7 18.c5 f6 (18...♖ed8 19.a6 b6 20.♕f3 ♘c6 21.♘d5 ♗g7 22.cxd6 cxd6 23.♖d3 ♘d4 24.♘f6+ ♗xf6 25.♕xf6 ♘xc2 26.♖xd6+−) 19.♘f3 ♖ad8 20.cxd6 cxd6±.

In this game everything Adams does fits in well.

17.h5!±

Finally the weakness on h6 is fixed! As far as the structure is concerned, this move would be less effective with the black h-pawn on h7. Black could then meet hxg6 with ...hxg6.

17...♖ad8 18.a6 b6 19.♘d5 ♖d7 20.hxg6 fxg6 21.♘h4!

This prepares the subsequent attack on g6. The pawn should in any case be forced into advancing!

21...c6 22.♘xe7+ ♖exe7 23.♖g3! g5 24.♘f5±

At last! Adams has been inventive in his play and has worked hard to get the knight on to its dream square. And now? Of course White is better and Black must face up to painstaking defence. But it is still far from a winning position, rather simply a clear advantage.

24...♖f7 25.♖d3 ♗f8 26.b3 d5 27.♕g4 ♔h7??

Onischuk breaks down under the weight of the knight (or perhaps of time trouble?) and gives away the game with this blunder. After 27...b5 28.c3 (28.♖ed1 d4 29.c5 b4 − not 29...♗xc5? 30.♖h3 ♖xf5 31.exf5 ♕f6 32.♕e4+−) 28...bxc4 29.bxc4± or 27...d4± nothing was finally decided.

28.cxd5 cxd5 29.♘xh6 ♕xg4 30.♘xg4 ♗c5 31.♖e2

And Black resigned.

Adams systematically linked his attempts to conquer the f5-square with threats in the centre and on the queenside. At the end he was successful.

Conclusion

Think twice before placing a pawn on the same colour of square as that of your bishop − even if it only appears to be 'temporary'. The mechanism with which Adams made use of the (slight) weakening ...h7-h6, in order to create the outpost f5, is worthy of thorough study.

Model games

Kasparov-Chiburdanidze (Baku 1980), the future World Champion fights for the knight outpost on f5 with his preferred means, tactics

Gurevich-Kazhgaleyev (Cappelle-la-Grande 1996), a pawn sacrifice for a square!

The structure of the King's Indian Exchange Variation

The diagram shows a structure which is frequently met with and which can arise from various openings, mostly after the exchange of central pawns d4xe5 d6xe5. The best known route is from the Exchange Variation of the King's Indian Defence, after the moves **1.d4 ♘f6 2.c4 g6 3.♘c3 d6 4.e4 ♗g7 5.♘f3 0–0 6.♗e2 e5 7.dxe5 dxe5**. The pawn skeleton very closely resembles our diagram, leaving to one side for the moment the position of the black g-pawn.

Characteristics

The position is almost symmetrical, the only imbalance is the advanced white c-pawn, which can have serious consequences for the judgement of the position. In return for White's advantage in space on the queenside he has weak squares on c5 and d4. Sensible pawn levers are nowhere to be seen.

Plans for White

Since the advance f2-f4 would weaken the structure, only play on the queenside and in the centre is worth considering. White can determine the timing of the pawn exchange on e5, which has already happened in the position in the diagram and thus exploit the greater rearspan on the d-file. Depending on circumstances, the open file can be relevant for an invasion of the black camp. It must always be borne in mind, however, that White's own king's bishop is a bad piece and that the squares c5 and d4 must not fall under permanent control by Black. Getting in c4-c5 would solve both problems at a stroke. A preponderance in space, linked with the new outpost on d6, can lead to an advantage for White.

Plans for Black

The permanent weakness of d4 is a clear structural advantage. The significance of the c5-square is just as great. Black is aiming for complete control of these points as well as play against the bad white king's bishop. It is worth making efforts to reduce the number of defenders of the dark squares – e.g. ...♗g4x♘f3 and exchanging dark-squared bishops so as to be able to occupy d4 with a piece. The d-file, often in White's possession, can be neutralised with the vis-à-vis of the rooks, or also ignored, as long as the entry squares are sufficiently well protected. He must prevent c4-c5 by White, since it overturns the then favourable evaluation.

Conclusion

If White cannot make anything of the d-file and if he cannot get in c4-c5, this structure should not be aimed for. The danger of losing the struggle for the dark-squared complex d4/c5 is too great.

57 King's Indian Defence
Silvio Danailov   2295
Garry Kasparov   2595
Dortmund 1980 (11)
1.c4 g6 2.♘f3 ♗g7 3.♘c3 d6 4.d4 ♘f6 5.e4 0-0 6.♗e2 e5 7.dxe5 dxe5

8.♕xd8 ♖xd8 9.♗g5

At first sight White's opening initiative is developing splendidly. In addition to the advantage in space sought by c2-c4 he is now threatening 10.♘d5, which would delay Black's development. Despite that, the Exchange Variation is nowadays a rare guest in grandmaster praxis. When it is played, nevertheless, White tries to use his initiative to bring about a change in the structure.

9...♘bd7

King's Indian theoretician Mikhail Golubev recommends as the simplest defence 9...♖e8. Then after 10.♗xf6 ♗xf6 11.♘d5 ♗d8 the white threats have been warded off and Black retains his superior pawn formation as well as the bishop pair. White should instead eliminate his structural weaknesses with 10.♘d5 ♘xd5 11.cxd5.

analysis diagram: position after 11.cxd5

The exchange cxd5 renders the weak d4-square inaccessible and burdens Black for his part with a backward c-pawn. The latter, however, is resolved by 11...c6 12.♗c4 cxd5 13.♗xd5 ♘d7, with level play: 14.♘d2 ♘c5 15.♘c4 ♗f8= (Golubev).

10.♘d5?!

This inaccuracy allows Kasparov to retain an unchanged pawn structure. The correct way was 10.0-0-0 ♖f8 (but not 10...♖e8? 11.♘b5+−) 11.♘d5! ♘xd5 12.cxd5, though with a certain white initiative, which Black must first neutralise.

10...c6 11.♘e7+ ♔f8 12.♘xc8 ♖dxc8 13.0-0-0 ♘c5∓

Kasparov has already taken over the initiative. How should the defence be conducted?

14.♗xf6?

But 14.♘xe5? is not possible on account of 14...♘fxe4∓. He would do better to sacrifice a pawn than allow himself to be paralysed. After 14.♗e3 ♘fxe4 15.♘d2 b6 16.♘xe4 ♘xe4 17.♗f3 ♘f6 18.g4 White's counterplay may not suffice for equality, but it does limit the disadvantage.

14...♗xf6 15.♗d3

Black to move

1. **Evaluate the black bishop.**
2. **Which plan should Black follow?**

A glance at the known model 'bishop on f6 behind its own blockaded pawn on e5' immediately convinces us that this must be a bad bishop. However, that is not quite correct! There are two halves to the board. The bishop, which is bad on the right-hand side, is good on the left. Moreover it has no counterpart which could contest any diagonal there. The bishop becomes strong (but by definition not the good bishop!) as soon as we transfer it to the queenside.

A plan immediately springs from this idea: the e5-pawn will be protected in a different way. Thereafter Black aims for manoeuvres such as ...♗e7-c5(b4) or ...♗d8-b6(a5). So that White cannot thwart this idea with a2-a3 and b2-b4, first of all these moves are blocked and the outpost on c5 secured.

15...a5∓

Please always bear in mind that in such situations a knight on c5 cannot be driven away with the immediate a2-a3 (renewing the threat of b2-b4)! Black replies ...a5-a4 and b2-b4 is off the agenda. The white structure is left with major weak squares. He is forced into the cautious plan of first b2-b3, intending to follow up with a2-a3 and b3-b4. So Black gains a tempo with ...a7-a5.

16.♖he1 ♖e8 17.♗f1 ♗d8 18.g3

With 18.b3 White prevents the advance ...a5-a4. The b6-f2 diagonal, however, is also attractive: 18...♗b6 19.g3 f6 20.♗h3 ♖ad8∓.

18...a4 19.♔c2 ♗a5 20.♖e3?!

This loss of tempo makes the defence more difficult. In any case, even after the more precise 20.♖e2 f6 (20...♖ad8 21.♖xd8 ♖xd8 22.♘xe5 ♖d4 23.f3 ♗c7 24.♘g4 ♖xc4+∓) 21.♗h3 ♖ed8∓, Danailov would not have been able to stir.

20...♖ad8 21.♖xd8 ♖xd8 22.♗h3

White is helpless, and with the move in the text he is more or less waiting until Kasparov transforms his superiority into a victory.

Just as in a won position we should not be looking for the shortest or even the most beautiful way to win, but the simplest and safest, so in a difficult or hopeless situation we must not choose the longest way to a defeat, but the one which gives our opponent the greatest practical difficulties! In line with this motto, 22.♘xe5 was preferable. With that move Danailov would at least have given his opponent the opportunity to miscalculate during the subsequent variations. Admittedly, his chances of success were slim: 22...♖d2+ 23.♔c1 ♖xf2 24.♖f3 ♖xh2 25.♖xf7+ (25.♘xf7 ♔e7) 25...♔g8 26.♖f3 ♖h1 27.♔c2 ♗c7 28.♘g4 ♔g7-+.

22...f6 23.♖e2?

After this, Kasparov wins without any great effort. 23.♗f1 (23...♘a6 24.♗e2) 23...♔e7 24.♗e2 would have prevented the subsequent incursion by the knight. Black can then make no further progress without employing his king. He has every chance in the long term of opening up the play decisively on the weakened white queenside. He would, however, be faced with a tough struggle.

23...♔e7?!

A simpler way was 23...♘d3 24.a3 ♘c5–+.

24.♗g2

Also after 24.♖e3 h5 with the threat of ...g6-g5 White can no longer sustain his defensive position.

24...♘d3!–+

This forces the following pawn move, after which Kasparov gets, in addition to all the rest, the b3-square for his knight.

25.a3 ♘c5 26.h4 h5 27.♖e3?! g5!

With the driving of the knight away from f3 the white position collapses.

28.hxg5 fxg5 29.♖e2 ♘b3 30.♔b1 ♔f6   **0-1**

The game shows that White has great problems and few chances for active play, if Black controls the dark squares on the queenside.

Model games
Teschner-Fischer (Stockholm 1962)
Karpov-Kasparov (Lyon/New York m 1990)
Beliavsky-Kozul (Gothenburg 2005)

Chapter 10
Pawn chains

When the others think we have reached the end, that is
when we must really start.
Konrad Adenauer

Fixing the central pawn structure often leads to constellations in which a white and a black 'pawn chain' dovetail. The most important cases are the 'French' structure (white pawns on d4 and e5 against black ones on e6 and d5) and the 'King's Indian' (white e4 and d5 against d6 and e5 for Black). They can arise from various opening systems.

The French chain is the mirror image of the King's Indian one: in the first one a white pawn has crossed the middle line of the board on the right (e4-e5). In the second the same thing happens on the left-hand side of the board.

The strategies for dealing with the centre are therefore very similar. There is however an important difference in the position of the kings, which mostly castle kingside. This affects the plans of both sides: if White attacks on the side on which he has an advantage in space, that implies in the French structure an attack on the king, in the King's Indian, however, simply action on the queenside.

In this chapter we will discuss both types of position and with the help of grandmaster games point to what they have in common and where they differ.

The French structure

Specific characteristics

The central pawn chain divides the board into a left and a right half. The position is closed in character. There is still no open or semi-open file for a rook and also the pieces on both sides mostly have little contact with each other.

White has an advantage in space in the centre and on the kingside. The e5-pawn, the 'head' of the pawn chain, cramps the black kingside by controlling the f6-square. At the same time the right-hand side of the board offers White a lot of space to bring his pieces into position for an attack.

The effect of the firm blockade of the central pawns is that the queen's bishops on both sides are bad, which can have serious consequences at a later stage.

Plans for White

You attack where you control more space, i.e. on the kingside. In other words: play on the flank to which the pawn chain is pointing.

A popular attacking plan here is the 'classic bishop sacrifice on h7': a piece is sacrificed for a pawn which forms part of the king position and a tempo. After that the white army attacks the exposed

black king, usually with ♘g5+ and then ♕h5 and a mating attack.

But also, if Black has managed to swap off the valuable white king's bishop at an early stage, White can get a strong attack on the right-hand side of the board.

As we search for a plan we are helped by another rule:

In general one would like to move the pawn next to the furthest advanced one!

The result of this is a typical pawn storm on the kingside: f2-f4, g2-g4 and the destruction of Black's castled position, e.g. by f4-f5-f6, or the opening of files for an attack by the major pieces.

Black is severely cramped by the white pawn chain. It represents the basis for an attack and should therefore be attacked and (ideally) completely cleared.

The obvious way is 'the attack on the base', i.e. d4, with the help of the pawn lever ...c7-c5. If White protects the latter with c2-c3, Black has two options: he can exchange on d4 and after ...c5xd4, c3xd4 both fight for the c-file and also exert piece pressure against the now weak pawn:

A second option (after ...c7-c5 and c2-c3) consists of 'laying siege to the base': Black plays ...c5-c4 and attacks the chain by means of ...b7-b5-b4(xc3).
(see next diagram)

In addition to this plan, the 'attack on the head' of the pawn chain is an important topic. In this case Black proceeds with ...f7-f6. If this happens at an early stage, White can usually not support the e5-pawn with f2-f4 and will react with exf6, which provides Black with a semi-open file as well as more squares for his pieces (d6 and f6). The cost he must accept for this is the backward pawn on e6. Black, however, obtains the possibility of activating the bad queen's bishop: ...♗c8-d7-e8-g6 or h5 is a typical manoeuvre.

In the attack on the pawn chain it is very important to achieve more than the simple disappearance of the opposing pawns. It is all about the domination of the centre! Nimzowitsch, who was the first to formulate the theory surrounding pawn chains, demonstrates in game 60 what power can emanate from white minor pieces on the blockading squares d4 and e5 which have been freed. In that game, his opponent Salwe should definitely have fought for control of d4 and e5. The black pawn chain e6/d5 should advance!

Conclusion

At first glance, the French structure conveys the impression that in a closed position everything is about play on the flanks. This, however, is deceptive. Both sides must keep their eye on the centre! Black would like to destroy the white pawn chain in order to raise the blockade of his central pawns e6 and d5. Often the bad light-squared bishop plays an important role. If Black manages to exchange or activate it he generally has equality. The structure is fundamentally more favourable for Black, since the base of his pawn chain is better secured. White, on the other hand, uses his advantage in space to attack.

58 Slav Defence
Pavel Eljanov   2687
Loek van Wely   2676
Dagomys 2008 (2)
1.d4 d5 2.c4 c6 3.♘f3 ♘f6 4.e3 a6 5.♗d3 ♗g4 6.♕b3 ♗xf3 7.gxf3 ♕c7 8.cxd5 cxd5 9.♘c3 e6 10.e4 ♘c6 11.♗e3 ♖d8 12.0-0-0 ♗e7 13.♔b1 0-0 14.♖c1 ♔h8 15.♘e2 ♖c8 16.♘f4 ♖fd8 17.♖hg1 b5?

A better move would have been 17...♕b8.

18.e5

White could also reach an advantage with the opening of the centre for the bishop pair: 18.exd5 ♘xd5 (18...exd5 19.♗f5) 19.♘xd5 ♖xd5 20.♗e4±. But Eljanov is aiming for a French central structure. The opposing pieces on the queenside are not contributing much to the defence of the cramped king position.

18...♘d7

Black would need only a few moves to obtain play on the queenside or to exchange major pieces on the c-file, which would clearly water down the attack. So Eljanov must act energetically.

White to move

Is there a tactical solution?

19.♗xh7

The typical bishop sacrifice! Possibly Van Wely's attention was diverted from this because it happens without the obligatory check.

19...♘f8

Accepting the offer leads logically to a mating attack: 19...♔xh7? 20.♕d3+ ♔h8 21.♖xg7 ♔xg7 22.♘xe6+! and Black must surrender the queen. However, returning the piece immediately with the destruction of the white centre offered more tenacious resistance: 19...♘dxe5 20.dxe5 ♔xh7 21.♕c2+ ♔g8 22.♘h5 ♕xe5 23.♖xg7+ ♔f8 24.♖h7 ♘a5 25.f4! ♖xc2 26.♖xc2 ♔g8 27.fxe5 ♔xh7 28.♗b6 ♘c4 29.♗xd8 ♗xd8 30.f4 and White still has some work to do to win the endgame.

20.♗d3

With queens on the board, the attack against the weakened king position plays itself. Van Wely can neither instigate sufficient counterplay on the queenside, nor can he manage to defend his king.

20...♕b6 21.♖g4 ♘a5 22.♕d1 g6 23.♕f1 ♔g7 24.♕h3 ♖xc1+ 25.♗xc1 ♖c8 26.♗e3 ♘c4 27.♘xg6   **1-0**

59 Queen's Indian Defence
Shakhriyar Mamedyarov   2752
Magnus Carlsen   2765
Baku 2008 (4)
1.d4 ♘f6 2.c4 e6 3.♘f3 b6 4.g3 ♗b7 5.♗g2 ♗e7 6.0-0 0-0 7.♖e1 ♘a6 8.♘e5 ♗xg2 9.♔xg2 c6 10.e4 ♕c7 11.♘c3 ♕b7

12.♘d3! d5

Mamedyarov suggests in *New In Chess* 4/2008 12...♘b4 13.e5 ♘xd3 14.♕xd3 ♘e8 15.d5 cxd5 16.cxd5 ♘c7 17.♕f3 'with freer play for White'. But with the tactical point 17...f6 Black can equalise: 18.dxe6 (18.d6? fails to 18...♕xf3+ 19.♔xf3 fxe5+!) 18...♕xf3+=.

13.e5 ♘d7 14.cxd5 cxd5

White to move

Work out a plan.

Carlsen has extremely cleverly exchanged the light-squared bishop before allowing the locking of the centre. An attack against h7 is therefore excluded.

Nevertheless, White has various options on the kingside. The knight on d3 can be transferred via f4, where it first prevents Black's attempts to free his position with ...f7-f6, to h5. There it supports the queen, which is coming to g4 in its attack on g7. The knight on d3 is thus a valuable attacking piece, which should be saved from a possible exchange if Black plays ...♘b4.

Another traditional plan begins with f2-f4, intending f4-f5. The black d-pawn is badly protected after ...e6xf5 and is won by ♕f3 and ♘f4. On the other hand, after f5xe6, f7xe6 the e-pawn has been weakened. The attack described above, with ♕g4 and ♘f4, is now directed not only at g7. The fact that the f-file has been opened, favouring the rook on f8, is hardly of any importance since it can be blocked by the knight on f4 and moreover the entry squares are protected. But with the continuation 15.f4 White would after 15...g6 still turn to his rook pawn: 16.h4, e.g. 16...♘b4 17.♘f2! ♖fc8 18.h5 and then ♖h1.

With the immediate advance 15.h4 White prepares for ♗g5. An exchange then opens the h-file, which the rook can occupy in a single move thanks to the king being on g2. In addition, the typical advance h4-h5 leads in any case to a typical weakening of the black king position, as will be seen in the game continuation.

15.h4

Mamedyarov is not very satisfied with this move in his analysis. He prefers the direct attack with pieces. However this leads to a very sharp series of sacrifices. He analyses 15.♕g4 ♖fc8 16.♗h6 g6 (16...♗f8 17.♘b5) 17.h4 ♘b4 18.♘f4!

♘c2 19.♘xe6 ♖c4 20.h5 ♘xa1 21.hxg6 hxg6 (21...fxg6 22.♘d8!+−) 22.♘f4! ♘f8! (22...♗f8 23.♖h1 ♘xe5 24.♕h4+−; 22...♘c2 23.♘xg6 ♘xe1+ 24.♔f1+−; 22...♖xd4 23.e6 ♖xf4 24.exf7+ ♔h7 25.♕xf4+−)

analysis diagram: position after 22...♘f8

23.♖h1!! ♖xd4 24.♕h3 ♕d7 25.♕h2 ♖xf4 26.♗xf4 f6 27.♕h8+ ♔f7 28.♖xa1± (Mamedyarov).

So, in the position after the 14th move various attacking plans are possible. The world-class grandmaster considers the attack with pieces starting with 15.♕g4 to be the best solution.

15...♘b4!

An exchange of knights was not on White's wish list. That decreases his chances on the kingside.

The attacking side should basically avoid exchanging material!

16.♗g5

16.♘f4 ♖ac8 17.a3 ♘c6 with counterplay.

16...♘xd3 17.♕xd3 ♗b4 18.♖ec1 a6 19.♘e2

The knight should be employed for the attack on the king. But according to Mamedyarov 19.a3 ♗xc3 20.♖xc3 ♖fc8 21.♖ac1 h6 22.♗d2 is better, with an advantage for White in view of his control over the single open file. As long as the knight does not get to c6, the bad bishop remains the stronger piece.

White is in any case in possession of the c-file.

Here we again see a typical scenario in the struggle between differing minor pieces. After the exchange of the major pieces we would have the clear case of 'knight against bad bishop'. Black manoeuvres the knight to c6, and White must fight for survival. With control of the c-file the question of the 'bad bishop', on the other hand, plays only a subordinate role. There are good chances of at some point invading the black camp down the open file. A sample variation is 22...b5 23.b3 ♘b6 24.♖c5 ♖xc5 (24...♘d7 25.♖5c2 ♘b6 26.♗b4) 25.♖xc5 ♖c8 26.♕c2 ♖xc5 27.♕xc5 ♘d7 28.♕e7 ♕c8 and Black is facing a laborious defence. Even here White still has attacking chances on the kingside. He can, for example, after some preparation, open the position with h4-h5 and g4-g5.

19...♖fc8

White to move

How does the attack continue?

20.h5

The advance of the rook pawn forces a weakening in the opposing camp. If Black allows h5-h6, then after ...g7-g6 a complex of weak squares is created. Carlsen works against this with

20...h6

But now he no longer has the possibility to use ...g7-g6 to prevent the advance of the white pawn to f5. This mechanism for weakening the g6-square is known to us from the previous chapter 'Weak squares'.

21.a3!

White fights to retain his bad bishop and not, for example, to swap it for the good black one. He is planning to play ♗c3 later to block black counterplay on the c-file.

21...♗f8 22.♗d2 ♖xc1 23.♖xc1 ♖c8 24.♖f1!

Of course Mamedyarov also needs the rook. But he had to calculate carefully that Carlsen does not get too much play on the c-file.

24...b5

This gives White an important tempo. It was preferable to play the pawn sacrifice 24...♕c6! 25.♕xa6 ♘b8 with sufficient compensation.

25.f4 ♕c6 26.♖c1 ♕b7 27.♖f1 ♕c6 28.♕f3

The attack with f4-f5 will come. Will it develop quickly enough before the black counterplay on the c-file becomes too strong?

28...♕b6 29.f5 exf5 30.♗c3!

Gaining time.

30...a5?!

30...♕c6 31.g4 ♔h8 32.gxf5 ♕b7 33.♔h1±.

31.♗xa5!

This diverts the queen. Mamedyarov could also have decided for an advantageous endgame: 31.♕xd5 ♕c6 32.♕xc6 ♖xc6 33.d5±.

31...♕xa5 32.♕xf5

Now the fall of f7 can no longer be prevented. After that the knight intervenes via f4 and g6.

32...♕d2 33.♕xf7+?

An inaccuracy which put White's win in question. The correct way was 33.♖f2 ♘xe5 34.dxe5 ♖c7 35.♘f4 ♕d4 36.♘e6! fxe6 37.♕xe6+ ♔h7 38.♕f5+ ♔g8 39.♕xf8+ ♔h7 40.♕f5+ ♔g8 41.♔h3 ♕e4 42.♕xe4 dxe4 43.♔g4+− (Mamedyarov).

33...♔h8 34.♖f2

34...♖d8?

But Carlsen goes wrong too and misses out on the chance he was offered. He could after 34...♘xe5 35.♕b7 ♕c2

(35...♖d8 36.dxe5 ♗c5 37.♕c7 ♕e3 38.♕xd8+ ♔h7 39.♔h3 ♕xf2 40.♘f4 ♕f1+ 41.♔g4 ♕d1+ 42.♔f5 ♕c2+ 43.♔e6+− Mamedyarov) 36.dxe5 ♕e4+ 37.♔g1 ♖c2 38.♕b8 ♔h7 39.♕xf8 ♖xe2 40.♖xe2 ♕xe2± reach a queen ending, in which a win for White cannot be taken for granted.

35.♕xd5+− ♕a5 36.♘f4 ♕a8 37.♘g6+

In view of 37...♔h7 38.♕xa8 ♖xa8 39.♖f7 ♖d8 40.♖xd7 Carlsen resigned. This game demonstrates the numerous attacking options for White on the kingside.

60 French Defence
Aaron Nimzowitsch
Georg Salwe

Karlsbad 1911 (15)

1.e4 e6 2.d4 d5 3.e5 c5 4.c3 ♘c6 5.♘f3 ♕b6 6.♗d3 ♗d7?!

The move 6.♗d3 has fallen out of fashion, since with 6...cxd4 7.cxd4 ♗d7 Black can fix and attack the weak d4-pawn. After it, 8.0-0 (8.♗e2, Nimzowitsch) 8...♘xd4 9.♘bd2 (9.♘xd4) is a risky gambit continuation.

7.dxc5!

Is Nimzowitsch surrendering the centre? Not really... he intends to occupy it with pieces instead of pawns. This plan was an innovation in its day.

7...♗xc5 8.0-0 f6?!

8...a5 is a suggested improvement by John Watson. After it, it is not simple to blockade the black central pawns.

9.b4 ♗e7 10.♗f4 fxe5 11.♘xe5 ♘xe5 12.♗xe5 ♘f6 13.♘d2 0-0 14.♘f3 ♗d6 15.♕e2 ♖ac8 16.♗d4 ♕c7 17.♘e5 ♗e8 18.♖ae1

White has obtained an ideal position. His pieces occupy the central blockading squares. He is ready to attack on the kingside.

18...♗xe5?!

Now White's dominance in the centre is written in stone. Salwe had to try to free himself from White's clutch, even at the cost of a pawn: 18...♘e4 19.♗xe4 dxe4 20.f4 (20.♕xe4 ♗b5! 21.c4±) 20...exf3 21.♘xf3±.

19.♗xe5 ♕c6 20.♗d4 ♗d7 21.♕c2 ♖f7 22.♖e3 b6 23.♖g3 ♔h8?

A mistake in a critical situation. He probably miscalculated the strike which

follows. After 23...a5 24.a3 ♕a4± nothing would have been decided yet.

24.♗xh7+− e5

24...♘xh7? 25.♕g6 loses immediately.

25.♗g6 ♖e7 26.♖e1 ♕d6 27.♗e3?!

Nimzowitsch could win more quickly: 27.♕e2 exd4 28.♕xe7 ♕xe7 29.♖xe7+−. With the move in the game Salwe still reaches a lost endgame.

27...d4 28.♗g5 ♖xc3 29.♖xc3 dxc3 30.♕xc3 ♔g8 31.a3 ♔f8 32.♗h4 ♗e8 33.♗f5 ♕d4 34.♕xd4 exd4 35.♖xe7 ♔xe7 36.♗d3 ♗d6 37.♗xf6 gxf6 38.♔f1 ♗c6 39.h4

Black resigned.

Nowadays, the 'surrender of the centre' demonstrated by Nimzowitsch, followed by the blockade of the central pawns by pieces, is a standard procedure.

61 Caro-Kann Defence
Ni Hua 2632
Viorel Iordachescu 2563
Moscow 2007 (7)
1.e4 c6 2.d4 d5 3.e5 ♗f5 4.♘f3 e6 5.♗e2 ♘d7 6.0-0 ♘e7 7.♘bd2 h6 8.♘b3 ♖c8 9.♗d2 ♗e4

The black queen's bishop was placed in front of the pawn chain so as not to be in the way on d7. It is supposed to be exchanged for the opposing king's bishop.

White has an advantage in space, though his pieces too are cramped. With the subsequent exchange of his bishop Ni Hua creates some space and eliminates the risk of ever ending up in an endgame with a bad bishop against a knight. However, in doing so he helps the Romanian grandmaster with his development.

10.♗b4 ♘g6 11.♗xf8 ♘gxf8 12.♘fd2 ♗h7

The black position shows no weaknesses. The bishop on h7 is good insurance against the standard white plan of an attack on the kingside.

13.f4

The advanced e-pawn must be supported.

13...♘g6 14.♗d3 0-0 15.♔h1 ♘e7 16.♗xh7+ ♔xh7 17.♘f3 c5

White to move

How do you evaluate the position? Which plan should White follow?

White still has an advantage in space. However, he cannot so easily use that for an attack on the king, since in the opposing camp everything is sufficiently well protected. After the exchange of two pairs of minor pieces Black has enough space for the coordination of his pieces. As usual, the white centre is a target to attack. Black is ready to fix a pawn weakness on d4, which he can attack with ...♘c6, ...♕b6 and possibly later ...♘f5. White could absolutely be forced on to the defensive. One of the quirks of the French and also the King's Indian structure: an advantage in space is an abstract concept – and no games are won with that alone.

The chances are roughly level. So as not to be forced into passive defence, White is almost obliged to attack on the kingside. Since his pieces can find no active squares there, Ni Hua sends forward the pawns to open files.

18.g4 ♕b6 19.c3

19...cxd4

Here it would be wrong to transfer the attack to the new base c3 with 19...c4? 20.♕c2+ ♔h8 21.♘bd2. Black loses too much time organising an attack.

20.♕c2+

After 20.cxd4?! ♖c4 Black's counterplay on the queenside would be too quick.

20...d3

20...♔g8 21.♘bxd4.

21.♕xd3+ ♔g8 22.♖ae1

The base of the chain has fallen. Now the head must be protected.

22...♕a6?!

After 22...♖c4 23.g5 ♖xf4 24.gxh6 gxh6 (24...g6 is also interesting) 25.♖g1+ ♔h8 26.♕d2 ♘g6 27.h4 h5 28.♖g5 ♖xf3 29.♖xg6= White can get a perpetual check. An indication that in the position in the previous diagram things were okay for Black. With the move in the game Iordachescu shows great respect for the opposing activity on the kingside. He had in 22...♘c5 and 22...a5 good alternatives, in each case with level but double-edged play.

23.♕b1?!

23.♕xa6 bxa6 gives Black with the semi-open b-file compensation for the pawn weakness. Nevertheless, this was preferable to Ni Hua's continuation.

23...f5

He braces himself against White's attacking efforts. Nevertheless, it is now easier for White to open files. Black should not touch the pawn constellation, but attack the weaknesses in the white position. One difficulty of the defence is working out on every move whether passive protection or active counter-attack is the best way. Here it was the counter-attack. After 23...♕c4 24.♘fd4 ♘c6 the pressure on the white centre would have put the brakes on the thrusts f4-f5 or g4-g5.

24.♖g1 ♘c5 25.♘xc5 ♖xc5 26.g5

26...♖c4?

The decisive mistake. After 26...hxg5 27.♖xg5 ♔f7 28.♘d4 the position was more or less level, despite the holes in the black king position. After the move in the game White wins an important pawn without his attack being slowed down.

27.gxh6+– g6 28.♘d4 ♔f7 29.♖e3 ♖h8 30.♖h3 ♖cc8 31.h7 ♔e8 32.♖h6 ♔d7 33.h4 ♖cf8 34.h5 1-0

Crossing the middle of the board with e4-e5 is committal! Ni Hua used his advantage in space for an attack, which with correct defence should only have been enough for equality.

Model games

Tarrasch-Teichmann (San Sebastian 1912)
Geller-Karpov (Moscow 1976)
Nakamura-Pelletier (Biel 2005)
Grischuk-Gurevich (France tt 2003)
Predojevic-Morozevich (Sarajevo 2008)

Every passably gifted player – in no way does he have to be outstanding – can become a master. But it is not at all necessary! The correct point of view is to play for one's pleasure, and no one should believe that enjoyment is in any way proportional to ability.

Siegbert Tarrasch

The King's Indian structure

Specific characteristics

Similarly to the French, the white position shows an advantage in space, but this time on the queenside. The black attack on the pawn chain proceeds according to known patterns.

An important difference is the aim of Black's attack: this time it is the opposing king. Black can uncompromisingly play for mate, often with considerable sacrifices. A successful white advance on the queenside, on the other hand, offers chances of a slow victory.

Plans for White

The queenside attack inevitably involves the advance of the pawn to c5. Usually the c-file is opened with c5xd6, after which White can lay siege to the black d6-pawn, e.g. with ♘c4, ♘b5 and ♗a3. Naturally an invasion down the open file is a possibility at any point.

Both after a successful c5xd6 exchange and after the advance of the pawn roller a2-a4, b2-b4, c4-c5, White's superiority on the queenside is frequently so great that Black must no longer consent to a transition to the endgame.

Since the opponent will not be idly watching these merry goings-on and will be working on his own play on the

other side of the board, White's plans must be adapted to what is happening on the kingside.

White can also attack the black structure at the head, e5: f2-f4 opens the f-file. In doing so he absolutely must take care not to let the stopping square for the backward e-pawn, e5, become a permanent outpost for black pieces. So the lever f2-f4 is played mostly only when the black pieces are badly coordinated.

Plans for Black

It is only in exceptional cases that White's queenside attack can be met with exclusively passive defence. In the game Anand-Carlsen the young Norwegian manages to neutralise the white occupation of the c-file and take control of all the entry squares. It can be seen, however, that his pieces are too cramped to ward off the surprise white attack on the other side of the board quickly enough.

The main plan for Black consists of the attack on the base of the pawn chain by means of ...f7-f5. After a possible e4xf5 exchange, Black obtains the semi-open f-file as well as the f5-square, via which a knight can be manoeuvred to d4. Also, the head of the white chain, d5, loses support. If after ...f7-f5 White protects the base e4 with f2-f3, Black gets the opportunity, after ...f5xe4, f3xe4, to attack the weak e4-pawn with pieces and obtains play against the white king down the open f-file. We see this happening in game 63, Gelfand-Radjabov.

Furthermore, the attack with ...f5-f4 can be transferred to the new base f3, and at the same time the advantage in space increased.

The white pieces are forced to defend their king in cramped conditions.

Conclusion

In the King's Indian structure the central pawn chain is often left standing even after the obligatory attack with ...f7-f5. Matters are often decided by what is more successful: the white advance on the queenside or the black attack on the king.

62 Ruy Lopez

Viswanathan Anand	2779
Magnus Carlsen	2690

Morelia/Linares 2007 (10)

1.e4 e5 2.♘f3 ♘c6 3.♗b5 a6 4.♗a4 ♘f6 5.0-0 ♗e7 6.♖e1 b5 7.♗b3 d6 8.c3 0-0 9.h3 ♘a5 10.♗c2 c5 11.d4 ♘d7 12.d5 ♘b6 13.♘bd2 g6

Black is threatening to attack the white pawn centre with ...f7-f5. If the base,

e4, falls, the head, d5, becomes very vulnerable. Supporting the e4-pawn with f2-f3 is of course out of the question after h2-h3 has been played. After 14.♘h2?! f5 then 15.f3?? would be a terrible positional block. The dark squares are suddenly irredeemably weak, so Black can go over to the attack with 15...♗h4. To maintain his pawn chain nevertheless, White exploits the somewhat shaky position of the two black knights.

14.b4

This gains Anand time for the development of his queenside. The c4-square would indeed be temporarily weakened, but Carlsen cannot exploit this.

14...cxb4 15.cxb4 ♘ac4 16.♘xc4 ♘xc4 17.♗b3!

White is fighting for c4 and at the same time protects the head of the pawn chain.

17...♘b6

White to move

On which side of the board should White become active?

The castled position, having been weakened by ...g7-g6, is just inviting 18.♗h6 – 'winning a tempo'. But it is not easy to achieve anything concrete there. Anand plays instead to occupy the c-file.

18.♗e3 ♗d7 19.♖c1 ♖c8 20.♖xc8
♗xc8 21.♕c2 ♗d7 22.♖c1±

Carlsen must not allow the major pieces to invade on c7.

22...♘a8 23.♕d2

This in any case protects an important square and delays the white attack. Of course no grandmaster likes to make such a move. But from time to time there are no alternatives and the bitter pill has to be swallowed. In what follows, the steed on the corner square bobs up and down. But it is not so easy for White to capitalise on this.

Black to move

What is wrong with the standard plan 23...f5 ?

We too frequently play according to 'general considerations' or follow plans we have learned without taking a sufficiently good look at the position! Attentiveness and a consideration of all the pieces and their effectiveness are indispensable in a tournament game! 23...f5 is positionally desirable but fails to 24.♘xe5+−. The white 'Spanish' bishop also has, as well as c4 and d5, its X-ray eye on the king on g8.

Tactics have priority over strategic thinking!

23...♕b8 24.♗g5

After Carlsen has secured the queenside, Anand focusses on the weakened dark squares on the right-hand side of the board and exploits his advantage in space. The white pieces can switch very rapidly from the occupation of the c-file to an attack on the kingside. Black is less flexible: his troops can hardly get back from the queenside. The knight on a8 has an especially long way to go!

24...♗xg5

And once again not 24...f6?? 25.♘xe5!, winning. Anand analyses the alternative 24...♗d8 25.♗xd8 ♕xd8. Now with the penetration of the queen on h6 White moves over to an attack on the kingside. In the following variations the Spanish bishop also plays an important part: 26.♕h6 ♕f6 (26...f6 27.♖c6! ♗c8 (27...♗xc6? 28.dxc6+ ♔h8 29.♘h4+−) 28.h4) 27.♘g5 ♕g7 28.♕h4

analysis diagram

and the threat of 29.♘e6! sets Black probably insoluble problems:

A) 28...♖c8? 29.♖xc8+ ♗xc8 30.♘xh7!;

B) 28...♖e8? 29.♘e6;

C) 28...♔h8? 29.♘xh7 ♕xh7 30.♕e7 (Anand) 30...♕h6 31.♖c2 ♗c8 32.♕xd6 ♔g8 (32...f6 33.♕c6) 33.♕xe5±.

The best defence consisted of 24...♕d8! 25.♕e3 ♗xg5 26.♘xg5 ♕e7 27.f4 with an initiative for White. We can see a situation in which Black is not well set up against the lever f2-f4. It would be ideal to be able to rapidly occupy the central outpost e5 with a piece. But the knight which would suit this role is indisposed.

25.♘xg5 ♖c8?

25...♘b6 26.f4 h6 27.♘e6 ♖c8 28.♖f1 'and White has the initiative' (Anand). That is really understating the case. Closer analysis does not reveal how Black can hold the position, e.g. 28...♘c4 29.♗xc4 bxc4 (29...♖xc4 30.fxe5 ♕e8 (30...fxe6? 31.♕xh6 ♕e8 32.♖f6+−) 31.exd6 ♖xe4 32.♘c5 ♖e2 33.♕xh6+−) 30.fxe5 ♕b6+ 31.♔h2 dxe5 32.♘c5+−.

26.♖f1 h6

27.♘e6!

The best positional play cannot work without tactics. It is only this combination which makes the difference between 'with a winning attack' and 'with a level game', which would be seen after 27.♘f3 ♔g7=.

27...♔h7 28.f4 ♕a7+ 29.♔h2 ♗e8 30.f5 gxf5

The slightly more tenacious defence consisted of 30...fxe6. The following variations make it clear that the opening of the black king position, together with the passed pawns which White gets in return for the knight he has sacrificed, represents more than sufficient compensation: 31.dxe6 gxf5 32.exf5 ♕d4 33.♕xd4 exd4 34.f6 ♘b6 35.e7 (35.f7 ♗xf7 36.exf7 ♖f8 37.♗e6±) 35...♘c4 36.f7 ♗xf7 37.♖xf7+ ♔g8

38.♖f4 d3 39.♗xc4+ bxc4 40.♖xc4 ♖b8 41.♖d4 ♔f7 42.♖xd3 ♔xe7 43.♖d4±.

31.exf5?!

There was an easier win with the alternatives 31.♘f8+ ♔g7 32.exf5 f6 (32...♔xf8? 33.f6+−) 33.♘e6+ ♔h7+− or 31.♘g5+ ♔g8 32.exf5+−.

31...f6 32.♖e1 ♘c7 33.♖c1 ♗d7 34.♖c3 e4 35.♖g3 ♘xe6 36.dxe6 ♗e8 37.e7 ♗h5 38.♕xd6   1-0

In this lively attacking game Anand made use of his advantage in space to create threats on both wings. What was decisive was the 'X-ray effect' of the (actually bad) Spanish bishop, which not only prevented the counterplay ...f7-f5, but was also the basis for some tricks on the a2-g8 diagonal.

63 King's Indian Defence

| **Boris Gelfand** | 2737 |
| **Teimour Radjabov** | 2735 |

Wijk aan Zee 2008 (11)

1.d4 ♘f6 2.c4 g6 3.♘c3 ♗g7 4.e4 d6 5.♗e2 0-0 6.♘f3 e5 7.0-0 ♘bd7 8.♗e3 ♖e8 9.d5 ♘h5

An interesting move, typical of the King's Indian. Black provokes a pawn move with the threat of ...♘f4. The knight will have to retreat from h5, but the tempi he has invested are outweighed by the weakening of the white structure.

10.g3 ♗f8 11.♘e1 ♘g7 12.♘d3 f5 13.f3

Radjabov's manoeuvres on the kingside are instructive: despite having the smallest amount of space he creates a function for each of his pieces. After the locking of the centre the king's bishop contributes nothing more to the play; it is to be exchanged on g5. The knight had to return to g7, but from there it supports the advance of the f-pawn. After White plays exf5 it can be activated with ...♘xf5.

13...♗e7 14.♕d2 ♘f6 15.c5 fxe4 16.fxe4 ♗h3

The holes provoked on h3 and f3 with loss of tempo make themselves felt here and in what follows.

17.cxd6 cxd6 18.♖fc1

18.♖f2.

After the exchange of pawns each of the players has created a weak point in the opposing centre. Now these have to be attacked with pieces. Radjabov proceeds cleverly here: with the next move he provokes the exchange of the – nominally bad – opposing bishop. In doing so he arranges for his own queen's bishop to dominate the weak light squares close to the opposing king.

18...♘g4 19.♗xg4

Of course there is no question of giving up the most important white piece, the dark-squared bishop.

19...♗xg4 20.♘b5 ♖f8 21.♖c3

With 21.♘xa7?! White would secure for himself a win in the endgame. However, with the pawn grab he loses a lot of time, which Black makes use of on the kingside: 21...h5 22.♘b5 h4 23.♖c7 hxg3 24.hxg3 ♖f3 and the attack takes shape. It is totally unclear whether White will ever reach the endgame. In any case, the text move is not the best continuation. As will be seen, the rook is badly placed on c3. Gelfand would have done better to continue with 21.♖c2 or 21.♖c4.

21...a6 22.♘c7 ♖c8 23.♖ac1 ♕d7 24.♘f2 ♗d8 25.♕c2?

The white knight sortie to b5 and c7 has achieved nothing specific. The black position is completely intact. Gelfand now had to accept the pin with ...♗a5. After 25.♘xg4 ♕xg4 26.♘b5! ♗a5 27.♘xd6 ♗xc3 28.bxc3 ♖c7 29.c4 he would not only have beaten off the attack, but also obtained compensation for the lost exchange.

25...♖f3∓

Now the black pieces fall upon the kingside.

26.♕b3?

26.♘xg4 ♕xg4 27.♘e6 ♖xc3 28.♕xc3 ♘xe6 29.dxe6 ♕xe4 30.♖e1 h5 offered better defensive chances.

26...♖xc7−+ 27.♖xc7 ♗xc7 28.♘xg4

28.♖xc7 ♕xc7 29.♘xg4.

28...♕xg4 29.♖xc7 ♘e8?

But Radjabov too makes a mistake. He coped well with the invasion of the white major pieces on the seventh rank, because his attack gets in more quickly. With 29...♘h5 he could not only keep g7 protected, but also set up the deadly threat of 30...♘xg3. There is no defence to it: 30.♕a4 (30.♕xb7 ♖f8! threatens 31...♕d1+ and then 32...♕f1 mate) 30...b5 31.♕c2 ♖xe3 32.♖c8+ ♔g7 33.♖c7+ ♔h6 34.♕d2 ♕e2−+.

30.♖e7 ♕xe4 31.♖xe8+ ♔f7 32.♖c8 ♖xe3 33.♕xb7+ ♔f6 34.♖f8+ ♔g5

35.♕xh7?

In the long run it is Gelfand who makes the infamous 'final mistake'. After 35.♕e7+ ♔h6 36.♕xd6 ♕d4 37.♔f1!= he could have reached the haven of the draw. Defending the king against queen and rook looks at first sight impossible. But the rook on f8 prevents the mate.

35...♖e1+ 36.♖f1 ♕d4+ 37.♔g2 ♖e2+ **0-1**

Each side obliged the other to defend the base of a chain, which was in need of protection. Radjabov managed, however, to provoke a weakening of the king position and to exploit the entry squares h3 and f3.

> *People do not stop playing because they become old, they become old because they stop playing!*
> Oliver Wendell Holmes

64 Ruy Lopez
Peter Leko	2713
Vladimir Kramnik	2809

Monaco (rapid) 2002 (4)

1.e4 e5 2.♘f3 ♘c6 3.♗b5 a6 4.♗a4 ♘f6 5.0-0 ♗e7 6.♖e1 b5 7.♗b3 d6 8.c3 0-0 9.h3 ♘b8 10.d4 ♘bd7 11.♘bd2 ♗b7 12.♗c2 ♖e8 13.b3 ♗f8

White to move

Would you lock the centre with 14.d5 ?

If you like this move, you find yourself in good company. Peter Leko (*1979), former Hungarian prodigy, has for years been one of the circle of top grandmasters and in 2004 only just lost to Kramnik in the battle for the title of World Champion.

Since he can later comfortably protect the head of the pawn chain d5 with c3-c4, Leko sets out to achieve a permanent advantage in space.

14.d5?!

As Vladimir Kramnik will show, this overstretches the position. Leko will not manage to defend the terrain he has conquered. A better way was 14.♗b2 or 14.a4.

14...c6 15.c4 ♘b6 16.♗d3 ♘fd7! 17.♗a3

A more prudent course was 17.dxc6 ♗xc6 18.♗a3 ♘c5 19.♗f1 with approximately level chances, but that was not Leko's idea when he advanced the pawn.

17...cxd5 18.cxd5

18...f5!

Kramnik accepts a weakening on the kingside in order to spring open the white centre.

19.exf5 ♘xd5 20.♘e4 ♘7f6 21.♘fg5 ♘f4!

All the elements in Black's game are in perfect harmony: the knight is protecting e6 and attacking the white king's bishop.

22.♗c1

But 22.♗f1 did not work on account of 22...h6 23.♘xf6+ ♕xf6 24.♘e6 ♘xe6 25.fxe6 ♖xe6 and Black is a pawn up.

22...♘xd3 23.♕xd3 ♘xe4 24.♘xe4 d5 25.♘g3 e4 26.♕d2 d4

The diagram is impressive evidence of why chess players aim to obtain connected pawns in the middle of

the board. The white pieces cannot find any outposts. In this case, the duo is additionally mobile and will be supported by the black pieces in its urge to advance.

27.♗b2 ♗c5 28.♖ac1 ♗b6 29.♕f4 ♕d5 30.♖c2?!

A better way was 30.♕g4.

30...e3 31.fxe3 ♖ac8 32.♖d2 ♖xe3 33.♖xe3 dxe3

34.♖e2?

Despite the overwhelming black position Leko could still have reached an endgame: 34.♖xd5 e2+ 35.♖d4 e1♕+ 36.♔h2 ♗xg2 37.♕d2 ♕xd2 38.♖xd2 with a big advantage for Black in view of the bishop pair and the open white king position.

After the text move Kramnik ends the game in style.

34...♖c2 35.♕g4

Neither 35.♕e5 ♕xe5 36.♗xe5 ♖xa2−+ nor 35.♖xc2? e2+ 36.♕f2 ♕xg2# would have changed the result.

35...♖xb2! 36.f6 g6

The 'finish for lovers of checks' was 36...♕xg2+ 37.♖xg2 e2+ 38.♔h2 ♗g1+. But there is no need for any checks.

37.f7+ ♕xf7

White resigned.

In this game Kramnik destroyed the white centre with the pawn sacrifice ...f7-f5 and obtained two mobile central pawns.

65 King's Indian Defence

Lubomir Ftacnik	2585
Ognjen Cvitan	2570

Germany Bundesliga 1997/98 (2)

1.d4 ♘f6 2.♘f3 g6 3.c4 ♗g7 4.♘c3 0-0 5.e4 d6 6.♗e2 e5 7.0-0 ♘c6 8.d5 ♘e7 9.♘d2 ♘e8 10.b4 f5 11.c5 ♘f6 12.f3 f4

Transferring the attack to the new base of the chain f3.

At the very first glance the cramped king position catches our eye. The monarch is the target for the black forces. Here Black has at his disposal several plans for an attack on the kingside, in which as quickly as possible all his pieces – apart from the rook on a8 – will take part. The manoeuvres which follow in the game, ...♖f7, ...♗f8, ...♖g7, ...g5-g4, ...♘g6, ...♘h7 and ...♕h4, are frequently encountered in this type of position. It is all very dangerous and White must devote his full attention to his opponent's intentions so as not to be mated. Grandmaster Ftacnik is, however, an experienced proponent of the white side. His success rate is so high that presumably many King's Indian lovers have been tempted to change to other openings.

Basically: the black attack is more dangerous than the white advance on the queenside. Mate takes precedence over a positional victory! Nevertheless, the King's Indian player is fighting here under a

great, long-term handicap – the bad bishop on g7, a sometimes ineffective piece. In the final analysis, that is the main reason for the slightly above average success of the white side in practice.

Ftacnik follows a standard procedure.

13.♘c4

The ideal square for the knight.

13...g5 14.a4 ♘g6 15.♗a3 ♖f7 16.b5 dxc5

Actually Cvitan would like to be playing only on the kingside.

The position should not be compromised by pawn moves on the side of the board on which the opponent is attacking.

However, after 16...♗f8 17.a5 or 17.b6 (Golubev) his queenside would rapidly collapse.

17.♗xc5

This should be considered a success for White. The bishop can now combine both defensive and attacking tasks on the f2-a7 diagonal.

17...h5 18.a5 g4 19.b6 g3

You would have to be a real survivalist not to panic here. The king position is being softened up and the black attacking forces are gaining entry. On the other hand, a king also needs only exactly one square on which it can stand. The corner offers it enough room.

20.♔h1!

But 20.h3? would be a clear mistake on account of the typical 20...♗xh3! 21.gxh3 ♕c8 and the black attacking

179

forces hit home. Eduard Gufeld, one of the 'venerable' players of the King's Indian, once wrote that the queen's bishop is in fact perfectly developed on c8. The long-range bishop does not have to be developed in order to play an active part. In view of the attacks taking place on both wings, here the classical connecting of the rooks for development is often irrelevant. The rook on a8 is doing good work in the protection of the queenside. If required, it can be activated later. And the bishop frequently has the honourable task of sacrificing itself on h3 so as to shatter the white king position.

20...♘h7 21.d6

Other interesting moves were 21.♖e1 and 21.♘b5. Golubev gives the following sample variation after the latter: 21...♕h4 22.♗g1 ♗h3 23.gxh3 ♕xh3 24.♖f2 gxf2 25.♗xf2 axb6 26.♘xc7 ♖xc7 27.♘xb6 and the threat is ♗f1, trapping the queen. White has a clear advantage.

21...♕h4 22.♗g1 ♗h3 23.bxc7?

But now the experienced Ftacnik makes a mistake. He had to continue with 23.gxh3! ♕xh3 24.♖f2 gxf2 25.♗xf2± (Khalifman). In view of White's great superiority on the queenside, the sacrifice of an exchange is a small concession if it stops Black's attack.

Black to move

The white king position is in tatters, material is no longer significant. How does the attack continue?

23...♗xg2+ 24.♔xg2 ♕h3+

Simply beautiful, isn't it?

25.♔xh3 ♘g5+ 26.♔g2 ♘h4+ 0-1

After the cramping of the white king-side with ...f5-f4, the mutual flank attacks were carried out to a great extent uninfluenced one by the other. The cramped white king position led to a beautiful tactical solution.

Model games
Najdorf-Gligoric (Mar del Plata 1953)
Taimanov-Najdorf (Zurich 1953)
Petrosian-Gligoric (Zurich 1953)
Averbakh-Kotov (Zurich 1953)
Tal-Fischer (Bled/Zagreb/Belgrade 1959)
Gligoric-Fischer (Monaco 1967)
Kortchnoi-Kasparov (Barcelona 1989)
Piket-Kasparov (Tilburg 1989)

'Modern chess worries about too many things like pawn structure etc. Forget all that, checkmate ends the game!'

Nigel Short

Index of Games

Index of Openings

(numbers refer to games)

Bibliography

Anand, Viswanathan
    Meine besten Schachpartien, Edition Olms 1998
Bronstein, David
    Zurich International Chess Tournament 1953, Dover New York 1979
Bronznik, Valeri and Terekhin, Anatoli
    Techniques of Positional Play, New In Chess 2013
Estrin, J.B.; Kalinitschenko, N.
    d4-d5 Der Angriff mit dem Damenisolani, frankh Schach 1989
Fischer, Robert
    Meine 60 denkwürdigen Partien, Verlag Dr.Eduard Wildhagen 1969
Karpow, Anatoli
    Wie ich kämpfe und siege, Rudi Schmaus Verlag 1984
Kasparow, Garri
    Von der Zeit geprüft, Walter Rau Verlag 1986
Kasparov, Garry
    My Great Predecessors Part I-IV, Everyman Chess 2003-2006
Kasparov, Garry
    Revolution in the 70s, Everyman Chess 2007
Kosten, Tony
    Mastering the Nimzo-Indian, Batsford 1998
Keene, Ray and Simpole, Julian
    Petrosian vs the Elite, Batsford 2006
Keres, Paul
    Ausgewählte Partien, 1931-1958, Variant 1983
Kmoch, Hans
    Die Kunst der Bauernführung, Verlag 'Das Schach-Archiv' 1967
Kramnik, Vladimir and Damsky, Iakov
    my life and games, Everyman Chess 2000
Marin, Mihail
    Learn from the Legends, Quality Chess 2006
Marovic, Drazen
    Geheimnisse der Bauernführung im Schach, Gambit 2003
Matanovic, A.
    Schach-Informator, Band 1-101, Sahovski Informator 1966-2008
Michaltschischin, A.; Srokowski, Ja.; Braslawski, W.
    Isolierter Bauer, Intelinvest 1994
O'Connell, Levy, Adams
    The Complete Games of World Champion Anatoly Karpov, Batsford 1976
Nimzowitsch, Aaron
    Mein System, Verlag 'Das Schach-Archiv' 1965

Sadler, Matthew
>   Queen's Gambit Declined, Everyman Chess 2000

Schereschewski, Michail
>   Strategie der Schachendspiele, Sportverlag 1985

Speelman, Jon
>   Endgame Preparation, Batsford 1981

Speelman, Jon
>   Jon Speelman's Best Games, Batsford 1997

Slotnik, Boris
>   Typische Stellungen im Mittelspiel, Rudi Schmaus Verlag 1987

Smyslow, Wassili
>   Meine 130 schönsten Partien, Rudi Schmaus Verlag 1988

Soltis, Andy
>   Pawn Structure Chess, McKay Chess Library 1995

Tal, Mikhail
>   The Life and Games of Mikhail Tal, Everyman Chess 1997

Watson, John
>   Secrets of Modern Chess Strategy, Gambit 2001

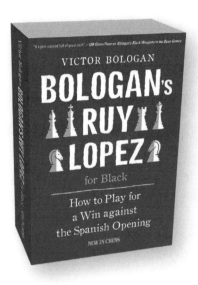
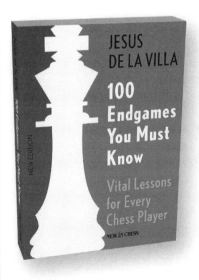

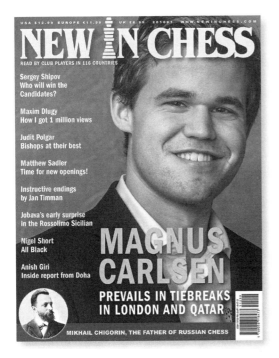
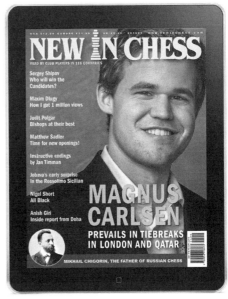

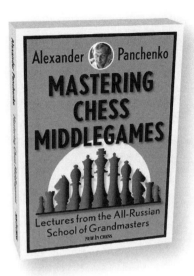
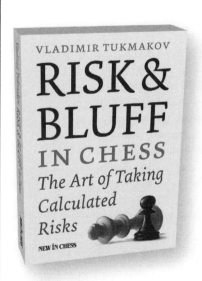

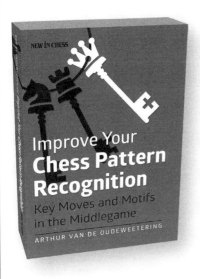